# WOKE GAMING

# WOKE GAMING

## DIGITAL CHALLENGES TO OPPRESSION AND SOCIAL INJUSTICE

EDITED BY
KISHONNA L. GRAY AND
DAVID J. LEONARD

UNIVERSITY OF WASHINGTON PRESS
*Seattle*

UNIVERSITY OF WASHINGTON PRESS
www.washington.edu/uwpress

LIBRARY OF CONGRESS CATALOGING-IN-PUBLICATION DATA
Names: Gray, Kishonna L., editor. | Leonard, David J., editor.
Title: Woke gaming : digital challenges to oppression and social injustice / edited
  by Kishonna L. Gray and David J. Leonard.
Description: Seattle : University of Washington Press, 2018. | Includes bibliographical
  references and index. |
Identifiers: LCCN 2018010422 (print) | LCCN 2018016086 (ebook) |
  ISBN 9780295744193 (ebook) | ISBN 9780295744186 (hardcover : alk. paper) |
  ISBN 9780295744179 (pbk. : alk. paper)
Subjects: LCSH: Video games—Social aspects. | Video games—Moral and ethical
  aspects. | Violence in video games. | Sex in video games.
Classification: LCC GV1469.34.S52 (ebook) | LCC GV1469.34.S52 W65 2018 (print) |
  DDC 794.8—dc23
LC record available at https://lccn.loc.gov/2018010422

*For those who are tirelessly working to transform gaming culture*
*We believe in you*
*We appreciate you*

# CONTENTS

*Acknowledgments*   xi

**INTRODUCTION.** Not a Post-Racism and Post-Misogyny Promised Land:
Video Games as Instruments of (In)Justice
KISHONNA L. GRAY AND DAVID J. LEONARD   3

**PART 1. ETHICS, VIOLENCE, AND OPPOSITIONAL GAMING**

**CHAPTER 1.** The Corporeal Ethics of Gaming: Vulnerability, Mobility,
and Social Gaming
ROB COVER   27

**CHAPTER 2.** Power, Violence, and the Mask: Representations of
Criminal Subjectivities in Grand Theft Auto Online
TIMOTHY ROWLANDS, SHERUNI RATNABALASURIAR,
    MELISSA HOBART, KYLE NOEL, SHAUN-PATRICK ALLEN,
    BRIANA REED, AND ANTHONY GONZALES   45

**PART 2. ECONOMICS OF GAMING**

**CHAPTER 3.** The Post-Feminist Politics of the "Everyone Can Make
Games Movement"
STEPHANIE ORME   65

**CHAPTER 4.** Smart Play: Social Stereotypes, Identity Building, and Counter Narratives of Gold Farmers in China
ZIXUE TAI AND FENGBIN HU   82


**PART 3: FEMINIST GAMING**

**CHAPTER 5.** The Sobering Reality of Sexism in the Video Game Industry
STANISLAV VYSOTSKY AND JENNIFER HELEN ALLAWAY   101

**CHAPTER 6.** The Perpetual Crusade: Rise of the Tomb Raider, Religious Extremism, and the Problem of Empire
KRISTIN BEZIO   119

**CHAPTER 7.** Nancy Drew and the Case of Girl Games
ANDREA BRAITHWAITE   139

**CHAPTER 8.** The Horrors of Transcendent Knowledge: A Feminist-Epistemological Approach to Video Games
STEPHANIE C. JENNINGS   155


**PART 4: GAMING AGAINST THE GRAIN**

**CHAPTER 9.** Playing with Pride: Claiming Space Through Community Building in World of Warcraft
KAREN SKARDZIUS   175

**CHAPTER 10.** Curate Your Culture: A Call for Social Justice–Oriented Game Development and Community Management
AMANDA C. COTE   193

**CHAPTER 11.** The Legends of Zelda: Fan Challenges to Dominant Video Game Narratives
KATHRYN HEMMANN   213

## PART 5: EMPATHETIC AND INCLUSIVE GAMING

**CHAPTER 12.** Avatars: Addressing Racism and Racialized Address
ROBBIE FORDYCE, TIMOTHY NEALE, AND
   THOMAS APPERLEY   231

**CHAPTER 13.** Activism in Video Games: A New Voice for Social Change
TAYLOR ANDERSON-BARKLEY AND KIRA FOGLESONG   252

**CHAPTER 14.** DiscrimiNation: A Persuasive Board Game to Challenge
   Discriminatory Justifications and Prejudices
MARESA BERTOLO, ILARIA MARIANI, AND
   ELEONORA ALBERELLO CONTI   270

*List of Contributors*   293

*Index*   296

# ACKNOWLEDGMENTS

Of course, first and foremost, we would like to thank the contributors to this collection. None of this would be possible had you not chosen to share your brilliance, your intellectual labor, and your scholarly insights in this collection. This collection is truly a team effort. In an environment where gamers and academics, for entirely different reasons, rebuff, scoff, and criticize critical game studies, you continue to courageously speak truths that demand more from gaming, from gamers, from the academy, and from society as a whole. Thank you for trusting us and for the work you continue to do inside and outside of game studies

Second, thank you to everyone at University of Washington Press who provided us with this important platform. Thanks especially to Larin McLaughlin for being the editorial G.O.A.T. You not only helped usher through this project but also did so in a way that you always asked the necessary questions to allow us and all the contributors to fulfil our purpose within and beyond gaming.

We would both like to thank the many scholars in game studies who paved the way for critical discussions about video games. We are grateful for the work and for your courage in carving out a space for important research on games, gaming communities, and gamers.

**From DJL:** I would like to specifically thank Dr. Kishonna L. Gray. Several years back, Kishonna asked me to write the foreword to her important book *Race, Gender, and Deviance in Xbox Live: Theoretical Perspectives from the Virtual Margins*. Before receiving this request, for a variety of reasons,

I had basically stopped writing and researching about video games. Her request brought me back to the work. More than this, her work inspired me to revisit past works and continue this research. The ability to collaborate with you on this project has been a blessing. So thank you. I am grateful to call you a collaborator and a co-editor; I am grateful because you are someone I learn from each and every day, because you are a friend for life.

DJL would also like to thank Rich King, Lisa Guerrero, Carmen Lugo-Lugo, Mary Bloodsworth-Lugo, Paula Groves-Price, Bryan Fry, Mark Anthony Neal, Ebony Utley, Danielle Heard, Stacey Patton, Aureliano Desoto, Theresa Runstedtler, Safiya Umoja Noble, Gaye Theresa Johnson, Jeffrey McCune, Nitasha Sharma, Ayana Jackson, Camille Dubose, Danielle Dirks, Jasbir Puar, Vernadette Gonzalez, Mark Padoongpatt, Sarah Jackson, Mary Yu Danico, Deborah Whaley, Heidi Renée Lewis, Darnell L. Moore, Jlove Calderon, Alexandro José Gradilla, Cindy Wu, Stephanie Troutman, Jared Sexton, and Dylan Rodriguez, who are not only peers and sources of support and inspiration but family.

I would also like to thank my students, whose work, whose daily contributions, and whose "freedom dreams" inspire me in so many ways. Everything I do, from the classroom to the scholarly workbench, is because of what I see from you each and every day. Thank you Basheera, Malik, Monae, Christina, Chijioke, Terlona, Bruce, Terlona, Kaila, Simone, Alexis, Cameron, Cammy, Jaade, Amber, Orion, Kendra, and so many others.

And finally, thanks to my family, whose support for the work here and elsewhere not only allows such research to happen but gives me hope that tomorrow will be better than today. Your work continues to raise consciousness and awareness, inspiring gamers and game studies to reimagine a world that we not only love but also want to love even more.

**From Kishonna:** I would first like to thank Dr. David J. Leonard. Without your amazing scholarship in race and video games, I would not have embarked on this beautiful journey. I remember being told that this scholarship didn't exist in the mid-2000s, and then I came across your piece, "Live in your World, Play in Ours." It literally changed my life. I saw what the possibilities were and knew that I could also be an innovator in this field. I would be remiss to not mention the other people I feel are pioneers in this field: André Brock, Lisa Nakamura, Samantha Blackmon,

TreaAndrea Russworm, Anna Everett, and so many others that I know I'm missing. Please forgive me! I thank you.

I would also like to personally thank Dr. T. L. Taylor for believing in me and my work and inviting me to come hang with you at MIT for a year! I would also like to thank the other amazing individuals who supported me and my research while at MIT: Helen E. Lee, Emily Neill, Sophia Hasenfus, and the entire SHASS family.

And also a special shout out to individuals at the Microsoft Research Collective: Nancy Baym, Mary L. Gray, Tarleton Gillespie, and all the other dope individuals who make up the Social Media Collective. I would also to thank my Berkmaster (LOL), Rebecca Tabasky, and the wonderful Berkman-Klein community for pushing the limits and effecting change. We will save the Internet!!!

To the amazing crew of "Not Your Mama's Gamer": Sam, Alex, Alisha, Charlotte, Bianca, Jynx, Lee, Ashley, and all the other dope folks that make NYMG great—I love y'all. I just have one question—what you drinking??!!!

And of course, my homies from the dark web!! LOL. Catherine Knight-Steele, Andre Brock, Sarah Florini, Jenny Korn, Khadijah Costley White, Miriam Sweeney, and Lois Scheidt. I appreciate y'all's never ending support!

I would also like to thank my beautiful family—Kayland, Anteaus, and Jay—for inspiring me every day. Game Over FAM!!!!

# WOKE GAMING

# INTRODUCTION

*Not a Post-Racism and Post-Misogyny Promised Land:*
*Video Games as Instruments of (In)Justice*

KISHONNA L. GRAY AND DAVID J. LEONARD

**B**REAKING NEWS: NOVEMBER 15, 2017
Amid the daily reminders on our social media feeds that racism and sexism remain defining forces in our culture, there are also moments of respite. Out of the constant turmoil that Black women experience around hair, the release of an immersive and interactive game provided a glimmer of hope in the fall of 2017. Created by Momo Pixel, *Hair Nah* allows players to customize an avatar who can "smack away as many white hands" as possible as they attempt to touch locs, twists, braids, and relaxed Black hair (Callahan 2017).

Not surprisingly, the game quickly went viral. Both the game and its resonance captured a convergence of powerful contemporary racial and gendered dynamics and histories, from Black hair politics to the history of white supremacy as it relates to the hyperpolicing and surveillance of Black women's bodies, from the daily toll of racial microaggressions Black women face to the exhaustion of our current political moment.

Yet the game's power reflects its rejection of these histories and its embrace of a virtual and physical clapback. As a game produced and developed by a Black woman, the shock, surprise, and hope resulting from the release of the game speaks to the whiteness of the video game industry and the systemic refusal to give voice to the experience of Black women. The game's intervention, centering of Blackness, and embrace of resistance all embody the game's refusal of erasure. From its conception to reception,

**I.1.** A screenshot of gameplay from Momo Pixel's game, *Hair Nah*, showing hands being swatted away from a Black woman's hair. Courtesy of Momo Pixel

*Hair Nah* exemplifies the yearning for transformative games. By centering the experiences of Black women, the existence of such a game is disruptive in itself as it illustrates the power and potential to use video games, online technology, and game culture to give voice to the experience of Black women and other marginalized communities, resisting and otherwise challenging dehumanizing representations. The game and its narrative construction locate structural oppression in the everyday. Playing this game highlights the power and potential of resistance of everyday and systemic violences within everyday cultural engagement. This game captured the essence of the *why* and the *how* of the current text.

### GAMERS, NOT HATERS

We, the editors of this collection, are gamers. We play video games; we enjoy games and have done so for a very long time. We are also scholars, teachers, and critics who have long been uneasy about the costs and consequences of the racism, misogyny, and xenophobia within game culture. As a Black female scholar (Dr. Kishonna Gray) and a white male scholar

(Dr. David J. Leonard) with varied experiences and different vantage points, we have both seen the toxicity and violence that pervade gaming as well as the individualized and systemic harm gaming culture sustains. From Gamergate to the white grievance politics of the 2016 US election, to the daily experiences of white female gamers and those of color, the ways gaming is entangled with mainstream cultures of systematic exploitation and oppression is clear. While video games may be a distraction to some communities and a source of power and pleasure to others, they can at times also be a source of violence, oppression, pain, and trauma. Our identities shape these complex and messy relationships with games.

Like the contributors to this volume, we enter into the world of video games with our own identities and experiences intact. Our disparate social locations and varied privileges shape our relationship to gaming and gaming's relationship to us. From the Internet to the constructive worlds of virtual gameplay, the digital world offers spaces of play and freedom in a post-ism promised land of equality and justice, but our experiences reveal the fissures found within those spaces.

## DO BLACK LIVES MATTER?

From stereotypical representations of hypersexual women to those depicting people of color in stereotypical ways, video games have the power to perpetuate injustice (Malkowski and Russworm 2017). Associated gaming communities across console and computer games of all genres also fuel toxic practices of antisocial behavior, racism, heterosexism, and misogynistic language in in-game chats. At one level, video games mirror and embody the injustices we see throughout popular culture and in society at large. For example, by signalling the impossibility of survival for Black and Brown men, the opening mission within *Battlefield 1* illustrates this trend. This first-person, World War I military shooting game allows the player to engage as a member of the Harlem Hellfighters. Given the erasure of soldiers of color within war games as well as popular culture as a whole, there was initially much praise around the inclusion of this regiment, comprised of Black men who identified mostly as African American and Puerto Rican. The game, however, still forces death upon the player, even remarking in the opening sequence that survival is not an option.

Upon the first death, a screen appears providing a fictional name and timeline of life for the gamer to preview.

The gamer then spawns the life of another Harlem Hellfighter, and he too succumbs to the violences of war. This trend continues throughout the game, causing many Black gamers on social media to reflect on their uncomfortableness witnessing and experiencing hypervisible Black Death. We liken this pattern within *Battlefield I* to the present era of consuming and sharing Black Death via associated hashtags, where we witness the final moments of Black and Brown life without context or a historic backdrop (e.g., #PhilandoCastile, #EricGarner, #TamirRice). The humanity of Black lives is lost, reducing life to the spectacle of Black Death. The pleasure in and normalization of Black Death is not limited to historical games. And the dialectics between gaming and entrenched social injustice is not limited to how games explicitly teach white supremacist ideologies.

Whether visible in the persistent color line that shapes the production, dissemination, and legitimization of dominant stereotypes within the industry itself, or in the dehumanizing representations commonplace within digital spaces, video games encode the injustices that pervade society as a whole. According to Williams, Martins, Consalvo, and Ivory, gaming is a space defined by the "systematic over-representation of males, white and adults and a systematic under-representation of females, Hispanics, Native Americans, children and the elderly" (2009, 815). The criminalization of Black and Brown bodies throughout society in general and video games specifically, and the profiling of Black and Brown gamers that is endemic to gaming culture, illustrates not only how race operates within video games but the dialectics between the virtual and the lived, the spaces of play and the spaces of the everyday.

Gaming imagines a world of good and evil, of domination and annihilation, where whiteness and American manhood characterize protectors and heroes—values not afforded the pixelated Harlem Hellfighters in *Battlefield 1*. In this way, games provide a training ground for the consumption of narratives and stereotypes as well as opportunities to become instruments of hegemony; they offer spaces of white male play and pleasures, and create a virtual and lived reality where white maleness is empowered to police and criminalize the Other. Games provide opportunities to both learn and share the language of racism and sexism, and the grammar of empire, all while perpetuating cultures of violence and privilege.

Yet despite the ubiquitous violence within video games, gaming also offers a potential space for change—for a different kind of gaming. As noted by Helen Young, in "Racial Logics, Franchising, and Video Game Genres: The Lord of the Rings," video games "can also be designed to address racial stereotyping and 'get a person to understand one's self-concept and aspects of a culture that may be different to one's own" (Lee 2013, 147). Fantasy video games, moreover, can challenge white hegemonies. Within online game worlds, the technology, communities of gamers, and digital reality itself are important and potentially powerful tools for broader fights for social justice.

## REIMAGING REALITY: VIRTUAL FREEDOM DREAMERS

We see the ample potential and possibility of gaming culture. We see the ways that people of color, women, LGBTQ people, and their allies have challenged the hegemony of whiteness and hetero-maleness within gaming culture in terms of both production and representation. Even as the mainstream industry continues to be dominated by heterosexual white men, a huge diversity of people outside the industry, on the margins, have been creating their own video games for years, beyond the focus of mainstream gaming culture.

Anna Anthropy, a transgender video game developer, took on game development and design because she was fed up with the AAA offerings of limited character development and clichéd story lines. Using Game Maker, a novice-friendly computer program, she began creating her own games. Accessible game design tools enable communities traditionally excluded from the power structures in gaming to participate and create their own innovative games. Anthropy has also employed Twine among other platforms for her games, which range in cultural and political context. They include *Keep Me Occupied*, a collaborative two-player arcade game featuring Occupy protesters in Oakland, California, who are subjected to tear gas and grenades, as well as *Dys4ia*, a game based on the creator's experiences with hormone replacement therapy. Her critically acclaimed games often repurpose traditional game mechanics and narratives in provocative ways. In a gaming context that often privileges battle and competition, and in an era where the term *social justice warrior* is often deployed as a slur and a rhetorical insult, it becomes imperative to shield oneself from the attacks of those threatened by diversifying content in gaming. Anthropy notes that her content has been influenced by queer scholars such as Audre Lorde and alternative comic writers like Diane DiMassa, with their focus on queer love and transidentity (Lipinski 2012). While not all her games feature queer content, Anthropy states that her queer identity is always visible and influences the narratives she constructs around her games.

These examples and others make evident some of the ways in which game makers have sought to tear down the walls of the hegemony of gaming and demand equity in each and every space. They demonstrate the potential of games as teachers of alternative narratives and histories, as challenges to the ideologies of hate, persistent inequalities, and violent injustices. They model the possibility of games giving voice to the experiences, (intersectional) identities, and histories of otherwise marginalized and erased communities. While current gaming culture systematically embraces ideologies that make clear that white males lives are the only ones that matter, it's clear that games can show that all lives matter, representationally and materially.

Games can also foster critical dialogue, as shown in the ways that discourse surrounding games and gameplay have opened up key conversations about the histories of minstrelsy and cultural appropriation, and around misogyny and rape culture. Calls to challenge gaming for its reliance on representations and narratives of Blackness as criminal, female as sexual object, Asian as exotic, Muslim as terrorist, and so much more, not only demand shifts in representations but also speaks to larger political, social, and lived contexts. To change gaming in an effort to change culture—to use gaming as an instrument and technology within larger social movements—is to bolster the toolbox for justice.

## MISOGYNY, RAPE CULTURE, AND GAMERGATE

Games are a significant cultural force, as is evident in the connective tissue between the gaming pedagogies of violence and the 2016 election. Rape culture, toxic masculinity, and homophobia are ubiquitous to gaming, not only reflecting these ideologies but also existing as teachers, pedagogies, and platforms for the dissemination of dehumanizing representations and ideologies of injustice and violence. The injustices that predominate gaming culture also sit at the core of the political, social, and communal arrangements of mainstream US culture.

We see the importance of games in examining the relationship between rape culture and the objectification of women as sources of male pleasure and domination (Malikowski and Russworm 2017; Benstein 2013; Fox, Bailenson, and Tricase 2013; Salter and Blodgett 2012; Dill, Brown, and Collins 2008). Gaming culture is rife with the realities of #MeToo. As noted by the New Jersey Coalition Against Sexual Assault in "Gaming Culture and Rape Culture: How #GamerGate's Misogyny Prevents a Safer Space,"

> In current gaming culture, the connection between sexuality and violence in games supports a misogynistic version of reality, in which the majority of heroes are males displaying their masculinity through violence, and women are serving as background characters to be objectified. As a result, gaming culture is mirroring, and perpetuating, rape culture. The problems that exist in gaming culture not only relate to the visual representation of women, but also through the language used by gamers in their interactions with their counterparts. Technology now provides ample opportunity to interact with others in the game, which has led to a normalization of violent language to match the game's level of violence. Name-calling is a standard practice, and studies show female gamers receive higher levels of taunts and sexually aggressive remarks while playing than men. As a bonding method, teams assert their dominance by using sexually violent language, often referring to winning or beating a player as "raping" them. Perhaps without knowing, their consistent use of this language minimizes the seriousness of sexual assault. With 1 in 5 women and 1 in 71 men experiencing sexual assault in their lifetimes, these violent interactions impact survivors in what should be a safe space.

These effects and the presence of rape culture and misogyny (Shaw 2015) within video games and gaming culture was fully realized during the 2014 controversy known as Gamergate (Quinn 2017).

During Gamergate, the divisions and fissures, inequalities and unspoken violences that were longstanding within video game culture bubbled to surface. Despite the civil war (Jilani 2014) trope that came to define Gamergate, the moment was not a battle between two equally powerful constituencies. In the face of criticism from feminists, people of color, and other critical voices, "'gamer culture and traditional conservatives" (Jilani 2014) sought to not only demonize but also silence those who sought to change gaming culture.

Lamenting political correctness, multiculturalism, and the betrayal of gaming tradition, Gamergate also empowered this narrative of white male victimhood. Gamergate was defined by such belief: It was not that women in the video game industry were unfairly treated; it was not that people of color were rendered invisible through stereotypes within game spaces; it was not that gamers of color and women endured mistreatment online. The injustices within gaming could be found in oppression and unfair treatment of white males. As such, the self-appointed heroes of Gamergate were white men who dared to challenge political correctness. They wanted to make sure games stayed great. Seeing change as a threat, they fought to preserve the hegemony of white male hetero gaming and gamers. Not surprisingly, the contested ground that lay at the foundation of the racial and gendered culture wars that became visible during Gamergate would become fully visible during the 2016 election. The white grievance politics that coalesced around the candidacy of Donald Trump propelled Gamergate as well.

In so many ways, Gamergate predicted and sowed the seeds that sprouted the Trump presidency. Two months before the 2016 election, Amanda Marcotte wrote:

> For those who survived Gamergate, a 2014 dustup over the place
> of women in the video-gaming world, the 2016 election is instill-
> ing a deep and unpleasant sense of déjà vu. It's not just that
> Republican presidential nominee Donald Trump and his acolytes
> are playing to the same grievance about "social justice warriors"

who dare to think that white men should share power with women and people of color. It's that Trump and his men are using the same tools as the Gamergaters: gaslighting, projection, working the refs and leaning heavily on often subconscious double standards that allow white men to have more benefit of the doubt than others.

What's really terrifying is that for a surprisingly long time Gamergate worked: For months, anti-feminists in the tech world were extremely effective at undermining feminists and creating the illusion that a bunch of bullies might have legitimate grievances. Eventually, most witnesses to Gamergate woke up and saw it for what it was. I have no doubt the same will happen with the Trump campaign. Even if many people don't get it right now, history will remember the campaign as a black mark on our democracy, forged in bigotry.

Similarly, in "What Gamergate Should Have Taught Us about the 'Alt-right,'" Matt Lees highlights the parallels between Gamergate, the rise of the alt-right, and the Trump presidency. The shared opposition to truth, the propensity to see themselves as victims of feminists, people of color, and the Other, and the embrace of bullying, can be seen within each "movement." Each has embraced online technology to not only articulate their grievance politics but to silence, demean, and terrorize opposition.

From this perspective and history, we can understand Gamergate as a movement that focuses on white men's anxieties over losing ground in a universe assumed to be homogenous. The rallying point that emerged was retaliation for the recent increase in feminist critiques of video games and gaming culture (Chess and Shaw 2014). This toxic technoculture and geek masculinity positioned itself as a victim in the social justice warrior era (Massanari 2017; Gray, Buyokozturk, and Hill 2017). As scholars have noted, the culture and subculture within gaming focuses on white men, targets white men, and is dominated by male perspectives (Gray 2012). Before Gamergate, when women and people of color breached this assumed norm, they were targeted using symbolic violence, which was generally relegated and contained as isolated incidents between a few individuals. The events of Gamergate, however, revealed that women, especially those who publicly oppose marginalization and symbolic violence, were met with real violence outside of these games. The public harassment of Zoe Quinn, Anita Sarkeesian, and Brianna Wu, among others, who endured highly publicized doxxing, rape threats, and death threats, serves a an example of this shift.

When Gamergate began, Zoe Quinn was the first woman who was targeted and experienced violence in both physical and digital settings. She was accused of trading sexual favors with journalists for positive reviews of her game *Depression Quest*. Initially the target of symbolic violence, Quinn was shamed for crafting a non-traditional game and for suffering from depression. Subsequently, her former partner, Eron Gjoni, created *The Zoe Post*—a website on which he published his experiences with Quinn and claimed that she had sexual relationships with multiple individuals during their relationship, potentially including gaming journalists (https://thezoepost.wordpress.com). Quickly thereafter, Quinn became the target of anonymous threats through Twitter and other social media outlets, and in August 2014 she was doxxed—meaning her personal information (including address, phone number, and bank information) was published online (Parkin 2014). These acts of violence jeopardized Quinn's safety, forcing her to flee her home.

Brianna Wu, also a video game designer, became another public, high-profile target of Gamergate when she shared a meme poking fun at Gamergate on Twitter. This meme was reworded to mock her instead, and came with a slew of death and rape threats. When asked about harassment from Gamergate, Wu stated "[t]he truth is, I'm a pretty visible woman in a very small field. I think they see the changes I'm advocating, and it scares them" (TransEthics 2016). As she was so public with her criticisms, the men of Gamergate embarked on a significant campaign to silence her. However, Wu has continued as an active participant in the game industry, reminding us of the potential and power of changing the gaming industry and how technology can be an instrument of justice and equality.

Similarly, feminist media critic Anita Sarkeesian, another target of Gamergate, has refused to be silent in the face of gaming injustices. Known for her "Tropes vs. Women in Video Games" video series, Sarkeesian has been accused repeatedly of promoting feminist gaming at the expense of white male gamers. In the aftermath of Gamergate, Sarkeesian faced greater threats for her work. In October 2014, Sarkeesian was scheduled to speak at Utah State University. Following anonymous emails and letters threatening harm to both Sarkeesian and those who attended her campus presentation, the event was cancelled. One threat promised that the lecture would become "the deadliest school shooting in American history" while another stated, "one way or another, I'm going to make sure they die" (McDonald 2014). Though no one was harmed, the threat of real violence was significant.

These attacks have come to define gaming culture. Challenges to the lack of diversity or the gross stereotypes promoted by mainstream games are often met with demonization and rhetorical violence directed at those who merely seek to help gaming reach its fullest potential (Everett 2017). While responding to attacks on specific individuals and acts of prejudice, discrimination, and microaggressions, we must also examine the structural and institutional factors that allow them to exist. The daily practices of gaming continue to sustain what Mark Anthony Neal calls *micro-nooses* and a violent lived reality for many on and offline. The stakes are too high to ignore the harm of games and turn our backs on the technological possibility of interventionist games.

## JUSTICE IN THE ASHES OF GAMERGATE

This collection grew from the ashes of Gamergate. We seek to follow in the footsteps of those who have challenged how games have furthered the military industrial complex, justifying our state of perpetual warfare (Payne 2016; Huntemann and Payne 2009; Leonard 2004). It moves forward in memory of #TrayvonMartin and #SandraBland, in this moment where Black Death is a source of white pleasure, where Black bodies have been a part of the entertainment structure for white audiences (Glenn and Cunningham 2009). This trend continues within video games and gaming culture. To be immune from violence, to be insulated from injustice, to be able to cash in on the privilege encoded by/in white supremacy, misogyny, and heteronormativity is a source of pleasure. The collective efforts of the authors of this text seek to move the conversation beyond the critical examination of the virtual pedagogies of racism, sexism, and homophobia to rightly examine the role of digital games as purveyors of violence, as spaces for the normalization of violence and domination, as sites for the consumption of worlds that privilege the American empire, militarism, and white male heroes. We seek to highlight and celebrate games and gamers that demand change from within games and beyond.

We find inspiration not simply in fighting these injustices and in identifying the connective tissue between gaming and lived violence, but in sites of resistance. We find hope in the growing number of "diversity-minded developers constructing game worlds around 'sheroes'" (Everett 2016, xii). And we see alternatives with Dean Chan's (2009) discussion of Joseph DeLappe "pacifist act of civil disobedience" while playing *America's Army*. According to Kathleen Greg (2006):

> Joseph DeLappe is careful about typos. In the multiplayer war game *America's Army* DeLappe can see the soldiers around him advancing, but he doesn't care to join them. Logged in as "Dead_in_Iraq," DeLappe types the names of soldiers killed in Iraq, and the date of their death, into the game's text messaging system, such that the information scrolls across the screen for all users to see. DeLappe's goal is simple: He plans to memorialize the name of every service member killed in Iraq.

Such interventions not only reveal the possibility of games and gaming technology, of "video games of the oppressed" (Frasca quoted in Dyer-Withford and de Peuter 2009, 197), but also hold the potential to redefine the gaming community. These sources of opposition are as much reflective of gaming as those individuals and games that perpetuate inequality and violence. People such as Joseph DeLappe, Anna Anthropy, and Anita Sarkeesian, or games like *Depression Quest, Never Alone,* and *We are Chicago* define games as much as *Grand Theft Auto* and Gamergate.

As such, this collection seeks to document the voices, games, and dreams that persist in the face of blockades, gatekeepers, and a culture of violence. These contributors and the world they illuminate give us hope, all while reminding us that we must not cede power or control to those who use tiki torches, virtual spaces, and hashtags for the sake of power and continued domination.

From these chapters, we see possibilities in the endless examples of "playing against the grain" (Chien 2009), whether as game modifications, cultural interventions, or the embracing of collective resistance. Despite the hegemony of gaming practices that "require algorithm-like behaviour from players" (Chien 2009, 250), change exists because of the agency and creativity of gamers (Everett 2016; de Peuter 2015; Meads 2015, Frasca 2004). From gamers to games themselves, we agree with Tanner Higgin (2009) who writes, "Video games do have the capability to generate emotional affect while tackling complex and controversial narrative material" (254). The chapters and the contributors reveal this truth not only in the gamers, games, artefacts, and discourses that they spotlight here but also in their own work and presence within the gaming community.

We find hope in games like *Sunset, Mafia III,* and *Watch Dogs 2* that create worlds where Black humanity is fully realized and even celebrated. We appreciate the destruction of the slave economy on the shores of Haiti by Adewale in A*ssassin's Creed: Black Flag Freedom Cry.* We praise the fierceness of Aveline de Grandpre from the same game, who becomes an assassin to destroy the slave trafficking enterprise in New Orleans and successfully liberates a slave community. We see possibility in characters like Marcus Halloway in *Watch Dogs 2,* whose existence gives voice and power in Black nerdom and hacking culture. We acknowledge Larae Barrett, who used her voice and platform to advocate for oppression in the police state in *The Division.* These interventions are reflective of the efforts put forth by individuals such as Tanya DePass and the #INeedDiverseGames initiative, which urged more diverse content and more inclusion of diverse voices within these development spaces. We shout out to podcasters and live streamers who make themselves vulnerable to harassment in spaces created by and for white men. Their digital practices illuminate innovative cultural practices of creating and delivering content. We find hope and possibility in the work of Safiya Noble and others who are challenging the ways that technology not only reflects racial injustice but also perpetuates it. Our dreams and reserved optimism emanates from the scholars, gamers, and games discussed in this volume, which collectively demonstrate how games can be change agents at multiple levels. It is our hope that this collection builds from these works and advances the work being done by so many gamers.

## WOKE CHAPTERS: THE WORK OF THE WAKENING

This volume gathers established and emerging scholars in the fields of games, media, and cultural studies to interrogate individual and collective experiences inside video games, gaming communities, and the industry as well as address the structural factors impacting the reality and outcomes of the same. Each of the authors considers the ways gaming holistically operates as a medium with the potential for positive impact as well as the replication and recreating of inequalities. Together, the essays in this collection look for hope; for the possibility in gaming, gamers, and in the industry to change not only the gaming world but the broader social inequalities that we experience both virtually and in everyday realities.

Part 1 of this volume highlights the nature of gaming violence and how alternative readings, counter play, and oppositional gaming not only alters game spaces but disrupts our collective relationship to destruction, mayhem, and pain. The section begins with Rob Cover's powerful focus on the precarity of the body within gaming communities, situating ethics at the core of the discussion of gaming and gamers. This essay rightfully acknowledges the trend to continue discussing disembodied digital experiences. By centering the body, this chapter makes the case for "the *obligation* of gamers to act ethically and non-violently towards other gamers, non-gamers, in care-of-the-self and care-of-all-others." Alternative narratives are essential to disrupt the power that the hegemonic structure has created, especially its violent overtones. Any broader transformation in gaming depends on highlighting alternate ways to envision traditionally violent games and narratives.

In chapter 2, "Power, Violence, and the Mask: Representations of Criminal Subjectivities in *Grand Theft Auto Online*," Rowlands, Ratnabalasuriar, Hobart, Noel, Allen, Reed, and Gonzales explore the opportunities of subverting typical violent play offered by the creator aspects of the game. While *Grand Theft Auto* is typically associated with violence against women and stereotypical representations of people of color, the authors focus on its mod culture, which showcases creator and maker spaces. The powerful narratives unveiled in the chapter demonstrate the potential to transform traditionally hostile spaces by identifying alternate content and integrating digital storytelling.

In part 2, we bring together two authors who focus on the economics of gaming and the business dimensions of the global enterprise of games. While recognizing profits, transnational capitalism, and the logics of neo-liberalism, these authors reflect on how access shapes the intervention possibilities of games. Directly challenging the structure of the gaming industry is one necessary step in transforming it. One key myth, rooted in unacknowledged privilege, is the notion that anybody can make games. In chapter 3, Stephanie Orme powerfully questions this idea, along with the question that has dominated critiques of equality and inclusivity: "If people don't like games the way they are, why don't they just make their own?" Orme explores the structural barriers that affect incorporation and a hegemonic culture that influences outcomes. In chapter 4 Zixue Tai and Fengbin Hu offer an important economic perspective within online gaming by highlighting the precarious existence of gold farmers in online gaming in China. While their work isn't specific to gaming alone, they reveal how economics effect how gamers produce, consume, and engage with gaming culture. While gaming concerns representation, including race, gender, and nation, capitalist inequities also shape the economics of gaming. This chapter demonstrates how gold farmers negotiate a volatile existence in the micro economy of gaming.

When we started this collection on the heels of Gamergate, we had no idea what was in store for this nation politically, culturally, and socially, including the rise of President Trump and the reinvigoration of feminist struggles. Part 3, on feminist gaming and counter representations, speaks to this moment. In chapter 5, Vysotsky and Allaway provide us with a glimpse of this ongoing struggle, especially for women within the gaming industry. The culture of video games is both a microcosm of our moment and the staging ground for a larger movement. While spotlighting these shared histories, this section also provides a roadmap toward gender justice inside and outside the world of video games.

In chapter 6, "The Perpetual Crusade: *Rise of the Tomb Raider*, Religious Extremism, and the Problem of Empire" Kristen Bezio continues the focus on addressing structural inequalities by reflecting on how players themselves can complicate narratives of colonialism and taking over space. Discussions surrounding *Tomb Raider* heroine Lara Croft usually highlight narratives that disrupt traditional gender norms and misogyny in games. Demonstrating an intersectional approach to gendered analysis, Kristin Bezio rightfully interrogates the continuation of Western imperial perspectives, Islamophobia, and colonial paradigms in video games.

Andrea Braithwaite examines the 1990s girls' games movement in chapter 7, "Nancy Drew and the Case of Girl Games." She simultaneously demonstrates the historic nature of the gendered culture war in gaming while elucidating the ways that resistance has produced alternative representations within gaming culture. Similarly, Stephanie Jennings provides a discussion on critical epistemologies in video game narratives by focusing on her own auto ethnographic approach in chapter 8. This approach to creating content and narratives in games disrupts traditional masculine narratives and essentialist gender binaries.

Amid a culture of sexism and misogynistic violence, the gaming industry has embraced the rhetoric of diversity and inclusion. In response to protests, game developers have incorporated statements asserting their commitment to producing diverse games and building an industry no longer dominated by white men. The push to diversify is not simply about demographics or public relations but building a culture of voices that imagine more just and empowering realities. Diversity for diversity's sake is insufficient and is instead a starting point in the struggle for justice inside and outside gaming.

Part 4, "Gaming Against the Grain," examines these counter narratives and alternative realities, highlighting how games can do more than simply contribute to brochure diversity. Specifically, this section focuses on whether gaming culture can foster critical consciousness, aid in participatory democracy, and effect social change. It centers the silenced and marginalized, offering counter narratives to those post-racial and post-gendered fantasies that so often obscure the violent context of production and consumption.

Despite the endless possibilities of gaming as spaces of disruption, interruption, and transformation, games and the gaming world—whether the industry itself or those inhabited by gamers—generally remains a space of violence, bigotry, and harassment. In chapter 9, Karen Skardzius looks at the supportive relationships for LGBTQ gamers in *World of*

*Warcraft* and explores norms established around sexuality and how those who identify as LGBTQ are not extended full citizenship in the *WoW* community. Further, in chapter 10, "Managing Online Game Communities: Lesson from Past Attempts, Players' Experiences, and Workplace Strategies" Amanda Cote moves on to a discussion of player experiences in gaming communities. This chapter examines women's responses to and strategies in coping with online harassment. The alternative games and alternative spaces that are created in gaming provide an engaging analysis highlighting not only the structural and institutional factors perpetuating inequalities that permeate gaming culture but also alternate versions of what reality can be within these spaces.

Chapter 11 continues to examine the power to disrupt traditional narratives with an examination of *The Legend of Zelda*. Here, Kathryn Hemmann explores fan fiction and fan generated content to reflect on what different content players would like to see. What kinds of stories might they tell? The fans who propel these industries have perspectives that are not valued by the gaming industry. Hemmann suggests that change will come through harnessing the creativity and voices of fans. In offering the above framework, this chapter adheres to the volume's purpose by being grounded in the concrete situations of marginalized members within gaming culture. It reveals that despite the violence and bigotry directed in the real world at commentators, academics, content producers, and gamers who have spoken out about the persistent sexism, racism, misogyny, homophobia and other injustices in the gaming space, counter narratives and alternative voices, games, and spaces for the articulation of "freedom dreams" (Kelley 2002) abound.

Given the post-racial rhetorical turn of the last eight years, it is important to push conversations about gaming and gamers beyond diversity to expose the disconnect between rhetorics of multiculturalism and the struggle for justice and equity. Persistent contradictions exist between ideals of inclusion espoused within the video game industry and society as a whole and continued injustices within structural and institutional contexts. This final section highlights work that intervenes in the culture of violence and inequity by focusing on how games have the potential to foster change through empathy and compassion. While recognizing the ways that racism, xenophobia, sexism, homophobia and power shape the potential for empathy, where certain bodies bestowed with the privileges of humanity are afforded compassion and the politics of understanding, these chapters reflect on the power, possibilities, and potential of humanizing games of social change.

Chapter 12 examines this potential through the game *Everyday Racism*, which attempts to generate empathy and pushes for more anti-racist content in games. As Fordyce, Neale, and Apperley outline, online spaces have proven to be effective venues in building and supporting old racist practices. To combat this, scholars, activists, and everyday people have been using these same technologies to thwart the effectiveness of racist organizing online. The *Everyday Racism* game explores how people of color experience discrimination, particularly conveyed through mobile devices, in order to elicit anti-racist responses. Fordyce, Neale, and Apperley offer an important bridge to Barkley and Foglesong, who, in chapter 13, "Activism, Awareness, and Sympathy in Video Games," examine the potential for persuasive and serious games to increase empathy and effect social change. This chapter also assesses the ability of these games to reach large audiences and have widespread appeal, concluding that negative opinions about games with social commentary limits their overall success. Anderson-Barkley and Foglesong note that simplistic narratives, aesthetics, and gaming playability can limit audiences for these social transformative games, at the same time that they suffer from unfair perceptions that conscious games are just not fun to play.

The collection concludes with a powerful demonstration of how inclusive design can improve outcomes for marginalized users and generate empathy as well. Illustrating that change and transformative possibilities can come from fans, diversity in games, aesthetics, and design, Bertolo, Mariani and Conti show how in *DiscrimiNation*, a persuasive board game that showcases a viable means to improve social inclusion and communitarian comprehension, games can inspire, inform, and enrich in the name of justice and equality.

In a moment of increased fear and the prospect of even more inequality in every aspect of American life, where the already vulnerable face a dangerous tomorrow, video games provide the language and tools to imagine the world anew. The games, gamers, technologies, and movements discussed here point to endless possibilities. They imagine worlds based in justice; they offer technology and other tools that can facilitate transformation. The public outcry associated with Gamergate has put *why* at the forefront of game studies. Gamergaters, who gained media attention through their misogynist and racist attacks on women gamers and developers, even tried to justify their campaign as an attempt to restore the ethics needed in video game journalism. This attack directed at gamers and fighters of social justice, those believers in a better tomorrow, brought the hidden reality of harassment, cyberbullying, sexism, racism, homophobia, transphobia, and other injustices to light. While the work continues to be met with resistance, we see the power in community, in the persistent demand to break down the virtual walls of segregation, in the challenges to the sources of inequality and injustice. Yet, being woke isn't enough. We must, as Angela Rye reminds us, always be awake and at work in our disruption of the injustice of gaming or the worlds we each inhabit.

WORKS CITED

Bernstein, J. 2013. "The Scientific Connection between Sexist Video Games and Rape Culture." *Buzzfeed*, October 23. www.buzzfeed.com/josephbernstein/the-scentific-connection-between-sexist-video-game-and-rape?utm_term=.gcloA7G8GK#.quyPqMrgrQ.

Callahan, Y. 2017. "If You're a Black Woman Who's Tired of White People Touching Your Hair, There's a Game for That." *The Root*, November 15. https://thegrapevine.theroot.com/if-youre-a-black-woman-whos-tired-of-white-people-askin-1820505693.

Chan, D. 2009. "Dead-in-Iraq: The Spatial Politics of Game Art Activism and the In-Game Protest." In *Joystick Soldiers: The Politics of Play in Military Video Games*, edited by N. B. Huntemann and M. T. Payne, 272–86. New York: Routledge.

Chess, S., and Shaw, A. 2015. "A Conspiracy of Fishes, or, How We Learned to Stop Worrying about #GamerGate and Embrace Hegemonic Masculinity." *Journal of Broadcasting and Electronic Media* 59 (1): 208–20.

Chien, I. 2009. "Playing against the Grain." In *Joystick Soldiers: The Politics of Play in Military Video Games*, edited by N. B. Huntemann and M. T. Payne, 239–51. New York: Routledge.

Consalvo, M. 2007. *Cheating: Gaining Advantage in Video Games*. Cambridge, MA: MIT Press.

Craig, K. 2006. "Dead in Iraq: It's No Game." *Wired*, June 6. www.wired.com/2006/06/dead-in-iraq-its-no-game.

de Peuter, G. 2015. "Online Games and Counterplay." *The International Encyclopedia of Digital Communication and Society*, 1–7. Hoboken, NJ: Wiley-Blackwell.

Dill, K. E., Brown, B. P., and Collins, M. A. 2008. "Effects of Exposure to Sex-Stereotyped Video Game Characters on Tolerance of Sexual Harassment." *Journal of Experimental Social Psychology* 44 (5): 1402–8.

Dyer-Witheford, N., and de Peuter, G. 2009. *Games of Empire: Global Capitalism and Video Games.* Minneapolis: University of Minnesota Press.

Everett, A. 2017. "Foreword." In *Gaming Representation: Race, Gender, and Sexuality in Video Games,* edited by J. Malkowski, and T. Russworm. Bloomington: University of Indiana Press.

Fox, J., Bailenson, J. N., and Tricase, L. 2013. "The Embodiment of Sexualized Virtual Selves: The Proteus Effect and Experiences of Self-Objectification via Avatars." *Computers in Human Behavior* (29): 930–38.

Frasca, G. 2004. "Video Games of the Oppressed: Critical Thinking, Education, Tolerance, and Other Trivial Issues." In *First-Person: New Media as Story, Performance, and Game,* edited by N. Wardrip-Furnin and P. Harrigan, 85–94. Cambridge, MA: MIT Press.

Glenn, C. L., and Cunningham, L. J. (2009). "The Power of Black Magic: The Magical Negro and White Salvation in Film." *Journal of Black Studies,* 40 (2), 135–52.

Gray, K. L. 2014. *Race, Gender, and Deviance in Xbox Live: Theoretical Perspectives from the Virtual Margins.* New York: Routledge.

Gray, K. L. 2012. "Intersecting Oppressions and Online Communities: Examining the Experiences of Women of Color in Xbox Live." *Information, Communication and Society* 15 (3): 411–28.

Gray, K. L., Buyukozturk, B., and Hill, Z. G. 2017. "Blurring the Boundaries: Using Gamergate to Examine 'Real' and Symbolic Violence against Women in Contemporary Gaming Culture." *Sociology Compass* 11 (3). http://onlinelibrary.wiley.com /doi/10.1111/soc4.12458/abstract.

Higgin, T. 2009. "'Turn the Game Console off Right Now!' War, Subjectivity, and Control in *Metal Gear Solid 2.*" In *Joystick Soldiers: The Politics of Play in Military Video Games,* edited by N. B. Huntemann and M. T. Payne, 252–71. New York: Routledge.

Huntemann, N. B., and Payne, M. T. (eds.). 2009. *Joystick Soldiers: The Politics of Play in Military Video Games.* New York: Routledge.

Jilani, Z. 2014. "'I Want a Straight White Male Gaming Convention': Inside the Culture War Raging in the Video Gaming World." *Salon,* September 8. www.salon .com/2014/09/08/i_want_a_straight_white_male_gaming_convention_how_a _culture_war_exploded_in_the_video_gaming_world.

Kelley, R. D. G. 2002. *Freedom Dreams: The Black Radical Imagination.* Boston: Beacon Press.

Lee, Joey J. 2013. "Game Mechanics to Promote New Understandings of Identity and Ethnic Minority Stereotypes." *Digital Culture and Education* 5: 127–50.

Lees, M. 2016. "What Gamergate Should Have Taught Us about the 'Alt-right.'" *Guardian,* December 1.

Leonard, D. J. 2004. "Unsettling the Military Entertainment Complex: Video Games and a Pedagogy of Peace." *Studies in Media and Information Literacy Education* 4 (4): 1–8.

Leonard, D. J. 2003. "'Live in Your World, Play in Ours': Race, Video Games, and Consuming the Other." *Studies in Media and Information Literacy Education* 3 (4): 1–9.

Lipinski, J. 2012. "Video-Game Designer Anna Anthropy Describes the Life of a Radical, Queer, Transgender Gamer." *Politico*, April.

Malkowski, J., and Russworm, T. M., eds. 2017. *Gaming Representation: Race, Gender, and Sexuality in Video Games*. Bloomington: University of Indiana Press.

Marcotte, A. 2016. "Donald Trump's Campaign Really Is Gamergate Being Played Out on a National Scale." *Salon*, September 15. www.salon.com/2016/09/15/gamergater.

Massanari, A. 2017. "#Gamergate and The Fappening: How Reddit's Algorithm, Governance, and Culture Support Toxic Technocultures." *New Media and Society* 19 (3): 329–46.

McDonald, S. N. 2014. "'Gamergate': Feminist Video Game Critic Anita Sarkeesian Cancels Utah Lecture after Threat." *Washington Post*, October 15.

Meads, A. F. 2015. *Understanding Counterplay in Video Games*. New York: Routledge.

New Jersey Coalition Against Sexual Assault. "Gaming Culture and Rape Culture: How #GamerGate's Misogyny Prevents a Safer Space." https://njcasa.org/news/gaming-culture-rape-culture-gamergates-misogyny-prevents-safer-space.

Payne, M. T. 2016. *Playing War: Military Video Games After 9/11*. New York: NYU Press.

Quinn, Z. 2017. *Crash Override: How Gamergate (Nearly) Destroyed My Life, and How We Can Win the Fight against Online Hate*. New York: Hachette Books.

Rye, A. 2018. "'WORK Woke!' WATCH Angela Rye's Breathtaking Stand AGAINST Trump." February 1. https://www.youtube.com/watch?v=KynElYjK7tU.

Salter, A., and Blodgett, B. 2012. "Hypermasculinity and Dickwolves: The Contentious Role of Women in the New Gaming Public." *Journal of Broadcasting and Electronic Media* 56 (3): 401–16.

Shaw. A. 2015. *Gaming at the Edge: Sexuality and Gender at the Margins of Gamer Culture*. Minneapolis: University of Minnesota Press.

TransEthics 2016. "Trans Gaming: Brianna Wu on Gamer Culture, Harassment, and Caitlyn Jenner." https://transethics.wordpress.com/2016/01/06/trans-gaming-brianna-wu-on-gamer-culture-harassment-and-caitlyn-jenner.

Williams, D., Martins, N., Consalvo, M., and Ivory, J. 2009. "The Virtual Census: Representations of Gender, Race and Age in Video Games." *New Media and Society*, 11 (5): 815–34.

Young, H. 2016. "Racial Logics, Franchising, and Video Game Genres: The Lord of the Rings." *Games and Culture* 11 (4): 343–64.

# PART 1

# ETHICS, VIOLENCE, AND OPPOSITIONAL GAMING

# CHAPTER 1

# THE CORPOREAL ETHICS OF GAMING

*Vulnerability, Mobility, and Social Gaming*

ROB COVER

**G**AMING HAS TRADITIONALLY been viewed in public-sphere accounts as an unethical activity, external or oppositional to social justice claims related to the equitable distribution of wealth and opportunity and the inclusiveness for all in terms of genders and minority status. Indeed, gaming is often broadly depicted within a masculine framework of violence and domination, whether that be the violence portrayed in single-person shooter games; the militaristic basis of the single-person mode of gaming (McKosker 2013, 157); the racialized and gender stereotyping in game content (Leonard 2006); the perceived risks to younger people participating in networked gaming and online encounters with strangers (Haddon and Livingstone 2014, 4); or the notions that playing short-term social games is an unproductive activity in which users expend unnecessary time while having finance or data extracted (Rossi 2009). In these cases, the focus on gaming as an unethical activity that excludes social justice is based on its *representation* and *content*: the narratives, the on-screen setting, the required actions to perform in the game, or the view that engagement with such narratives and content is unproductive because it is seen as uneducational or without utility.

In a different way, gaming is sometimes understood as unethical as a result of the way in which gaming converges with a different media form—reporting, journalism, and public commentary. The Gamergate scandal, for example, emerged as a result of the active, unethical attempts to use violent language to marginalize women from gaming culture in both online and offline settings (Tomkinson and Harper 2015). The connection between gaming and a hypermasculinity performed through unethical behavior toward women results from a view of gaming itself as the province of masculine players, enacting violences of exclusion, obstruction of play, and online and offline verbal abuse toward women.

Gamergate has also, importantly, been understood to have significant ethical implications due to its relationship with alt-right, populist voices, particularly in relation to those who have been central in the presidential campaign of Donald Trump (Lees 2016). By implication, gaming itself is understood in some respects to be tainted by the masculinist and exclusionist voices of those articulating such views in the Gamergate controversy. Much of the game content and scandal writing that is targeted as being unethical or antithetical to social justice is more often focused on massively multiplayer online games (MMOs) and single-person games of longer-term temporal play. However, it would be unhelpful to discount social games and casual games from concerns around ethical gaming. Social, mobile, and casual games tend to be single-player short-term events, although there has been considerable growth over the past decade of mobile gaming that involves multiple players and play extending across weeks and months rather than minutes. Arguably, there is a continuum between social games and the MMOs more often related in scandal, since all forms of gaming incorporate concepts of play, a tenuous separation of gaming activities from "real life," and interactions with other players in both digital and geographically local settings.

An aspect that is missing, however, from a consideration as to the ethical or just potential of gaming is one that focuses not on its content, but on the act of *play* as a social activity that occurs in the interface between the site of the body and the formation of the game. This is to take a new angle on attempting to understand the relationship between ethics, social justice, and games by turning away from both content/representation and scandal/public discourse, and instead considering the sociality of play itself, particularly as that which is not an artefact but an activity that, indeed, more importantly, is a *corporeal* activity, with all the implications for sociality and ethics that emerge in a consideration of bodies. I am interested here in exploring social justice aspects of contemporary digital gaming by thinking through gaming's role in fostering interpersonal interactivity and ethical relationality. For analysis, I will deploy Judith Butler's (2004; 2009) ethics of nonviolence, which is grounded in a notion that all subjects are vulnerable as *corporeal* and *embodied* subjects prior to subjectivity, and therefore obliged to act without violence toward one another. Such subjects, here, might be understood to include the identity figure of the avid, devoted, or everyday "gamer" who communicates in a shared gaming cultural space, sometimes outside the bounds of the game itself.

A perspective that re-focuses attention on corporeality in the context of gaming and, particularly, mobile social gaming, has valuable potential to refigure the conceptualization of the entire gaming assemblage within more ethical frameworks that prevent such unethical violence. While a common distinction between social and hard-core gaming is that the former has the potential to be "intermeshed in the practices and considerations of everyday life" (Willson 2015, 16), hard-core games are correlative to smaller-group avid players and/or to specific temporal activities—choices to sit down and play, for example. While important distinctions in terms of practice, an alternative framework is to instead figure digital gaming *per se* as a unified activity no matter the gaming type, and (temporarily, at least) perform a "forgetting" of genre in order to see that what unifies that continuum is the fact that digital game players are corporeal, embodied subjects playing in a context that draws attention to the nuanced, networked, and interactive relationship between on-screen and off-screen bodies, bodies in spaces, bodies in movement, and bodies in particular kinds of temporalities.

I will make a case for the *obligation* of gamers to act ethically and nonviolently toward other gamers and non-gamers, in care-of-the-self and care-of-all-others social justice frameworks. In order to demonstrate some of the nuanced, corporeal relationalities that operate in gaming, I will use the example of the recently introduced social game *Pokémon Go* which, fad-like, became temporarily very popular in July and August 2016 internationally. *Pokémon Go* provides some important examples of the complex interweaving of on-screen and off-screen corporeality, mobility, spatiality, and movement in which players interact not only with the game but each other (as well as non-players) in very real, embodied social spaces. I argue here that once we begin to understand all kinds of gaming as sets of activities that cannot exclude the body, and once—as I will demonstrate—we see the body and digital gaming as a mutually constitutive assemblage, we are better positioned to understand how gaming can be re-figured in terms of socially just, ethical relationalities. *Gaming, it can therefore be argued, teaches us about social justice not in its content but in its play as a corporeal and social activity.*

I will begin with an introductory discussion of the body as radically central to the activity of digital gaming followed by an elucidation of some of the ways in which we can understand the body and gaming technologies as in a mutually constitutive assemblage such that *all* gaming activities (whether ethical or unethical, socially just or unjust) can *never* be understood as separate from bodies or as relegated to a separate ethical or unethical cyberspace. I will end by arguing that some of the ways in which gaming, as an endemically corporeal experience, can be understood through Butler's approach to ethics to oblige gamers to act with responsibility and responsiveness in ways that disavow the violence of misogyny, racism, homophobia, and other kinds of violence as an approach to social justice in gaming culture.

## GAMING BODIES, BEYOND REAL/VIRTUAL DISTINCTIONS

Thinking about *bodies* in the context of digital games remains novel in the sense that our contemporary approaches to digital communication and entertainment across activities in both offline and online gaming (both single-person and multiplayer) remain grounded in a radical separation of the body and the mind. This mythical separation, beginning from a Cartesian framework and extending into 1990s, Web 1.0 conceptualizations of cyberspace, relies on and reproduces a reductive, normative discourse in which an over-simplified representation of digital communicative, interactive, and engagement activities is separated into "real" and "virtual," typically favoring the "real" as the site of physical, corporeal, embodied, face-to-face, and ethical; and the site of the "virtual," "online," or "game space" as that which is represented as false, dangerous, risky, or addictive (Cover 2012). Or, in a reversal of Descartes' hierarchicalization of mind over body: the "real body" and the "virtual-less-than-social" mind-space of non-ethical digital behavior, as much public-sphere depiction of gaming articulates. This binary informs almost all scholarly writing on games and online play in the context of bodies. It extends not just to gaming but to gaming culture and online communication focused on gaming, possibly the result of the replication of adversarial behavior inculcated by gaming narratives that spills over to other gaming-related activities. Importantly, this false dichotomy not only reduces the capacity for understanding the ways in which behaviors, norms, activities, engagements, and relationalities are produced through digital work of gaming but turns public-sphere attention away from the radical and interesting possibilities of socially just gaming behaviors grounded in a *corporeal* ethics of mutually shared vulnerability, vulnerable bodies, responsiveness, and non-violence (Cover 2004). Indeed, much of the public-sphere response to any kind of questionable gaming behavior focuses on norms and a perception that gamers are somehow operating outside normative behaviors in ways that result in misogyny, racism, lack of care of the self, lack of care of others, risky or addictive digital activities, and violence against others (Cover 2007). In other words, a return to consideration of the corporeality of game players, in a general sense, opens the door to considering a new ethical perspective that has value for the production of ethical gaming environments built on care and self-care.

Useful, therefore, to a future perspective on gaming culture is to understand precisely how misogyny, racism, lack of care of the self and others, risky digital activities, and violence can be challenged through new approaches to ethical relationalities that oblige gamers to act toward themselves and others without the violence of misogyny, racism, lack of care, or risk. This is not to suggest that all gamers are unethical nor to suggest that the narratives or activities of gameplay themselves should be altered to promote a liberal code of justice; rather, it is to draw critically upon contemporary and emergent gaming practices in order to make a claim to an ethics that is *prior* to the performative process of gamer identification, categorization, self-categorization, and adversarial subjectivities. Such a view can open the possibility of new, non-regimentary normativities of gaming culture grounded in social justice through recognition of the mutual vulnerability of the body of the gamer and the vulnerability of the bodies of those others around us who might be affected by behaviors (all behaviors, whether in-game or not).

The way the body is understood in media theory, cultural studies, social psychology, and the social sciences was adapted during the 1990s, differing from the common public and pedestrian views of the body as a machine controlled by the mind of the subject (Gatens 1995). What has been referred to as the *corporeal turn* has informed much recent scholarship by investigating how Western philosophy and culture had been premised on a profound separation or disregard of the role of the body in lived experience and thought (Grosz 1994, 5). Following the important work on corporeality of Elizabeth Grosz (1994), we can understand the body to be constituted and produced within frameworks of social, cultural, and psychic representation, discourse and language (x–xi), which, for us, includes mediated and digitally communicated discourses of embodiment and corporeal normativity. For Grosz, "bodies must take the social order as their productive nucleus. Part of their own 'nature' is an organic or ontological 'incompleteness' or lack of finality, an amenability to social completion, social ordering and organization" (xi). Grosz (1995) defines the body as a material, animate organization of "flesh, organs, nerves and skeletal structure, which are given a unity, cohesiveness, and form through the psychical and social inscription of the body's surface. This body is so to speak, organically, biologically 'incomplete'; it is indeterminate, amorphous, a series of uncoordinated potentialities that requires social triggering, ordering, and long-term 'administration'" (Grosz 1995, 104).

Put in the context of subjectivity, it might then be argued that the practice of gaming is one specific site which simultaneously, first, provides the codes and conventions by which a body will be inscribed to make bodies both intelligible and recognisable and thus able to participate socially as culturally determinate bodies (Butler 1993, 4–5); and second, through the practices of interactive and participatory engagement are, as Grosz puts it, "administered" by being channelled, rehearsed, performed, and made sensible over time as racially "docile bodies" (Foucault 1977). For example, in the context of playing *Pokémon Go*, a user typically engages with the game while in the process of walking in public spaces, engaging through an avatar but simultaneously engaging with a fictionalized map that mirrors the map of the real-world space, both of which are only proximately indexical with the space in which the body moves. However, drawn to *Poké* stops and *Pokémon* gyms, and to tracking and capturing the pocket monsters, the body performatively produced through a particular kind of theatrics of gameplay—the avatar walks and so too does the body (Grodal 2003, 130). At a deeper and more complex level, of course, subjectivation occurs not because there is a false mirroring between the space of the game's movement and the space of the geo-locationally tagged movement among the public, but because the limitations set by the game—such as certain kinds of walking, certain kinds of tracking, certain spaces to which one is drawn –provide a regimentation that effectively materializes a particular kind of corporeality. *Pokémon Go*, more so than other social, desktop, and networked games, draws attention, of course, to this regimentation by ensuring the body is itself a practitioner of gameplay, collapsing the real/digital distinction more ostensibly than other, previous games that rely on the notion of a game space differentiated from the real.

Put another way: rather than the pretence of the body-less subject floating in the digital ether, or the idea of the subject who can express an on-screen identity differently from that which is coded and constituted in a "real body," it remains digital gaming is insistently *about* the body. Even among the precursors to *Pokémon Go*, the embodied nature of all gaming includes representations of the self in gaming as a visual presentation, the drawing-together of bodies and digital interactivities through new relationalities that focus on the body such as in the *Pokémon Go* example, citations of bodily practices, and norms from online representation in the materialization of the body (Cover 2016, 103–40). The potentialities for critique of the culturally constituted ways in which the body is conceived, framed, interpreted, gendered, racialized, and articulated in everyday life is a central, ongoing benefit of earlier perspectives on the relationship between bodies and perceptions of digital gameplay. In other words, if there is to be an ethics grounded in corporeality, no digital gaming conceptualization can be exempt from the embodied nature of gaming relationality, and the more recent games point most adamantly to this.

## AVATARS, IMMERSION, AND IDENTITY

The idea of immersion has regularly been used in connection with digital gaming experiences in which it is often argued that the gamer's identity extends into and beyond the screen into a conceptualization of cyberspace, whereby the user either leaves the body behind while engaging in the imaginative, digital world or extends the body into an amalgamation of corporeal self (real) and gaming avatar (digital). In an older game setting, for example, *Grand Theft Auto 3*, a set of avatars and on-screen representations both mirror and are wholly distinct from the body, establishing the physicality of the screen as a point of radical distinctiveness that effectively brings into imagination the "Other" (digital) side and the Othered body. This, again, works with the out-dated notion of a real/virtual or real/digital divide; a distinction that is, in today's culture of ubiquitous connectivity and digital interactivity, both outdated and unhelpful (Cover 2016, x). In some cases, this notion of immersion is one characterized by becoming (Other), by becoming that which the user has created as an articulation on screen. For example, Miroslaw Filiciak (2003, 91) has argued that rather than an identification with an on-screen character or avatar, the player is introjected across the screen to become one with it, losing his or her own identity in the process. This is a useful account of gameplay that describes some of the ways in which the player's identity is not necessarily to be understood as fixed while only ever performing an interactive non-real playful theatrics; rather, identity is conditioned by performances that include the performance of on-screen play, whether in real time or recorded (Cover 2012). However, problematically, here is, again, the persistence of the real/virtual distinction, presented through a corporeal real (the subject) and an avatar (object) that, in the act of playing, are seen to unify and fuse.

What this distinctiveness in contemporary understandings of gamer identity does is open up a possibility for *two identities with two, separate and potentially unrelated sets of ethics and ethical obligations.* For example, one might imagine an ethical injunction against violence in the site of the "real body" while an unethical set of behaviors emerge in which killing, in the context of the narrative of the game, is allowable. Indeed, this would be a normative way of understanding game-play in which, for example, in a first-person shooter, a subject quite rightly takes pleasure in shooting at an enemy and winning, while never dreaming that such an activity would be considered socially just in the site of real world and really vulnerable bodies.

In the social game *Pokémon Go*, following the broader *Pokémon* universe, the player does—perhaps—engage unethically and violently toward others: capturing, training, trading and fighting pocket monsters; engaging in adversarial forms of *Pokémon* combat in the gyms. In this context, a separation of ethics occurs because the knowable "real body" is vulnerable while the images and avatars on screen are plainly and rightly understood *not-as-bodies* and therefore not vulnerable, and therefore not obliging an ethical responsiveness. This is endemic and marks the earlier games that, in light of the recent *Pokémon* experience, are a separation that becomes less sensible or speakable over time. This is not, of course, to suggest that collapsing corporeality with digital avatars in *Pokémon Go* is itself necessarily socially just: at a more meta level, a *Pokémon Go* player becomes a more adapt and higher-level player as the result of the purchase of tools that improve capabilities within a financially inequitable economy, bringing real-world and game-world economies together. Nevertheless, it is the myth of the cyberspatial separation of the body and the avatar that submerges the injustices of real-world violences and inequities through a notion of separate worlds in which one immerses oneself *as if* there is no effect of one on the other.

Such a separation-yet-immersion of body/mind and ethics/non-ethics, however, comes in the knowledge that what it is that invokes affect is the context of the game's narrative. Just as it is no longer helpful to think in terms of a real/virtual distinction, it is likewise unhelpful to understand digital media as comprising a new, separate space or cyberspace behind the screen, as many writers on gaming, following William Gibson's (1984) coinage of the term in his cyberpunk book *Neuromancer*, have done so (Lahti 2003, 157). What, instead, is at stake is the process of narrative in the form of the game that is at a distance from the narrative through which we articulate and move our corporeal selves in everyday life. The parent of ludology, Johan Huizinga (1949), made clear that all "play" must be understood as separate from the everyday with its own boundaries of time and space: "A closed space is marked out for it, either materially or ideally, hedged off from the everyday surroundings. Inside this space the play proceeds, inside it the rules obtain" (19). That is, the conceptual space of the game—which I relate here as a narrative—is consciously understood as being radically different from the narrative spatiality of everyday life; in an era of digital games, it is not that the body is left alone in a space radically separate from the space of play, but that the player is aware of the narrative's difference and yet open to the affective and, subsequently, emotional formations that produce particular responses, articulated corporeally. Gaming, in that sense, may not necessarily disrupt the identity of the subject, but gaming itself is not clearly demarcated between the ethical shooting, for example, that occurs in the context of an online multi-user game and the unethical, for example, shooting down of other subjects in the context of gaming culture at the margins and edges of the activity of gaming.

Where the question of social justice emerges, then, is not in understanding there to be a wholesale collapse of the "real" and the "digital," despite the ubiquity of digital connectivity and digitally interactive entertainment. Rather, it is in thinking through the complexification of distinctions of relationality in a digital world based on sociality. For example, the kinds of misogyny that emerged in the 2014 Gamergate scandal or the kinds of racism, homophobia, discrimination, and exclusion that are seen in online gaming that is built around insistent sociality (Humphreys 2003) such as *Pokémon Go* present additional and sometimes complex sites in which there *are* real bodies to be made vulnerable by the actions of a subject. But those bodies—much like the online avatars in the context of gameplay—are at a remove, connected with gaming culture but not necessarily available within an interpretative frame (Butler 2009) that understands such subjects as vulnerable to discriminatory or socially unjust behavior by virtue of their not having been physically and geographically knowable as vulnerable bodies.

In thinking this point in terms of the *Pokémon Go* experience, there are differentiations between which bodies can access the game, which bodies are permitted to play, and how those bodies are represented—hard limitations on the choices of avatars being an example of a co-creativity that is regimented from the beginning in such a way as to produce sets of exclusions that may themselves be violently enacted on the subject of the player (or the one who cannot play). However, where *Pokémon* differs from other networked, online gaming is that bodies of other players are, indeed, brought into the visual frame and proximity of the player—around *Poké* stops, for example. The context of face-to-face engagement here might include the capacity to share a "lure," which one player has paid for and deployed at a *Poké* stop but which is beneficial to other, unknown, stranger-players who happen to be in proximity.

## BODIES AND GAMING ASSEMBLAGES
## AS A FOUNDATION FOR ETHICS

If part of the critical task in ethically grounded game studies is to think about how social justice can be imagined, then there is utility in thinking alternatively about the acts of play in the context of critical discourses of the body. Indeed, it may be a productive way of addressing and approaching unethical behaviors in the context of the border-points of gaming to restore corporeality to gaming culture beyond any framework that relies on the out-dated and unhelpful real/virtual distinction. This is particularly important where the "virtual" has sometimes been misunderstood to include not only gaming characters but characters of vulnerable subjects encountered in gaming culture but not in physical proximity and settings made "real" by virtue of geographic visuality. That is, one might articulate an ethics of care and nonviolence toward other game players, for example *Pokémon Go* players who have arrived bodily at the same *Poké* stop, or those non-playing bodies we encounter along the way. There is, in this context too, a broader population of bodies that we will never meet and never know but who will be affected by decisions both ethical and unethical. This is to point to the very complex "assemblage" between bodies, gaming, technologies, socialities, and relational engagements that may occur in both local and digitally defined spaces but primarily also outside of it—for example, women who are made vulnerable to violence as a result of the Gamergate name-calling but who themselves are not participants in gaming of any kind. An assemblage basis allows us to approach and apprehend an ethical perspective grounded on bodies, no matter where those bodies might be. If we are to understand the body as materialized in the terms given by Butler (1993) as described earlier, and if bodies of players are materialized as racialized and ethnic bodies through categorizations that occur in the narrative, representation and visual depiction of game space, then that materialization occurs in the context of the hidden everydayness of contact with the technology in ways that bring us closer to those representations as assemblage. Our bodies are given intelligibility and matter *as bodies* by virtue of the spatial, temporal movements and boundaries that come to lend the illusion of a fixed, stable, and unchanging corporeality, hiding the fact that we only have those bounds by virtue of the knowledges and prac-tices that are at stake in how the body is perceived, used, moved, and engaged with, and how it engages with others. If gaming technologies— which represent a kind of "seam" between the space of corporeality and the space of the game's representations and interactive participation—are part of the everyday experience of how bodies move, engage, and gain intelligibility, then it is necessary to consider the experience of gaming as an experience based in corporeal assemblage and relationality.

Grosz' conceptualization of the relationship between the body and the city (a distinct technology from gaming, but nevertheless still one that is *spatial, relational,* and *temporal*) provides some important ideas that are useful in helping to understand our subjectivities as assemblages of body and digital technology without having to resort to the out-dated notions of the cyborg or the disembodied subject. For Grosz (1995), the city is too often problematically seen as a reflection or projection of the body, in which bodies are understood mythically to pre-date the city and be its cause for design and construction, whereby the human subject is pre-sented as sovereign, responsible for "all social and historical production" (105). If we were to replace the notion of the city here with the idea of gaming technologies (controllers, screens, narratives, avatars) as sites through which digital activities are carried out in specific times and in certain temporal contexts, then this view would suggest that digital tech-nology is always knowingly produced by subjects with agency over that space and time and in which digital spaces and networks are only ever the effect of a willed creation and human creativity. This might include, for example, choosing one's *Pokémon Go* avatar in such a way as to match one's self-perception of a gendered, racialized, or ethnic body in terms of available discourses of categorization—alternatively, of course, to provide a *counterplay* and reflexively choose against the grain (Willson 2015, 20). Like other digital applications, games are regularly produced with particular categorizations of racialized and gendered bodies, presenting the appearance of a choice for which there may not necessarily be a pre-existing "fit." Since subjects are at least in part constituted by those choosing activities in those spaces in ways we cannot always know in advance, this is not to say that *we* are digital technologies' *effects*, but that the relationship is more than simply determined and causal.

In the case of bodies and cities, Grosz' critical contribution was to shift understanding of the relationship between the two as neither causal nor representational and, instead, as assemblages (though not necessarily in a state of permanency):

> Bodies and cities are not causally linked. Every cause must be logically distinct from its effect. The body, however, is not distinct from the city for they are mutually defining. Like the representation model, there may be an isomorphism between the body and the city. But it is not a mirroring of nature in artifice; rather, there is a two-way linkage that could be defined as an *interface* . . . This model is practical, based on the productivity of bodies and cities in defining and establishing each other . . . their interrelations involve a fundamentally disunified series of systems, a series of disparate flows, energies, events, or entities, bringing together or drawing apart their more or less temporary alignments. (108)

If we once more replace the notion of city in this quotation with the terms related to digital gaming technologies and techniques of digital interactivity, we can see that there is a framework here for understanding bodies within an interface that is mutually determining of the communicative cultures of gaming spaces (for example, the *Pokémon* goal operating as narrative, extra-game communication with strangers at a *Poké* stop, gaming culture journalism, risk-related panics over young *Pokémon* players in the street) and activities subjects who are bodies *actively materialized* and given coherence in the context of the relationalities of gaming culture. Linkages, communicative flows, collective actions, and activities over global spaces that come to resemble machines, temporary sites of group-work, in a disunified series of systems and flows becomes not only normative in the everyday engagement of embodied subjects with others but produces meanings in ways that mutually define bodies and technologies. It is in rethinking that relationship between bodies and technologies as assemblages that involve a seam that new opportunities emerge for considering racialization of bodies, in the sense that it is not possible to think racialization of bodies as separate from the racialization of (stereotyped) representation of diverse bodies. Here, the assemblage points to the opportunities for opening new diversities in the complexity of this relationship beyond merely inclusion and counter-stereotypical representations in games.

## A CORPOREAL ETHICS OF GAMING

I will now show some of the ways in which Butler's (2004; 2009) ethics of nonviolence built on the embodied and corporeal primariness of vulnerability can be a mechanism impelling gamer-subjects to apprehend themselves as necessarily obliged toward ethical relations and responses. This obligation is grounded in Butler's (2004) reading of Emmanuel Levinas' ethical responsibility. Butler extended Levinas to account for the responsibility to recognize the *vulnerability of others* as a condition that precedes subjectivity and selfhood on the basis of the endemic and primary violability of the body and the thrownness of bodies into a sociality in which care is necessary from the very beginning of life itself. Butler's work can contribute powerfully to fostering *ethical reflexivity* in gaming cultures by demonstrating how ethical relations can be achieved through understanding how the recognition of selfhood and others as commonly vulnerable occurs in contemporary cultures. This is not merely to argue that better and more pragmatic forms of preventative education, training, or imperatives for socially acceptable behavior are needed but that, at a conceptual level, Butler's work provides an in-road into how an ethics of nonviolence can be related to the ongoing performance of masculine identity itself in ways which do not depend on the subjugation of women and other men.

Butler's framework presents an ethical perspective based on the key concept of *recognition*. She has argued that an ethics of nonviolence can be grounded in a conceptual understanding that, as embodied, living beings, all human subjects are vulnerable in our exposure to one another; that is, all life is precarious, all bodies are easily harmed, and from the very beginning of life we are all dependent upon relationality with others for the ongoingness of life and bodies (Butler 2004, 44). Through perceiving the commonality of vulnerability for ourselves and for the Other whom we encounter, we are compelled to engage with others in ways that are responsible and responsive to that vulnerability; that is, in relations of nonviolence.

What Butler thus articulates is a means by which the human subject is conceived as predicated on a primary vulnerability through dependence upon others, meaning that all our identities are built on relationality. This is marked by the fact that we are vulnerable to the violence of others and yet we are always, from the very beginning of our lives, dependent on others for physical support. Re-reading Levinas, she proposes an ethical position through the notion that one has a *responsibility* to others that emerges in a conceptual act of *encounter* and *recognition* of the Other. This ethics is not, for either Levinas or Butler, a simple injunction to *behave* in a particular way such as in terms of an ethical and non-violent relation between subjects (as men and women; gamers and other gamers; diversely racialized bodies and other frameworks for discrimination). Rather, it produces a quandary, a requirement persistently to question ones' actions and a situation that can re-constitute the subject anew in the encounter with the Other. In conceptual terms, using the Gamergate example, when men come to encounter women in the digital spaces of gaming culture— whether in-game or out-game communication is involved—they are required in an ethics of recognition to consider *how* to treat women in the context of scandal reporting/information.

This is an encounter that requires that one is open to having one's identity re-configured in ways that acknowledge the primary *mutual* vulnerability of each party and thereby not to make one another more vulnerable in an act of violence, including misogyny, discrimination, exclusivity, bullying, or otherwise. Importantly, the requirement here is that we give *recognition* to the Other in the encounter: that we recognize the Other as human and therefore worthy of being in a relation of nonviolence; that we give recognition to the Other as a subject who is vulnerable—not merely a recognition of responsibility to the Other, but a re-cognition of the subject himself or herself as a way of coming to a more ethical understanding of the Other.

*How is this done? By beginning with knowing the self—as a corporeal being and therefore having been vulnerable as a corporeal life from the very beginning of life itself* (Butler 2004). Such a framework acknowledges that all parties are vulnerable because they are embodied and therefore have lives, which are precarious, even though there are varying degrees of vulnerability. Butler's framework for ethics draws attention to vulnerability as the condition for perceiving and recognising others as human and therefore worthy of being responded to without assault (or objectification, exclusion, or other forms of violence related to the physical, cultural, and linguistic).

It is obliged here, then, that it is ethically just to respond to or relate to another without violence in order to care for that person because that person is vulnerable, in that it is right to respond without violence in order to take care of the self. In the *Pokémon Go* context as much as in hard-core gaming, then, it is socially just to respond without violence (or the violence of discriminatory or non-inclusive language) to all parties that comprise that social space, which includes those who are not players and therefore definitive of the categorization of players. What *Pokémon Go* opens, however—through its re-conceptualization of bodies, spaces, and societies in the very tightly networked framework in which gameplay occurs in the context of others—is the capacity to draw the links between the different subjects, all of whom are worthy of an ethical relationality, across the streets of gameplay, which are represented both on-screen and in the geolocational visuality in front of us. By making this obvious, the "setting" for an ethical recognition of the Other is not, of course, assured; but it is opened in its potentiality.

CONCLUSION

If part of the activity of receiving a socially just world requires us first to imagine an ethical way of relating (Kelley 2002), such acts of imagining may not necessarily be limited to representation, content, public discourse or reaction to content in the context of gaming, but to how we might apply a complex ethical analysis of the *act* of gameplay through thinking about bodies and their relationality to games, game spaces, networks, and each other. Where dichotomous real-life bodies versus virtual-life play have resulted in attention on social justice concerns in gaming turning away from the question of bodies-at-play, in thinking about the example of *Pokémon Go*, we see a different framework for corporeality emerge, whereby avatars and immersion are not simply the pale shadow of real-world bodily sensation, nor its extension into the realm of the digital as if space is separate. Rather, the body is put at front and center in this perspective, which opens the possibility of considering a framework that obliges ethical behavior based on shared corporeal vulnerability itself. What matters here is that if there is to be an ethics based on corporeality that is to be sensitive to social justice causes and, indeed, lead toward the fruition of social justice, undoing the distinction between real and virtual is the most significant and important element. If the virtual is to teach us socially, we cannot have two ethics running in parallel, whereby a real world might exclude bodily violence while a virtual world might be seen to permit it among avatars *as if* this setting is not "properly real" or, in Huizinga's terms (1949), bounded off from the real. Rather, it is vital to think through how an ethics of shared but unevenly distributed vulnerability extends from the body not *into* a digital space as immersion but in the body's assemblage with gameplay.

WORKS CITED

Butler, J. 1993. *Bodies that Matter: On the Discursive Limits of "Sex."* London: Routledge.
Butler, J. 2004. *Precarious Life.* London: Verso.
Butler, J. 2009. *Frames of War: When Is Life Grievable?* London: Verso.
Cover, R. 2004. "Digital Addiction: The Cultural Production of Online and Video Game Junkies." *Media International Australia* 113: 110–23.
Cover, R. 2007. "Gaming Addiction: The Role of Narrative and Play in the Production of the Addiction Myth." *Game Studies: International Journal of Computer Game Research* 6 (1). www.gamestudies.org.
Cover, R. 2012. "Performing and Undoing Identity Online: Social Networking, Identity Theories and the Incompatibility of Online Profiles and Friendship Regimes." *Convergence* 18 (2): 177–93.
Cover, R. 2016. *Digital Identities: Creating and Communicating the Online Self.* London: Elsevier.

Filiciak, M. 2003. "Hyperidentities: Postmodern Identity Patterns in Massively Multiplayer Online Role-Playing Games." In *The Video Game Theory Reader*, edited by M. J. P. Wolf and B. Perron, 87–101. New York: Routledge.

Foucault, M. 1977. *Discipline and Punish: The Birth of the Prison.* Translated by Alan Sheridan. London: Penguin.

Gatens, M. 1995. *Imaginary Bodies: Ethics, Power and Corporeality.* London: Routledge.

Gibson, W. 1984. *Neuromancer.* New York: Ace Books.

Grodal, T. 2003. "Stories for Eye, Ear, and Muscles: Video Games, Media, and Embodied Experiences." In *The Video Game Theory Reader*, edited by M. J. P. Wolf and B. Perron, 129–55. New York: Routledge.

Grosz, E. 1994. *Volatile Bodies: Toward a Corporeal Feminism.* St. Leonards, NSW: Allen & Unwin.

Grosz, E. 1995. *Space, Time and Perversion: The Politics of Bodies.* London: Routledge.

Haddon, L. and Livingstone, S. 2014. *The Meaning of Online Problematic Situations for Children: The UK Report.* London: EU Kids Online.

Huizinga, J. 1949. *Homo Ludens: A Study of the Play-Element in Culture.* London: Routledge & Kegan Paul.

Humphreys, S. 2003. "Online Multi-user Games." *Australian Journal of Communication* 30 (1): 79–91.

Kelley, R. D. G. 2002. *Freedom Dreams: The Black Radical Imagination.* Boston: Beacon Press.

Lahti, M. 2003. "As We Become Machines: Corporealized Pleasures in Video Games." In *The Video Game Theory Reader*, edited by M. J. P. Wolf and B. Perron, 157–70. New York: Routledge.

Lees, M. 2016. "What Gamergate Should Have Taught Us about the 'Alt-right.'" *Guardian*, December 1.

Leonard, D. J. 2006. "Not a Hater, Just Keepin' It Real: The Importance of Race- and Gender-Based Game Studies." *Games and Culture* 1 (1): 83–88.

McCosker, A. 2013. *Intensive Media: Aversion Affect and Media Culture.* Basingstoke: Palgrave Macmillan.

Rossi, L. 2009. "Playing Your Network: Gaming in Social Network Sites." *Proceedings of DiGRA2009: Breaking New Ground: Innovation in Games, Play, Practice and Theory.* www.digra.org/dl/db/09287.20599.pdf.

Ruberg, B. 2010. "Sex as Game: Playing with the Erotic Body in Virtual Worlds." *Rhizomes* 21 (Winter). www.rhizomes.net/issue21/ruberg.html.

Tomkinson, S., and Harper, T. 2015. "The Position of Women in Video Game Culture: Perez and Day's Twitter Incident." *Continuum: Journal of Media and Cultural Studies* 29 (4): 617–34.

Willson, M. 2015. "Social Games as Partial Platforms for Identity Co-creation." *Media International Australia* 154: 15–24.

CHAPTER 2

# POWER, VIOLENCE, AND THE MASK

*Representations of Criminal Subjectivities*
*in Grand Theft Auto Online*

TIMOTHY ROWLANDS, SHERUNI RATNABALASURIAR,
MELISSA HOBART, KYLE NOEL, SHAUN-PATRICK ALLEN,
BRIANA REED, AND ANTHONY GONZALES

C HALLENGING ASSUMPTIONS ABOUT the role of catharsis in video games, Gonzalo Frasca, a Uruguayan ludologist, ambitiously challenged game designers and gaming communities in 2001. He asked: How can we make (or mod) games to raise awareness, help instill a critical consciousness in players, and, by doing so, encourage critical thinking about real-world issues relating to equality, fairness, and freedom? This was a call for the maturation of the medium, an attempt to see if we could move beyond games as toys, pastimes, or virtual social hubs to think of them instead as art, capable of (and responsible for) evoking and provoking thought on serious, real-world issues. Since then, a wide range of game designers, activists, and scholars have embraced the "serious games" movement (Michael and Chen 2006; Ritterfeld, Cody, and Vorderer 2009), exploring the possibilities of using this versatile medium to engage important questions facing us all in a rapidly changing world. As a renewed interest in thinking about how games can fit into social justice movements has emerged in the wake of the Gamergate scandal (Hathaway 2014; Lees 2016), returning to Frasca's challenge can prove useful. In this chapter, we join the discussion by looking to Frasca's original proposal for non-immersive, alienating games, *The Sims of the Oppressed*, as inspiration for a series of experiments in creating games for social change within the multiplayer mode of Rockstar Games' 2013 smash hit, *Grand Theft Auto V (GTA5)*.

Through the Creator Mode in *Grand Theft Auto Online (GTA Online)*, players are given the option to design, test, and publish races, death matches, capture-the-flag missions, and last-man-standing (LTS; one-life death match) scenarios of their own creation. As early as 2014, players had already created over 9.8 million such "jobs" (R*Q 2014; Rockstar North 2013), a good indication that users have found this to be both a versatile and rewarding game-maker nested within the greater *Grand Theft Auto* experience. Not surprisingly, many such player-made jobs follow similar frames and formats as existing, designer-made content. As some measure of this, if Rockstar approves of players' job designs, they will officially endorse them with a "Rockstar Verified" label and incorporate them into the online game. While, as Terranova (2000) warns us, we should always be cautious of the potentially exploitative relationship between coding authorities and their prosumer players (Novak 2005; Toffler 1980) generating player-made content for free that nevertheless brings profits to the publisher, we should also celebrate player ingenuity and propensity to take the tools provided to build things never imagined by their creators. In this regard, it is important to notice that many players have embraced the possibilities of the game-makers to create new and unique experiences, many of which break the immersion of the game. At the time of this writing, popular examples of such experimental jobs include those focusing on parkour, car-bowling, "snipers/RPG (rocket-propelled grenade) vs. stunters," "jets vs. base," as well as wall-ride and super-jump races.

In light of the success and popularity of these player-made jobs, we approached the Creator Mode with the goal of testing the possibilities and constraints of this system. We sought to answer two major questions: 1) Building on the analyses of Leonard (2003, 2006a, 2006b, 2009, 2016), Gray (2014), and Polasek (2014), how can we rewrite/remix existing *GTA*

*Online* game modes and tropes to foster critical consciousness to help players think about social justice in terms of race and gender? 2) How can we use these game modes to offer counter narratives to the post-ironic glorification of transnational, organized crime so prevalent in the game?

As researchers, we have often been content to analyze others' games. However, at the heart of this project was an attempt to move beyond the descriptive level of *what* is going on in gameplay to begin to better understand *why* predictable frames and formats of gameplay have emerged in player-created content by delving into game design ourselves (if only in a very small, tentative, and basic way). We sought to think about the limitations of genre, representation, and social justice in this medium as we worked to develop culturally responsive jobs, hack some inequalities, and maybe even present some solutions to eliminate bias. In particular, we wanted to see if we could use these missions to help players move beyond simplistic, "post-racial," color-blind (Bonilla-Silva 2013) notions of the concept of diversity as new markets and laborers (Hardt and Negri 2000) to a more complex understanding of how diverse groups of people are represented in games. By stressing the game modes to their breaking points, if not technologically then at least conceptually, we were able to rethink how structural and institutional factors shape both the creation and reception of games.

## VIDEO GAMES OF THE OPPRESSED

Frasca (2001) grounded his challenge upon a foundational assumption that simulations offered in some games allow those who use them to analyze the ideology being presented as factual reality in games (Swinfen 1984). To emphasize and foreground this potential in video games, Frasca (2001) suggested designers abandon the Aristotelian poetics which commonly structure traditional video game narratives. Instead, he proposed using the alienating and potentially consciousness-raising effects found in the dramaturgic philosophies and practices of Bertold Brecht (1964), especially as adapted by Augusto Boal in his techniques for the *Theater of the Oppressed* (1979). These techniques are aimed at breaking the audience's immersion— understood as the active creation of belief (Murray 1998)— with the goal of intentionally denying the potential for the emotional release (and resultant pacification) of catharsis. Using techniques to keep both audiences and actors acutely and self-consciously aware of their interaction and involvement with a re-presentation of life opens space to disrupt, challenge, and rethink oppressions reified and naturalized in everyday discourses of hegemonic masculinity, patriarchy, white supremacy, and consumer capitalism.

In our research in and around *GTA5* and *GTA Online*, we have often wondered how players experience and make sense of the representations of transnational crime that play out in the game. This can be an uncomfortable question for game designers, who often see their creations first and foremost as problems to be solved (Greenfield and Cocking 1996; Koster 2004), in which the narrative and aesthetic elements are the shiny trappings for the really important stuff, the game mechanics beneath. As Frasca (2001) notes, for both game designers and frequent gamers, like the operator watching the code fall across his screen in the Wachowskis' *The Matrix* trilogy (Silver 1999; 2003a; 2003b), after a while, the metaphors fall away, leaving behind only abstract, symbolic logic. In this situation, having become unproblematic, taken for granted, reified, and naturalized through familiarity (in the sense of Schutz 1970), it is understandable why players often don't recognize games as having any symbolism despite the fact that video game worlds are mythic realms of pure symbolism, where every inclusion (and exclusion) is an intentional design decision (Rowlands 2012; Taylor 2003).

In our attempts to see if we could turn *GTA Online* on its head, we were particularly aware of the representations of serious transnational crimes devoid of consequences or social commentary. From the jobs available, the average *GTA* player is well accustomed to engaging in murder-for-hire (and killsports), the eponymous grand theft auto, grand larceny, drug trafficking, gun running, racketeering, human smuggling, and sex trafficking. An example of how un-problematically these scenarios are presented can be found in the job titled, "Cleaning the Cathouse," a so-called Contact Mission offered to players by the non-player character (NPC) Martin Madrazo, head of a Mexican drug cartel. Here, the mission description is illustrative. Inviting players to participate, Martin texts the players the following message:

The Lost have set up a brothel at an abandoned motel in Grand Senora. We have our own operations, and I don't like to think how this one is being run. If it's not up to standards, the cops will come down on everyone. Can you go down there and take out the bikers. Bring the girl they're using to me, and we will see she's looked after. (Rockstar North 2013)

While written in a rather civil, business-like tone, to think through what this mission really represents can be quite disturbing. Player characters go to the derelict motel, kill members of the Lost outlaw motorcycle club, and then escort "the girl," Anna, out of the motel, across the desert and through the mountains, to finally drop her off at Martin's stilt-house in the hills. Not only are players engaging in mass murder (as gang warfare), they are kidnapping a sex worker from one criminal organization to transport her across county lines to deliver her to another criminal organization which plans to exploit her in the same way, just in nicer digs.

Habituated by hundreds of hours of gameplay, most players likely see this mission simply as a series of puzzles to be solved: how to (quickly) navigate to the derelict motel, how to kill the biker NPCs without being killed, how to safely escort Anna back to Martin's house while the bikers are in pursuit. However, the language is suggestive and disturbing. At best, Martin's reference to Anna as "the girl" is an example of the sort of misogynist language that demeans women as being childlike and provides rationalization of their control and abuse. At worst, it is direct reference to the fact that the average age of entry for girls into prostitution in the United States is between twelve and fourteen years old (Adams, Owens, and Small 2010). Added to this is the fact that Martin has the player characters drop off Anna at his house, not a brothel.

While we fully admit experiencing and understanding the pleasures of this sort of fast-paced and emergent gameplay—collectively, we have murdered thousands of Lost MC bikers and kidnapped and personally ensured Anna's continued victimization dozens of times—we also wonder how we might subvert this and similar narratives presented in *GTA Online*.

To do so, first, we identified recurrent themes in the representation of transnational crime. Similar to the main single-player campaign in *GTA5*, the activities of criminal organizations in *GTA Online* break down into three major categories: the provision of illicit goods (drugs, stolen property, counterfeits, etc.), the provision of illicit services (human trafficking for sex or forced labor, human smuggling, cybercrime, and fraud, gambling, etc.), and the infiltration of legitimate business and government (corruption, extortion, racketeering, etc.) (Rockstar North 2013). In creating jobs that would try to address these areas, we looked to Frasca's (2001) discussion of Augusto Boal's (1979) alienating techniques. Frasca writes, "The scene always enacts an oppressive situation, where the protagonist has to deal with powerful characters that do not let her achieve her goals," and is "enacted without showing a solution to the problem" (64–65). In this method of Forum Theater, the scene is then repeated, and members of the audience are encouraged to "interrupt the play and take over the place of the protagonist and suggest, through her acting, the solution that she envisions would break the oppression" (Frasca 2001, 65). Again, given the complexity of the issues, the goal is not to provide workable solutions. Rather, it is to raise consciousness about these issues of oppression and encourage critical thinking and the imagining of other possible worlds in which the oppression did not exist.

## MANUFACTURING OPPRESSION

Creating immersion-breaking missions proved more difficult than we imagined. Excerpts from the team's field notes illustrate:

> The thing heard most often during brainstorming sessions about the various scenarios we might create is that involuntary "ohhh!" of both delight and disgust that all human beings emit when they are both truly disturbed by an idea but also unable to hide the glee that thinking about that idea creates. The more we talk, both in a large group and in pairs and smaller groups, the more unhinged the ideas become. It certainly wouldn't look and sound like academic research to an outsider walking by the conference room, and yet we have to let ourselves go there in order to determine where the line is; where does a mission stop being a mission and start being something harmful?

As our research team brainstormed ideas for missions, it became keenly apparent that many of the scenarios could very quickly devolve into nothing more than hate-crime simulators. One LTS scenario that was discarded fairly quickly was the idea of creating a kind of Pride Day street festival, set in front of Pitchers, the gay bar in Downtown Vinewood. This would pit gay bashers against the so-called social justice warriors (Ohlheiser 2007) who would be there to make sure that all who wanted could celebrate in peace (even if it meant busting a few skulls). Another potential LTS scenario left on the cutting-room floor was tentatively titled "Anita Speaks," a mission set in the amphitheater where a representation of game researcher, host of YouTube channel Feminist Frequency, and target of Gamergate ire Anita Sarkeesian is scheduled to speak. In the end, the fact that we would be offering up "Anita" as a potential sacrifice pushed that scenario off the table as well. Although Frasca notes that, with the goal being awareness and critical thinking, nothing should be off the table, he also admits:

> Still, it would be a major problem for the company that produces the software package. No matter how much you stress the fact that the content is created by the users, I do not think that there is any company on Earth that wants to be known as the one that provided a platform for creating a simulator where you force young children to work in factories for ten cents a day. (2001)

Nor are we a research team who wants to be known for offering gamers with a grudge yet another chance to symbolically beat up Anita or, far worse, a chance to kill her outright.

To reframe these missions while still offering the opportunity to think critically about the oppression therein, we attempted to set up missions in which both sides were ultimately "equal," competing with each other for the same social justice goal as the good guys or the bad guys. The following scenarios were what emerged after our experiments with the Creator Mode:

"The Lost and the Ballas" is a capture mission. A Balla East gang member's sister has fallen victim to the sex trafficking ring of The Lost Motorcycle Club. One of the ways that sex traffickers maintain control over their victims is by confiscating their victims' passports, IDs, and other identifying documents. In this scenario, the two rival gangs fight for the documents of the gang member's sister throughout Sandy Shores.

"America's Next Top Trafficker" is a land race to see who the drug kingpin will pick to be his main human trafficking coordinator on the next job. Players must navigate through obstacles and rival gangs that simulate checkpoints while making decisions about alternate routes and avoiding police blockades.

"The Rent Is Too Damn High" is a deathmatch focusing on rent affordability and gentrification. The tenants in one of the last rent-controlled buildings in the area are threatened with a rent hike of three times the original price in the hope that they will leave to make way for a central business district construction project. The player's job is to "convince" the building contractor to move the project elsewhere by beating up the contractor's bigwigs at the construction launch party.

"Saving Private Ryan's Remains" is another capture mission. Paleto Bay is hiding a secret: a small group of Westboro Baptist Church (WBC) supporters. The WBC's plan is to protest a military funeral being held at the Fundamentalist Church by stealing the hearse containing the soldier's body. The Fundamentalists are prepared to fight back.

The difference between some of our original ideas—ones that we worried would become hate-crime simulators—and these are that in each one of these scenarios, players, no matter what side they choose, are "equal." Whatever your own label may be, the opposing team or opposing players fall under that same category. Whether you're a Balla or a Lost, you're still a gang member. Win or lose the race, you are trying to become a human trafficker. You are a heartless contractor or a violent tenant; in the end, you're both wrong. Whatever religious group you're affiliated with, you are fighting over a dead body in front of a church.

However, we felt that these scenarios might not be enough to break immersion. Although, at least in "The Rent Is Too Damn High," there is the expectation that the contracting company are the bad guys and the tenants are the good guys, and perhaps in "Saving Private Ryan's Remains" the thought is that the WBC is bad and the Fundamentalists are good, nevertheless these opposing forces are still quite similar to those contained in the main story of the game. One way to think about whether these things will break immersion is to imagine how uncomfortable players might be to be cast in these roles. Given that, throughout the story mode of *GTA5*, the player is everything from a bank robber to a meth-making murderer, perhaps it stands to reason that casting players in these typical bad-guy roles will not make enough of a difference to encourage players to observe the events from a distance, rather than from their in-game perspective.

Beyond the framing of the missions, we also ran into a number of technical difficulties in getting the look and feel right, mostly because we are either too limited by Creator Mode or too unfamiliar with it to make the creation process itself run smoothly. Hobart explained some of these challenges in her field notes:

> There are six members of the research team and we have brain-stormed far more than just six missions. We have to start some-where, so each team member chooses a favorite scenario from the extensive list and vows to not only learn GTA Online's Cre-ator Mode but to have a close-to-finished mission ready for review in one week. It seems feasible to assemble this collection in that time. We are all intelligent critical thinkers with strong gamer backgrounds. We have used controllers with buttons and sticks for more than a combined century. We all try our best. We all come back in one week realizing that our best is not even close to good enough. But why? Why can't a roomful of smart adults take an open world and create representations of reality that force players to think about larger social issues? Why are we coming back to the table, seven days later, with an odd combination of frustration and self-deprecation rather than the awesome mis-sions we intended to make?

We all very quickly found that the interface of the Creator Mode was not particularly well-suited to creating our missions. Our research team was playing across different generations of both PlayStations and Xboxes, and all of us experienced difficulty, but the level of difficulty and the number of problems eventually made the task of mission creation seem insurmountable. Indeed, sometimes the difficulty was so great that we weren't able to finish making a mission.

In this case, a tutorial was not available for the capture mission, and turning to YouTube was both time-consuming and frustrating, particularly because there was no solution that ever became apparent. In other cases, there were glitches in characters that caused them to flicker and jerk—nothing that prevented the mission from being playable in a technical sense, but certainly something that prevented the mission from being watchable.

Despite playing on different systems, one of the common problems in Creator Mode was the text limitation. Ratnabalasuriar explains some of these difficulties in her field notes when first attempting to make a mission:

> "The Rent Is Too Damn High" is my first attempt at writing up the 500 character limited mission description using the PS4 controller. It goes well until I hit "X" and lose the entire block of mission text because I can't count 500 characters in my head to make sure I'm not over the limit. I try again to enter my mission text. I realize I should have typed it out in another word processor with a character count in the first place. I try doing this, have what I think is a character count under 500 (according to the word processor) and painstakingly type it in again, word for word. I hit "X." The damn thing gets deleted for being too long. Again! At this point, I throw the controller on the coffee table and get up to grab a beverage.

This 500-character limit makes it nearly impossible for anyone to feel as if he or she has truly set the scene. This small block of text is the only way of setting up the social issue at hand, and 500 characters, including every single space and punctuation mark, is woefully inadequate. To add insult to injury, the system has nothing built in to alert you that you have reached the maximum number of characters. It simply deletes the entire block of text if you have exceeded your limit. Even if we were able to squash all of the information, emotion, and oppression to which we were calling attention into that one small box, we are also assuming that players will bother reading the mission description. Without the set-up, there is no impact; it is a swing and a miss. Any consciousness-raising and critical thinking that might have occurred just goes rushing past, and players are never jarred out of immersion by the resultant smack.

The steep learning curve for Creator Mode was certainly evident in the physical set-up of the missions themselves, and the frustration was clear at nearly every step of the creation process across every team member. Limitations on model memory placed unforeseen restrictions on all manner of things, from the number of NPCs to the number of dynamic objects (items that players can interact with, like traffic cones that can be knocked over or gas cans that can explode when fired upon). There are strict limits on how many of these things you can place, and an excess of one lowers the available number of the others. Thus, there is simply no way to manufacture a true crowd of people, which makes representing reality tricky. For example, our soldier's funeral looked woefully under-attended and sad.

It also became apparent that game design is something that is very easy to enjoy but very difficult to master. Again, Ratnabalasuriar's field notes provide an illustration:

"The Rent Is Too Damn High": I start placing the spawn points
for the team and immediately start getting annoyed about having
so many spawn points. 16 damn spots per team? I only picked two
teams! I sigh and start placing them in a horizontal line next to
one another. At the team meeting later, a colleague explains that
having a variety of spawn points helps prevent corpse camping
from the other team, where once they figure out the spawn points,
they camp their character there to kill you the moment you pop
back into the world from your most recent death experience.
Crap. Game design is a bit more complicated than anticipated.
    . . . In hopes of offering some escape routes or access to effec-
tive cover elements like barricades, boxes, pallets, etc., I've placed
some of my spawn points directly near the edge of stairwells and
buildings. At this point, I have not realized that the spawn points
have directional arrows (this is what happens when I text and
design missions, missing crucial tutorials on this very issue), so
when I hit the test run button, I am treated to my first epic design

fail. An NPC on my team pops into existence on the building edge only to take a step directly off the edge and plummet to his death. I am heartily cackling at this and after running it again to see if it would happen again (it did!) I go back to the Creator and fix the spawn point directions, so my teams don't make their direct action a suicidal one.

Hobart's field notes document additional technical difficulties we encountered:

"Saving Private Ryan's Remains": There is a slight hiccup as I realize that I have placed the maximum number of dynamic objects (traffic cones). Trying to delete these, I inadvertently place an enormous wall in the middle of the church parking lot and can't get rid of it. Even choosing "delete all" keeps the wall where it is. I end up exiting the Creator and coming back later. Luckily, when I do, the wall is gone.

. . . The WBC headquarters is at the shady motel at the edge of town. It is, I imagine, their temporary headquarters—easy to set up, easy to abandon, and fake names and cash payment for rooms seem like things that will be just fine to the motel's owner. The Fundamentalist Church is meeting (spawning) in the local grocery store parking lot. This parking lot is where they're taking the hearse if they wrest control away from the WBC, while the WBC is trying to get the hearse to the motel. When I test my mission, it's hilarious in its wrongness. And then it gets even more hilarious when I realize that while I've gotten the spawn points for the two groups as I intended (WBC at the motel, Fundamentalists at the grocery store), once a side has the hearse, I've set it up so that they need to deliver it to the opposing team's location. This would be so much easier if you could name each of your teams instead of just relying on the orange and blue circles of Team 1 and Team 2.

Perhaps the hardest tightrope to walk was the one strung between two opposing poles, one called "fun missions" and the other called "meaningful missions." Hobart explained how the first iteration of "Saving Private Ryan's Remains" was originally an LTS mission, and a terrible one at that:

> After about an hour and a half (two and a half, including the hour break I took in the middle to ease my frustration), the scenario is done, the test has been successful, but the mission itself . . . is dreadfully boring. I've given it far too small of a radius. I likely haven't put enough weapons, health, and armor around. I placed a few cars, but I actually parked them in parking spaces in the parking lot, worrying more about realism than creating an interesting mission.

Is it even possible to create a fun mission that is also meaningful?

CONCLUSION

Our attempts to create game scenarios that rewrite/remix existing game modes to foster critical consciousness by offering counter narratives to those embedded within the games helped reveal some important limitations as well as possibilities that exist in these and other open-world type games. Though largely failures, our experiments did not dissuade us that video games can be used to help players think about serious social justice issues in terms of representations of race, gender, and other identity categories. Instead, our experiences within the *GTA5* Creator Mode helped us gain a greater understanding and appreciation of the time, labor, experience, resources, and training that go into the creation of a successful and highly entertaining mainstream game title. By unpacking the limitations of the game scenario modes, we began to better understand how such restrictions channel players' efforts into uncritical repetitions of existing game mechanics. The Creator Mode successfully facilitates the quick duplication of existing game modes in the main *GTA5* storyline and online, and thus represents an opportunity for the generation of endless jobs, an extension of what appear to be the game's most entertaining gameplay mechanics and mission modes provided, for free, by players themselves. Working within these proscribed parameters presented significant barriers to the creation of game scenarios that featured more culturally responsive jobs or explored social inequalities and helped to break immersion from the main gameplay mechanics.

Despite these limitations, the project helped push forward some alternative ideas for using the Creator Mode to foster discussions and dialogue around these issues. As our research team worked out problems and kinks encountered in the Creator Mode, we began to discuss how various group identities were represented (or not featured at all) in the game. After these discussions, we noticed in our individual gameplay that some of us began to play the games with a more critical eye, paying closer attention to the elements in games that reproduced stereotypical representations and erasures of various identities in the game. In other words, as Frasca (2001) proposed, we began to pay closer attention to the structure of the game and wonder more about how the structure might be imagined differently to become more inclusive and more critical, and offer a platform to spark discussions. That is, while our missions may not have broken immersion, for us, the act of creating them did.

Boal's *Theater of the Oppressed* (1979) is a series of theater games, unique as a form of theater because it breaks immersion, denies catharsis, and provokes audience participation. The Creator Mode experience explored the potential of using *GTA5* as a setting for running a series of scenarios meant to provide the player with a set of potential outcomes around a specific social justice issue such as gender (human trafficking) as well as race (gentrification and housing cost, drug trafficking, etc.). This presents researchers with some potential tools for answering Frasca's (2001) challenge. However, with the current Creator Mode setup, there are few gameplay mechanics available to facilitate storytelling.

Observations by Gee (2007) help us understand these limitations by explaining how content and gameplay are not always necessarily connected. He explains how this works as applied to an earlier iteration of the *Grand Theft Auto* series:

> The content of a game like *Grand Theft Auto: San Andreas* involves poverty, an African-American community, and crime. However, the game play involves solving problems strategically, problems like how to ride a bike through city streets so as to evade pursuing

cars and follow a map to end up safely where you need to go. In games like this, elements of content could be changed without changing the game play—for example, in some cases, taking pictures of people instead of shooting them or secretly planting a message rather than a bomb in their car would leave the problem solving and its difficulty pretty much the same. Critics of games need to realize that players, especially strategic and mature players, are often focusing on game play more than on content *per se*. (Gee 2007, 19)

Gee's observation of how changing small aspects of the gameplay content would be minimally disruptive to the gameplay mechanics offers some interesting opportunities for creating game scenarios that break immersion.

Based on these observations, future research will focus on identifying alternate content which nevertheless does not change the mechanics. Integrating storytelling and facilitation elements into gameplay may be a way to add in these missing elements and produce non-immersive gameplay by literally breaking the fourth wall. We plan to continue our experiments by adding a facilitator who plays alongside the participant, taking him or her on a guided tour of Los Santos. Using extra narrative layers and scripts similar to pen-and-paper, role-playing game adventure supplements, the goal of this facilitator will be to try to break immersion and encourage players to think critically about structures of inequality represented within the game.

We are encouraged in such efforts by forms of this immersion-breaking meta-commentary already occurring with gameplay broadcasting and commentary in online video platforms such as Twitch, Ustream, YouTube, and console-specific streaming services offered through PlayStation 4 and Xbox One. While Gamergaters have tried to shut down such social commentary about games, with a community of tens of millions of players, it is clear that even relatively small niches in the game ecology can attract considerable interest. Developing tools to better unpack its messages may be a fringe interest within the GTA player community. Creating tools to begin to use the game for consciousness raising may seem even more marginal a pursuit. However, regardless of popular interest, continuing such experimentation with this incredibly popular video game can help us understand how to use existing, open-world games as platforms for building better, more just games in the future.

WORKS CITED

Adams W., Owens, C., and Small, K. 2010. "Effects of Federal Legislation on the Commercial Exploitation of Children." *Juvenile Justice Bulletin*. United States Department of Justice, Office of Justice Programs, Office of Juvenile Justice and Delinquency Prevention. www.ncjrs.gov/pdffiles1/ojjdp/228631.pdf.

Boal, A. 1979. *Theater of the Oppressed*. New York: Urizen Books.

Bonilla-Silva, E. 2013. *Racism without Racists: Color-Blind Racism and the Persistence of Racial Inequality in America*. Lanham, MD: Rowman and Littlefield Publishers.

Brecht, B. 1964. *Brecht on Theatre: The Development of an Aesthetic*. Translated by J. Willett. New York: Hill and Wang.

Frasca, G. 2001. "Videogames of the Oppressed: Videogames as a Means for Critical Thinking and Debate." Master's thesis, Georgia Institute of Technology. www .ludology.org/articles/thesis/FrascaThesisVideogames.pdf.

Gee, J. P. 2007. *Good Video Games + Good Learning: Collected Essays on Video Games, Learning, and Literacy*. New York: Peter Lang.

Gray, K. 2014. *Race, Gender and Deviance in Xbox Live: Theoretical Perspectives from the Virtual Margins*. London: Routledge.

Greenfield, P. M., and Cocking, R. R. 1996. *Interacting with Video*. Norwood, NJ: Ablex Publishing Corporation.

Hardt, M., and Negri, A. 2000. *Empire*. Cambridge, MA: Harvard University Press.

Hathaway, J. 2014. "What Is Gamergate, and Why? An Explainer for Non-geeks." *Gawker*. October 10. http://gawker.com/what-is-gamergate-and-why-an-explainer -for-non-geeks-1642909080.

Koster, R. 2004. *Theory of Fun for Game Design*. Scottsdale, AZ: Paraglyph Press.

Lees, M. 2016. "What Gamergate Should Have Taught Us about the 'Alt-right.'" *Guardian*, December 1.

Leonard, D. 2003. "Live in Your World, Play in Ours": Race, Video Games, and Consuming the Other." *Studies in Media and Information Literacy Education* 3 (4): 1–9.

———. 2006a. "Not a Hater, Just Keepin' It Real: The Importance of Race- and Gender-Based Game Studies." *Games and Culture* 1 (1): 83–88.

———. 2006b. "Virtual Gangstas, Coming to a Suburban House Near You: Demonization, Commodification, and Policing Blackness." In *The Meaning and Culture of Grand Theft Auto*, edited by N. Garrelts, 49–69. Jefferson, NC: McFarland.

———. 2009. Young, Black (and Brown) and Don't Give a Fuck: Virtual Gangstas in the Era of State Violence. *Cultural Studies <=> Critical Methodologies*, 9 (2): 248–72.

———. 2016. "Grand Theft Auto V: Post-Racial Fantasies and Ferguson Realities." In *The Intersectional Internet: Race, Sex, Class, and Culture Online*, edited by S. U. Noble and B. M. Tynes, 129–44. Bern, Switzerland: Peter Lang.

Michael, D. and Chen, S. 2006. *Serious Games: Games That Educate, Train, and Inform.* Boston: Thomson Course Technology.

Murray, J. H. 1998. *Hamlet on the Holodeck: The Future of Narrative in Cyberspace.* Cambridge, MA: MIT Press.

Novak, J. 2008. *Game Development Essentials: An Introduction.* 2nd ed. Clifton Park, NY: Thompson/Delmar Learning.

Ohlheiser, A. 2015. "Why 'Social Justice Warrior,' a Gamergate Insult, Is Now a Dictionary Entry." *Washington Post*, October 7.

Polasek, P. M. 2014. "A Critical Race Review of Grand Theft Auto V." *Humanity and Society*, 38 (2): 216–18.

R*Q. 2014. GTA Online Census: The Story So Far. *Rockstar Games*. www.rockstar games.com/newswire/article/52349/gta-online-census-the-story-so-far.

Ritterfeld, U., Cody, M., and Vorderer, P. (eds.). 2009. *Serious Games: Mechanisms and Effects.* New York: Routledge.

Rockstar North. 2013. *Grand Theft Auto V.* [Computer software].

Rowlands, T. 2012. *Video Game Worlds.* Walnut Creek, CA: Left Coast Press.

Schutz, A. 1970. *Reflections on the Problem of Relevance.* New Haven: Yale University Press.

Silver, J. (Producer), Wachowski, L., and Wachowski, L. (Directors). 1999. *The Matrix* [Motion picture on DVD]. United States: Warner Bros.

———. 2003a. *The Matrix Reloaded* [Motion picture on DVD]. United States: Warner Bros.

———. 2003b. *The Matrix Revolutions* [Motion picture on DVD]. United States: Warner Bros.

Swinfen, A. 1984. *In Defense of Fantasy: A Study of the Genre in English and American Literature since 1945.* London: Routledge & Kegan Paul.

Taylor, T. L. 2003. "Intentional Bodies: Virtual Environments and Designers Who Shape Them." *International Journal of Engineering Education*, 19 (1): 25–34.

Terranova, T. 2000. "Free Labor: Producing Culture for the Digital Economy." *Social Text* 18 (2): 33–58. http://muse.jhu.edu/journals/social_text/v018/18.2terranova .html.

Toffler, Alvin. 1980. *The Third Wave: The Classic Study of Tomorrow.* New York: Bantam.

# PART 2

# ECONOMICS OF GAMING

CHAPTER 3

# THE POST-FEMINIST POLITICS OF THE "EVERYONE CAN MAKE GAMES MOVEMENT"

STEPHANIE ORME

I N THE SPRING of 2015, I was invited to give a talk at Johns Hopkins University on the topic of women and gaming culture. The talk was followed by a game night during which undergraduate students were invited to play games featuring or developed by women. Following my talk, a group of about eight students dragged some chairs into a circle in the middle of a room filled with the sounds of *Mirror's Edge* and *Child of Light* and where they discussed some of the issues from my talk. They expressed frustrations over the lack of diversity in games, the prevalent misogyny and racism in online gaming spaces, and the dearth of women working in game development. They framed discrimination against women and people of color in the gaming industry as a social justice issue—the belief being that representation of white female and minoritized characters in games reflected those working in game production. Then one white male student ventured, "If people don't like games the way they are, why don't they just make their own?"

This answer points to a misunderstanding about how accessible digital game production is. His assumption is understandable given that even a quick Google search yields hundreds of websites promising opportunities to make games. The past five years have seen an explosion of school curricula, scholarships, summer camps, and workshops designed to encourage females and people of color to learn to code and program their own games. Thus, this student underscored a mantra rather than a new idea in suggesting that, "everyone can make games." Desperate to refute the narratives of a toxic gaming culture perpetuated by Gamergate, many in the industry are taking action to boost diversity—interventions I call the "Everyone Can Make Games Movement"[1] (or ECMGM, as I will refer to it henceforth). Although such initiatives are beneficial in many ways (i.e., bringing attention to the industry's lack of diversity, sparking interest in game design), I wish to challenge the use of the ECMGM as a viable "solution" to the game industry's concerns regarding diversity. While more diversity in game development promises to bring fresh perspectives to a community saturated with narratives of white, cisgender men, ECMGM may also obscure systemic forms of oppression that female game makers and game makers of color experience.

In this chapter, I argue that the discourse of ECMGM is built on a post-feminist/post-racial understanding of the video game industry, one that fails to acknowledge institutionalized sexism and racism. Drawing on published reports and experiences of industry workers, I discuss the promise and peril of ECMGM, highlighting the ways in which the culture of sexism and racism is built into the work culture of much of the game industry. In order to eschew racism and sexism in gaming, however, the industry is in need of widespread, systematic change. I suggest starting with a restructuring of work cultures so that they stop privileging white, cisgender male employees and disempowering members of marginalized communities that the industry claims to embrace. This type of social justice and feminist project is necessary to making the vision of ECMGM a reality.

## THE ARGUMENT FOR ECMGM

The most significant contribution of ECMGM is in calling attention to and attempting to resolve the gender and racial inequalities that persist in game development. The movement achieves this through a variety of initiatives that are designed to encourage members of marginalized groups to pursue careers in game development. Under the umbrella of ECMGM are both training-based initiatives such as *Girls Make Games*, a series of workshops that teach young girls programming, art design, and other game-making skills (http://girlsmakegames.com), and Internet-based do-it-yourself initiatives. For example, female game developer Zoe Quinn maintains a curated list of websites that offer resources for learning to program games, distribute your games, and other information aspiring game designers might be interested in (http://gamesareforeveryone.com). Internet searches turn up dozens of similar outlets; all are aimed at helping users learn to make games. I see these "incubator" projects as existing separately from larger-scale organizations such as Women in Games International (WIGI), which sponsors lecture series and professional development events, and even has a peer-mentoring program for industry professionals and students (http://womeningamesinternatioanl.org). These types of programs provide more long-term support for individuals working in the game industry, as opposed to DIY resources or short-term workshops on game design. Hence, when I refer to ECMGM projects, it is the latter type of inclusion-based initiatives that I am discussing.

There are a myriad of reasons why feminist gamers and game developers support ECMGM initiatives. Although different ECMGM projects go about it in their own ways, the central premise of the movement is that there is a need to recruit more women and members of other minoritized groups to the game development industry. While more women are pursuing careers in games, they remain vastly outnumbered by men, who are more likely to choose to be trained in high-tech computer skills (Legewie and DiPrete 2014). According to the 2015 survey of approximately three thousand game industry professionals from around the world conducted by the International Game Developers Association (IGDA), 75 percent of the industry workforce identified as male while 22 percent identify as female. Just over 1 percent identified as male-to-female transgender, 0.2 percent identified as female-to-male transgender; another 1 percent selected "Other" as their response, and 9 individuals listing "non-binary" for their gender identity (IGDA 2015).

There is a similar disparity in the industry workforce in terms of race. Respondents to the aforementioned IGDA survey overwhelmingly identified as White/Caucasian/European, comprising 76 percent of the global game development workforce. The survey allowed for respondents to select up to three categories for this question. Even when respondents only selected White/Caucasian/European for this question, the percentage was still high—67 percent. The next most frequently selected responses were East Asian (9 percent), Hispanic/Latino (7.3 percent), and Black/African/African American (3 percent) (IGDA 2015).

These gender and racial disparities in the workface are not reflective of minorities' interest in video games. Females now represent 44 percent of gamers, with women 18 years or older (33 percent) significantly outpacing boys under the age of 18 (15 percent) (Entertainment Software Association 2015). Furthermore, Black and Latino individuals average more time playing video games than white or Asian individuals (Northwestern University 2011). Clearly, there are demographic gaps between those who play games and those who make them. This is further troubling given that Kafai (1998), Denner and Campe (2008), and Heeter et al. (2009) have found that the gender of game designers seems to influence how audiences perceive the games. In each study, young boys were found to strongly prefer games that were designed by male game makers while girls preferred titles designed by females.

One motivation behind ECMGM projects springs from the hope that a diverse industry workforce will produce a more diverse repertoire of games that appeals to a diverse gaming audience. Despite diversity among the gamer population (Entertainment Software Association 2015), the majority of mainstream games continue to cater to an assumed male, white audience. Williams et al. (2009) found that male, white, adult characters are dramatically overrepresented in video games, compared to actual census data on their representation in the US population. Dozens of studies have highlighted the ways in which female characters in video games are routinely portrayed as passive, peripheral characters (Dietz 1998; Haninger and Thompson 2004) and sexually objectified (Beasley and Standley 2002; Ivory 2006). When Black characters are present, they tend to be stereotyped as athletes in sports games or as violent criminal characters (Burgess et al. 2011) similar to the sparse portrayals of Latino and Hispanic characters

(Leonard 2003). ECMGM initiatives aim to diversity the workforce, hoping it will lead to more equitable representations of these groups in games.

While formal education does not guarantee employment (as is the case with any industry), formal training in game design provides prospective developers with skills that will make them not only successful game designers but also successful employees. Sought-after work skills such as critical thinking, problem-solving, time management, and communication are equally important in securing a job in the industry. Many game design studios have established relationships with schools that offer degrees in game design programs, which can make obtaining an internship or full-time position in the industry easier (Sinclair 2014). Likewise, programs like WIGI offer networking opportunities for aspiring developers. Those who opt for the ECMGM approach instead are forced to navigate the job search largely on their own.

While the number of female developers has been on the rise in the past five years, women are still very much a minority in the field. Women account for only 11 percent of game designers and 3 percent of programmers (Burrows 2013). The majority of women employed in the game industry hold more stereotypically "feminine" positions such as marketing specialists or administrative support, as opposed to the more technical roles like programming, developing, and art design (Prescott and Bogg 2011). These more "female-friendly" positions in the industry also tend pay lower wages than the male-dominated fields. Even among the high-paying technical fields, women tend to earn less than their male colleagues performing the same roles. For example, female game programmers and engineers reportedly earned $14,000 less than their male peers in 2014 (Gamasutra 2014).

This "occupational ghettoization[2]" is the result of a "duel-queuing process." Employers rank desirable workers based on their skills and knowledge; however, gender and race may influence their evaluation, in either a discriminatory fashion or in a deliberate effort to recruit individuals of a particular gender or race. At the same time, workers may self-select certain occupations that are considered "sex-appropriate" or "race appropriate" (Reskin and Roos 1990; Kaufman 2002; Kadowaki 2014).

Research has consistently shown that boys are socialized to embrace math and engineering, while girls are encouraged to pursue literature and biological sciences, each of which reflects the stereotypical assumptions about gender and ability. This results in lower self-concept in girls and women in math-related disciplines, making them less likely to pursue a career in that area, even if they earn grades similar to their male peers (Sáinz and Eccles 2012). One of the core missions of ECMGM is to challenge this gendered professional socialization.

Despite promoting diversity in the gaming industry, ECMGM needs to do more to encourage individuals who have traditionally been excluded from the conversation surrounding careers in game development. What is lacking, specifically, from ECMGM is a critique of the systematic inequalities game makers of color and women game makers experience and that may stop prospective game makers from entering the industry. Tearing down institutional barriers require that, in addition to promoting diversity, ECMGM embraces feminist interventions in the gaming industry, ones that challenge the culture and beliefs that marginalize women and people of color.

## THE PERILS OF ECMGM

I cannot overemphasize the importance of the "anyone can make a game" message as a nudge of encouragement to young girls or children of color who grew up playing games but were never themselves able to create them. ECMGM, however, oversimplifies the struggles of women and people of color who seek to enter the white, masculinist world industry of gaming. "Boot-strap" rhetoric predicated on neoliberal economic assumptions centered on individual ability and sheer determination overlook institutionalized barriers to equality such as racism and sexism by suggesting that women and people of color are responsible for achieving equality (Steeves 1987). While these neoliberal logics operate in other industries, the gaming industry—steeped in a long legacy of masculinity—is arguably one of the most fraught ones for women and other minority groups.

In this regard, ECMGM can be seen embodying a post-feminist discourse of the gaming industry—one in which "everyone" has the equal opportunity to be successful. Angela McRobbie (2004) has written about how popular culture now frames women's achievements as obvious, stable fixtures, both socially and culturally. In the words of Susan Douglas (2010), "women's achievements . . . are simply part of the cultural landscape" (9). The ideas of McRobbie, and those of Douglas, can be applied to the hundreds of online seminars, workshops, and resource guides promoting the increasingly popular narrative of ECMGM. This "postfeminist" sensibility, however, runs the risk of blind-siding the individuals who adopt the rhetoric of ECMGM as an unquestioned truth and enter the gaming industry unaware of and unprepared for dealing with racism and sexism.

The promise of the independent game market, a booming sector of the gaming industry characterized by innovative games that try to provide players with new types of gaming experiences, also augments illusions that individual game makers are responsible for scaling institutional barriers. Indie games, like their film industry counterparts, are created and financed by individual developers (or small development teams), hence they are not accountable to a larger game studio. On the one hand, the indie market enables new voices to tell new stories beyond the narratives and characters that have long dominated the AAA[3] game industry. However, without a major studio backing a project, the onus of publishing and marketing a game falls on indie developers. Even with platforms like Steam, an Internet-based platform that allows developers to digitally distribute their games, indie developers are competing with thousands of other indie developers and established franchises with loyal markets ("7 Reasons" 2015). Additionally, indie game makers' earnings appear to be plummeting. According to the 2014 Indie Salary Report that surveys non-salaried game developers, solo indie developers earned an average of $11,812 in 2013, a 49 percent drop from 2012's $23,130 average (Gamasutra 2014).

Many self-taught developers get their start with programs like Twine or Game Maker, accessible game design software that often requires little to no programming knowledge. While great for learning the basics of how game code functions, these programs have limitations. Twine, for instance, restricts users to developing text-based games only. Game Maker allows for slightly more complex games without needing any programming proficiency, relying on visual scripting and programming instead. Like Twine, Game Maker is highly useful for understanding and visualizing how game code functions; however, in order to be competitive in the games industry, more advanced design skills are necessary. The relatively low-cost Unity engine allows for much more sophisticated games (including AAA titles) but requires significantly more technical knowledge and effort. In an era where we are told anyone can release a game, the market becomes filled with inexperienced developers competing against full-time professional developers (and their larger budgets), a reality that is often overlooked by the rhetoric of ECMGM.

Further complicating attempts to enter the industry for game makers of color and women game makers are commonly accepted hiring practices. Hiring managers are powerful gatekeepers. Unfortunately, some such gatekeepers also hold stereotypical notions about what a programmer looks like (Guo 2014). This has cultivated the widespread expectation for what a game developer looks like and to reproducing gaming as a cultural preserve for white males. Although today's ECMGM and STEM education programs challenge such beliefs, the imbalance between growth in minority game design graduates and their representation in the workforce suggests there are still prejudices in hiring.

As the gamer population diversifies, so, too, must the culture surrounding the games workforce. For the industry to become more diverse, the culture of game making must make room for women and people of color. Today's typical industry employee is a 32-year-old college-educated white male living in North America. According to the 2015 IGDA survey, 46 percent of employees are single, 78 percent have no children, and 83 percent are not responsible for providing care for elderly family members. As such, the work culture of the industry tends to be modeled after a young single man's perceived ideal lifestyle (Kelan 2008). The gaming industry, in other words, seems to assume that its young male workforce is not burdened with childcare, an assumption that further reinforces the gaming industry's gendered division of labor. Indeed, many of the 20- to 35-year-old men who work in game development do not have children, leaving some to speculate that ageism is also a factor in the industry's hiring practices (Serrels 2015).

Moreover, women in the gaming industry often cite "crunch time" as a particular challenge. Crunch time—during which developers put in as much as 90 hours of work a week to ensure a game is completed by its scheduled deadline—is embedded in the corporate culture of game design. The "long hours" culture is justified by rhetoric of "passion" for game design—the logic being that if you are committed to your work, you can endure crunch (Consalvo 2008). For industry employees who have families to care for, industry norms like crunch pose enormous burdens. Single parents, who are statistically more likely to be female and people of color (United States Census Bureau 2014), must find ways to balance the demands of the workforce with childcare responsibilities or, as Consalvo (2008) found, decide to leave the industry prematurely.

ECMGM also suggests part-time work as a solution to balancing parenthood with game development. Across industries in the United States, women are more likely than men to work part-time jobs, especially if they have children—38 percent of mothers compared to 4 percent of fathers (Allard and Janes 2008). Part-time work, however, is rare in the gaming industry. As a result, female employees with children tend to take jobs in areas of the industry that offer more predictable hours. While this response to working constraints may enable working mothers to balance work with childcare demands, working part-time frustrates career development. Part-time workers are less likely to land promotions and raises (Prescott and Bogg 2014). Additionally, because of the lack of affordable childcare and paid leave in the United States, many mothers cannot work in full-time positions that would offer career advancement. For these reasons familial labor deters women from entering or remaining in the industry. Studies have shown that women who choose careers in game design are more likely than males to leave the field (Prescott and Bogg 2014). While this is also the case in other industries, for heavily male-dominated sectors such as game development that already struggle to attract and retain women employees, the lack of part-time opportunities can be particularly detrimental. Challenges including unequal pay, workplace harassment, and difficult co-worker relationships have also been cited as common factors in women's decisions to leave game development (Brandeis-Hepler 2016). Male-dominated industries tend to cultivate workplace cultures that are more tolerant of sexual harassment or gender bias in hiring and treatment of employees (Maggs 2017). Women in the games industry receive a disproportionate amount of criticism and hostility than do men. Prior to the anti-feminist bullying that received public attention amid Gamergate, female developers have long endured discrimination and harassment in the industry. Women have reported insubordination from male colleagues, a lack of respect or consideration of their opinions or suggestions, a persistent "frat boy" culture in the office and at industry events, questioning of their technical ability, and overt sexual harassment (IGDA 2014). For example, female developer Filamena Young described how industry conventions have become unsafe spaces for her, having been sexually assaulted by male colleagues in attendance (Burrows 2013). And yet, there is a staunch refusal by many in the industry to acknowledge that there is anything problematic with the way women are treated (McIntosh 2014). Before inclusion-driven initiatives like ECMGM can be successful, the industry must acknowledge the need for a cultural shift regarding women's right to be in this space.

Unfortunately, there is far less documentation (or poor documentation) of racism in the gaming industry. Gray (2014) has observed the routine racism experienced by people of color in the online gaming community Xbox Live. People of color are sometimes "linguistically profiled" via auditory cues that signal they are of a particular racial background. They are then harassed and verbally abused, to the point where many marginalized gamers have been "ghettoized" into separate communities within Xbox Live. Moreover, Xbox's parent company, Microsoft, has taken no action to combat racism in their gaming community, declaring that racism is not an issue in Xbox Live (Gray 2014). Gray's work highlights the need for more analysis on racism and games and the systemic effects of micro-aggressions that racist representations in games encourage, which manifests in the hiring prejudices that affect people of color in the game industry.

## WHAT ECMGM MUST DO TO SUCCEED
## AS A SOCIAL JUSTICE PROJECT

If Gamergate has proven anything, it is that the gaming industry is in dire need of diverse perspectives. ECMGM is one way of helping the industry achieve that. Yet, it is not without its limitations and challenges. In order to be the successful movement that it can be, there needs to be a cultural shift in gaming as an industry. Attitudes about who plays games and who can make games must change before hiring for development jobs can be free of gender or racial biases. The general industry work culture needs an overhaul that better reflects the real-world needs of increasingly diverse development teams. I recognize that calling for a massive shift in the structure and culture of an industry that has existed for decades, with firm roots in male- and white-dominated practices, is an enormous challenge. Yet, I believe we are starting to see this shift, in part due to the work of ECMGM. More men in the industry and the gaming community have begun speaking out against the mistreatment of women in the industry and many are calling for the very diversity initiatives this chapter has focused on (Schreler 2014; Tsukayama 2014). However, until these overarching structural changes happen, ECMGM's progress will be stymied.

One way ECMGM can bolster its effects is to focus on strategies that better prepare people from oppressed groups for entering a work climate that can be, at times, resistant to their presence.[4] Earlier in this chapter, I referenced Women in Games International (WIGI), an organization that specializes in professional socialization for women. Seminars and training programs that not only provide prospective developers with tech-based skill sets but also tools for dealing with and combatting the types of barriers and challenges previously enumerated can help set up minority developers for a successful and long-term career in gaming. Online mentorship programs like the one offered by WIGI, which is open to both men and women, are an invaluable source of support for new developers navigating hurdles in the industry. Established programs like WIGI that have connections throughout the industry can also provide insight into which studios foster the most welcoming climates—something aspiring game professionals would have a tough time finding out on their own. For those who wish to become an indie game professional, having a mentor to teach them to design, publish and market a new game can be the difference between a commercial success and the all-too-common indie game failure.

So that such suggestions do not encourage game makers to operate in isolation from each other, however, collective organization is also necessary. Thus, ECMGMs should strive to foster partnerships with the gaming industry. Girls Who Code, a summer workshop designed to teach young girls coding skills, recently announced that twenty industry-leading technology companies have pledged to offer paid internships and other opportunities with alumni from the program (http://girlswhocode.com). Although Girls Who Code is not game-design specific, the program's "Hire Me" campaign serves as an excellent model for other diversity-focused initiatives. Fortunately, many in the gaming industry have expressed interest in diversity, including the heavily male-dominated eSports scene. In early 2015, Intel announced its partnership with the Electronic Sports League (ESL) and the video game criticism series Feminist Frequency to bolster diversity in the ESL industry (Vara 2015). The collaboration aims to promote both gender and racial diversity in game development, a goal that has long been a project of IGDA but now has the steam of large technology firms behind it. In spite of this, Intel recognizes the cultural challenges to their project:

> The doors are open for everyone; there aren't barriers to entry in the common sense . . . The problem isn't in getting people in; it's in accepting them once they've arrived. Sadly not everyone will be supported equally by the community along the way. That's the gaming and eSport community's problem. That's what we're trying to change. (Crecente 2015)

One of the greatest challenges for ECMGM's success, however, might actually stem from female members of the game industry. Harvey and Fisher (2015) highlight the tensions underlying women-in-games (WIG) projects, post-feminism, and the neoliberal culture of game production. They observed that many women working in the North American games industry—as developers, journalists, or other high-profile roles—embody a post-feminist ethos regarding WIG initiatives. These women's visibility in the conservative production culture of gaming places them in a precarious position: while they may be the best positioned to champion a feminist agenda like ECMGM, they must also navigate potential backlash from colleagues, the player base, and other key figures who could threaten their job security. Because of this, Harvey and Fisher note the tendency of some WIG initiatives to avoid self-branding as feminist, "often danc[ing] between what is implicitly a feminist agenda and a context that is, by and large, deeply unfriendly to anything that is labelled or characterized as feminism" (580), instead rallying behind the neoliberal logic that the only thing holding back anyone from pursuing a career in games is themselves.

## CONCLUSION

If Gamergate and the rising prominence of the alt-right post-2016 have taught us anything, it is to not underestimate the far-reaching influence that gaming culture can have. Gamergate, which began as a harassment campaign started by a male designer looking for revenge on an ex-girlfriend, quickly snowballed into a full-scale witch-hunt for feminist-identifying figures in gaming culture (Lees 2016). In time, the rhetoric of Gamergate morphed into an all-out war on social justice warriors and anyone invested in diversity and inclusion in everyday life. The conservative website Breitbart, one of the loudest pro-Gamergate voices in the movement, also became a key player in the 2016 US presidential election, with Breitbart's executive chair, Steve Bannon, eventually becoming White House Chief Strategist to Donald Trump. As Lees (2016) notes, "[The Gamergate] hashtag was the canary in the coalmine, and we ignored it."

Retrospectively, game studies scholars should be asking, "Could we have prevented this? Mitigated it in some way?" Given that white nationalists are, in fact, celebrating the white-, cis-gender-, male-ness of gaming culture, there is clearly a problem with the status quo of gaming. As Gray (2014) argues, all video game narratives serve some ideological project, with story often masking hegemonic portrayals of racial and gender identities. Such ideologies, which cater to the assumed white, heterosexual, male-dominated audience, maintain their prominence largely due to the composition of the industry workforce, which embodies its target and presumed audience, as opposed to the actual audience of players. Fron et al. (2007) describe how the predominately white, male elites of the industry produce a "hegemony of play," an exclusionary framing of video gameplay that upholds gaming culture's status quo. The industry's elites not only determine which technologies and games will be produced but also serve as the taste adjudicators for what games are "good," disparaging players who do not fit within the "hard-core gamer" demographic.

ECMGM is a rallying cry for those who feel unspoken to/for in games in an effort to have a voice themselves. However, if the industry refuses to hear those voices, how much change can we truly expect? Everyone may be able to make games; yet can we say that everyone has the same opportunity to make a career in games? This is a fundamental reality that ECMGM must come to terms with in order to devise strategies that will set developers up for success. The late game development legend Satoru Iwata is often quoted as saying, "Above all, video games are meant to just be one thing: Fun for everyone." It will take a great deal of reform from within the industry itself, and pressure for the industry to make radical change. Toward this end, it is my sincerest hope that someday the idea that "everyone can make games" is not merely a truism but is true for the gaming industry as a system.

NOTES

1    Alison Harvey and Stephanie Fisher (2015) use the phrase "Everyone can make games" to refer to the post-feminist articulations voiced by women working in the North American gaming industry. I specifically use this phrase to refer to what I see as a collective rhetoric of inclusion-based game development projects.
2    Barbara Reskin and Patricia Roos first used the term "occupational ghettoiza-tion" in their book *Job Queues, Gender Queues* (1990) to explain how jobs are organized in ways that segregate certain individuals in the workplace.
3    AAA refers to the major, big-budget studios that produce commercial digital games.
4    Although this is an individual-level strategy, I will also suggest how to link this approach with changes in the organization of game making.

WORKS CITED

Allard, M. D., and Janes, M. 2008. "Time Use of Working Parents: A Visual Essay." *Bureau of Labor Statistics*. www.bls.gov/opub/mlr/2008/06/art1full.pdf.
Beasley, B., and Standley, T. C. 2002. "Shirts vs. Skins: Clothing as Indicator of Gender Role Stereotyping in Video Games." *Mass Communication and Society* 5 (3): 279–93.
Black Shell Media. 2015. "7 Reasons Why Most Indie Developers Fail." April 7. http://blackshellmedia.com/2015/04/7-reasons-why-most-indie-game-developers-fail.
Brandeis-Hepler, J. 2016. *Women in Game Development: Breaking the Class Level-Cap.* Boca Raton, FL: CRC Press.

Burgess, M. C. R., Dill, K. E., Stermer, P. S., Burgess, S. R., and Brown, B. P. 2011. "Playing with Prejudice: The Prevalence and Consequences of Racial Stereotypes in Video Games." *Media Psychology* 14 (3): 289–311.

Burrows, L. 2013. "Women Remain Outsiders in Video Game Industry." *Boston Globe*, January 23.

Consalvo, M. 2008. "Crunched by Passion: Women Game Developers and Workplace Challenges." In *Beyond Barbie and Mortal Kombat: New Perspectives on Gender and Gaming*, edited by Y. B. Kafai, C. Heeter, J. Denner, and J. Y. Sun, 177–91. Cambridge, MA: MIT Press.

Crecente, B. 2015. "Intel Initiative Leads to Big Goal: Doubling of Women in Game Development by 2025." *Polygon*, January 20. www.polygon.com/2015/1/20/7863077/intel-initiative-leads-to-big-goal-doubling-of-woman-in-game.

Denner, J., and Campe, S. 2008. "What Games Made by Girls Can Tell Us." In *Beyond Barbie and Mortal Kombat: New Perspectives on Gender and Gaming*, edited by Y. B. Kafai, C. Heeter, J. Denner, and J. Y. Sun, 129–44. Cambridge, MA: MIT Press.

Dietz, T. L. 1998. "An Examination of Violence and Gender Role Portrayals in Video Games: Implications for Gender Socialization and Aggressive Behavior." *Sex Roles* 38 (516): 425–42.

Douglas, S. 2012. *Enlightened Sexism: The Seductive Message That Feminism's Work Is Done*. London: Macmillan.

Entertainment Software Association. 2015. "Essential Facts about the Computer and Video Game Industry." www.theesa.com/wp-content/uploads/2015/04/ESA-Essential-Facts-2015.pdf.

Flowers, L. O. 2012. "Commentary: Programs Are in Place to Help Minorities Successfully Pursue STEM Graduate Degrees." March 7. http://diverseeducation.com/article/16883/#.

Fron, J., Fullerton, T., Morie, J. F., and Pearce, C. 2007. "The Hegemony of Play." In *Situated Play: Proceedings of the 2007 DiGRA International Conference*, volume 4, edited by Akira Baba, 309–18. University of Tokyo, September 24–27.

Gamasutra. *Gamasutra Salary Survey*. 2014. www.gamesetwatch.com/2014/09/05/GAMA14_ACG_SalarySurvey_F.pdf.

Gray, K. 2014. *Race, Gender, and Deviance in Xbox Live: Theoretical Perspectives from the Virtual Margins*. New York: Routledge.

Guo, P. 2014. "Silent Technical Privilege." *Slate*, January 15. www.slate.com/articles/technology/technology/2014/01/programmer_privilege_as_an_asian_male_computer_science_major_everyone_gave.html.

Haninger, K., and Thompson, K. M. 2004. "Content and Ratings of Teen-Rated Video Games." *Journal of the American Medical Association* 291 (7): 856–65.

Harvey, A., and Fisher, S. 2015. "'Everyone Can Make Games!' The Post-feminist Context of Women in Digital Game Production." *Feminist Media Studies* 15 (4): 576–92.

Heeter, C., Egidio, R., Mishra, P., Winn, B., and Winn, J. 2009. "Alien Games: Do Girls Prefer Games Designed by Girls?" *Games and Culture* 4 (1): 74–100.

International Game Developers Association. 2014. "Developer Satisfaction Survey 2014 Summary Report." https://c.ymcdn.com/sites/www.igda.org/resource /collection/9215B88F-2AA3-4471-B44D-B5D58FF25DC7/IGDA_DSS_2014-Sum mary_Report.pdf.

International Game Developers Association. 2015. "Developer Satisfaction Survey 2015 Summary Report." https://c.ymcdn.com/sites/www.igda.org/resource /collection/CB31CE86-F8EE-4AE3-B46A-148490336605/IGDA%20DSS%20 2015-SummaryReport_Final_Sept15.pdf.

Ivory, J. D. 2006. "Still a Man's Game: Gender Representation in Online Reviews of Video Games." *Mass Communication and Society* 9 (1): 103–14.

Kadowaki, J. 2014. "Professional Ghettoization: The Clustering of Workers at the Intersections of Gender, Race, (and Class)." In *Routledge International Handbook of Race, Class, and Gender*, edited by S. A. Jackson, 184–94. New York: Routledge.

Kafai, Y. B. 1998. "Video Game Designs by Girls and Boys: Variability and Consistency of Gender Differences." In *From Barbie to Mortal Kombat: Gender and Computer Games*, edited by J. Cassell and H. Jenkins, 90–117. Cambridge, MA: MIT Press.

Kaufman, R. L. 2002. "Assessing Alternative Perspectives on Race and Sex Employment Segregation." *American Sociological Review* 67 (4): 547–72.

Kelan, E. K. 2008. "Emotions in a Rational Profession: The Gendering of Skills in ICT Work." *Gender, Work and Organization* 15 (1): 49–71.

Lees, M. 2016. "What Gamergate Should Have Taught Us about the 'Alt-right.'" *Guardian*, December 1.

Legewie, J., and DiPrete, T. A. 2014. "The High School Environment and the Gender Gap in Science and Engineering." *Sociology of Education* 87 (4): 259–80.

Leonard, D. 2003. "'Live in Your World, Play in Ours': Race, Video Games, and Consuming the Other." *Studies in Media and Information Literacy Education* 3 (4): 1–9.

Maggs, B. 2017. "More Women Are Becoming Game Developers, but There's a Long Way to Go." *The Conversation*, July 24. Retrieved from https://theconversation. com/more-women-are-becoming-game-developers-but-theres-a-long-way-to-go -79843.

McIntosh, J. 2014. "Playing with Privilege: The Invisible Benefits of Gaming While White." April 23. www.polygon.com/2014/4/23/5640678/playing-with-privilege -the-invisible-benefits-of-gaming-while-male.

McRobbie, A. 2004. "Post-feminism and Popular Culture." *Feminist Media Studies* 4 (3): 255–64.

Northwestern University Center on Media and Human Development. 2011. "Children, Media, and Race: Media Use among White, Black, Hispanic, and Asian American Children." http://web5.soc.northwestern.edu/cmhd/wp-content /uploads/2011/06/SOCconf ReportSingleFinal-1.pdf.

Prescott, J., and Bogg, J. 2014. *Gender Divide and the Computer Game Industry*. Hershey, PA: IGI Global.

Prescott, J., and Bogg, J. 2011. "Segregation in a Male-Dominated Industry: Women Working in the Computer Games Industry." *International Journal of Gender, Science, and Technology* 3 (1). http://genderandset.open.ac.uk/index.php/genderandset/article/viewFile/122/259.

Reskin, B., and Roos, P. A. 1990. *Job Queues, Gender Queues: Explaining Women's Inroads into Male Occupations.* Philadelphia: Temple University Press.

Sáinz, M., and Eccles, J. 2012. "Self-Concept of Computer and Math Ability: Gender Implications across Time and Within ICT Studies." *Journal of Vocational Behavior* 2: 486–99.

Schreler, J. 2014. "Thousands Rally Online Against Gamergate." *Kokatu*, April 15. http://kotaku.com/thousands-rally-online-against-gamergate-1646500492.

Sinclair, B. 2014. "Should Developers Go to School?" *Game Industry Biz*, April 22. www.gamesindustry.biz/articles/2014-04-22-should-developers-go-to-school.

Steeves, L. H. 1987. "Feminist Theories and Media Studies." *Critical Studies in Media Communication* 4 (2): 95–135.

Tsukayama, H. 2014. "The Game Industry's Top Trade Group Just Spoke Out against Gamergate." *Washington Post*, October 15.

United States Census Bureau. 2014. *America's Families and Living Arrangements.* www.census.gov/hhes/families/data/cps2014.html.

Vara, V. 2015. "Can Intel Make Silicon Valley More Diverse?" *New Yorker*, January 11.

Williams, D., Martins, N., Consalvo, M., and Ivory, J. D. 2009. "The Virtual Consensus: Representations of Gender, Race and Age in Video Games." *New Media and Society* 11 (5): 815–34.

CHAPTER 4

# SMART PLAY

*Social Stereotypes, Identity Building, and Counter Narratives*
*of Gold Farmers in China*

ZIXUE TAI AND FENGBIN HU

W E HAVE WITNESSED the mainstreaming of video games as a
formidable social, cultural, and economic force in the global media
landscape in the past two decades or so. Alongside this development is
the rise of moral panics among constituents ranging from academics to
pundits to the general public inciting widespread fears and concerns about
the alleged but often speculative role of video games and influence of
gameplays in inducing a variety of antisocial behaviors, aggressive tenden-
cies, health hazards, and other risks (Bowman 2016, 23–34). In tracking a
thirty-year period of major news magazine portrayal of video games, Dmitri
Williams (2003) notes "marked phases of vilification followed by partial
redemption" packaged in frames of a vast array of social hopes and fears
reflecting the socio-political climate of the time (543). Likewise, as a constant target of tirade and denunciation in popular rhetoric, video games and
gameplay are commonly lumped in with the consumption of "junk food"
and linked to prevalent social malaise such as "cultural decline, falling
standards of literacy and educational achievement" (Newman 2008, 4).

This chapter offers a critical interrogation of a special type of online
gamers in China commonly known as gold farmers who, as a marginalized

player group, have no legal recognition in Chinese society and must negotiate a living in a volatile game environment caught in between the fast-changing industry and an unpredictable transaction mechanism, coupled with ever-present government regulators. Our analysis is informed by two-plus years of in-depth field interviews with practitioners of gold farming in multiple cities in China.

## THE PRACTICE OF GOLD FARMING: AN OVERVIEW

We define gold farming as the practice of playing networked online games with the specific purpose of harvesting virtual loot, in-game currency, and other game assets that are then sold to other players or vendors for real money. It is an important component of the burgeoning secondary online game industry that "has grown out of the interaction between the gaming industry and gamers within China's unique sociopolitical context," and it thrives on "gamer-initiated business and services that emerged to fill the gaps in the chain of game production and consumption, which occupy a gray area that often merges consumption with production, and play with profits" (Zhang and Fung 2014, 39). Gold farming—which remains a highly controversial practice (Jin 2006; Nakamura 2009, 138–41; Steinkuehler 2006, 208–9)—is certainly not unique to China (Dibbell 2006). But it is fair to say that Chinese gold farmers have practiced the trade to a level of monetization and sophistication that is unrivalled in the rest of the world.

It is useful to foreground gold farming in the broad context of China's online game industry. Propelled by the explosive growth of the Internet sector and the state-supported online game industry in the past decades, network games have established an invasive and pervasive presence in Chinese society. Unlike major Western nations where console games dominate gameplay, networked online gaming virtually monopolizes China's video game world. With the largest gamer population as well as by far the biggest online game market in the world, China has cultivated a unique video game culture of its own. In particular, online gaming has exerted a prominent influence on Chinese youth culture from consumer products to everyday conversations.

While the gaming industry has relentlessly promoted a variety of ever-expanding services to diverse players, there has been a persistent mainstream discourse as typified in the popular media chastising online games for degrading and corrupting the mental and physical health of the younger generation in the nation. Because networked games are the main leisure activity for adolescents and youth across China, popular media and the public discourse exert a lopsided focus on the alleged pathological, addictive aspect of gameplay among this demographic primarily framed in the lens of an ongoing moral crisis in a society that is caught in a pro-tracted transformation to a Western-style consumerist culture (Golub and Lingley 2010, 462–63). Meanwhile, government regulation of online games is designed to foster the development of a nascent industry on the one hand, and to monitor modes of play (e.g., limiting the length of continuous gaming) and cleanse "unhealthy" content mostly in the area of porno-graphic and politically sensitive materials on the other (Ernkvist and Ström 2010, 63–65). Noticeably, the widely mentioned (albeit often dis-puted) impact of video games on aggressive behaviors, which dominates Western media's tirade against the game industry, has never been an issue of public concern in China, despite the heavy presence of violent content in China's online game space as typically represented in the popular genre of battlefield combat and *kung fu* titles.

The rise of gold farming as a special type of gameplay—or what we can call the professionalization of gold farmers—raises all sorts of chal-lenges for the players, the game industry, and society at large.

## FAN LABOR AND PRODUCTIVE PLAY

Contemplations of theoretical issues in video games have been under the heavy influence of two classic texts by Johan Huizinga and Roger Caillois on human play. Caillois (1961) defines play as "creating neither goods, nor wealth, nor new elements of any kind" (10). Huizinga (1964), whose ideas were the main sources of inspiration for Caillois, declares that play "is an activity connected with no material interest, and no profit can be gained by it" (13). This characterization of gameplay as "unproductive," however, has been increasingly challenged in the context of today's networked game environment.

In the broad conditions of the digital economy, immaterial labor has taken center stage (Hardt and Negri 2000, 29). Much of this labor, as

Terranova points out, is deemed "free labor" for its voluntary nature and for not directly generating monetary reward; but this should not be taken as possessing no value, because individual (most often voluntary and pleasurably embraced) participation in the production of immaterial labor increases the financial and utilitarian value of the creative industries over-all (Terranova 2004, 73). A similar concept is "playbour," which collapses the hitherto "relative temporal and spatial separateness of work and play," and incubates "recreation that generates value, consumption that is productive, play that is labour" (Fuchs 2014, 270). Playbour, as Christian Fuchs highlights, brings about economic value and begets financial profits; the designated beneficiary, however, turns out to be global capitalism.

Video games sit squarely at the generative forefront of this co-creative culture. Specifically, Taylor (2009) classifies video games as "co-creative media," in which players are "social laborers" and "co-productive agents" in maintaining the vitality of the game (159). Similarly, Celia Pearce (2006) argues in favor of treating video game culture as a hybrid entertainment form that crosscuts the boundaries "between play and production, between work and leisure, and between media consumption and media production" (68–71).

Gold farming takes advantage of player production by accumulating and transmitting prized assets and valued items within the game space, and these transactions typically materialize into real money (Dibbell 2006, 293). Toward that end, the practice of gold farming—by explicitly embracing the goal of cashing in on gameplay and prioritizing profit over fun—runs counter to most academic discussion on playbour and co-creative production in which users/consumers voluntarily contribute content for its affective value while the content is capitalized by global capitalism and corporate giants such as Google, Amazon, and Alibaba.

Whereas the online game industry has been very successful in branding games as fun as part of its marketing efforts, gold farmers reverse the conventional mode of play by placing money-making above entertainment and can thus be viewed as an act of subversion against the hypercommercialized game culture. In other words, gold farming is a type of profit-driven, transgressive gameplay that sabotages normative, predesigned modus operandi of working within game mechanics and rules. As we show later through player narratives, although the fun aspect of gameplay gives way to monetary aspirations, this does not necessarily mean that gold farmers cannot find enjoyment in the process.

## THE NEED FOR INSIDERS' PERSPECTIVES

This chapter offers a critical interrogation of this special type of online gamer from the vantage point of their personal perspectives on a variety of issues regarding their perceptions of the occupation, social bias, and the routines of practicing this trade. Our analysis is informed by two-plus years of extensive fieldwork primarily built on the in-depth interviews of practitioners of gold farming in five cities in China. This is much needed for two main reasons: first, there is precious little scholarly literature following any systematic mode of inquiry shedding light on gold farming. And second, in the limited scholarship that we found deliberating on gold farming, there is an unfortunate lack of in-depth, insiders' perspectives from the gold farmers themselves.

While it used to be a disaggregated, anarchic, and individualized underground cottage craft in the early years, gold farming has now evolved into a highly organized and discreetly coordinated enterprise seamlessly embedded in the current e-commerce environment. An efficient ecosystem for player recruiting and training, information sharing, and e-trading between players and clients has developed. We conducted an extensive preliminary investigation into the status quo of gold farming in China both online and offline, and recruited research participants thereafter. There are certainly still individuals who practice gold farming in China today outside an organization, but it is much more common for the practitioners to work in squads in dedicated workspaces and with a high degree of organization and coordination. The main reasons are threefold. First, most of the games that gold farmers target are *massively multiplayer online role-playing games* (*MMORPGs*), and playing in an organized group provides the most efficient way to strategically harvest game loot. Second, collaborating in coordinated groups makes it easier to bid for gold farming projects and facilitate online transactions; it is also easier for unified groups (mainly in the format of work studios) to earn client rankings and peer recognition through comments and ratings in the online transaction system. Third, keeping up to date with the latest gaming gadgets and computing equipment typically requires a hefty upfront investment, and it is more economical to invest in multiple stations and more feasible for resourceful investors to run this as a business operation. Most individual gold farmers would not be able to afford state-of-the-art playing stations on their own without external assistance.

Therefore, it is most common to find gold farmers working in a centralized work spaces—called gold farming studios (代练工作室)—where they coordinate tasks and responsibilities in play errands and missions. Most often, players live very close to their studio, or they sometimes convert residential apartments into small work studios, which can be simultaneously used for play, sleep, relaxation, and kitchen in designated areas. Studio managers, who typically pay the rent and are responsible for investing in the studios, hire individual gold farmers and serve as the liaison to bid for gold farming tasks and make final deliveries of completed missions. The managers naturally keep an eye on the profit throughout the process.

We made site visits and studied a total of fourteen studios, which, in an effort to maximize representation, spanned five cities, including one megacity (Shanghai), two mid-sized cities (Qingdao and Zhengzhou), and two small cities (Jinhua and Kunshan). Each site visit included in-depth interviews with managers and players, which usually lasted about one hour each. Interviewees were compensated in cash for their time. All together, we completed interviews with fifty-eight participants and our following analyses were based on the portion of the interview questions inquiring about interviewees' perceptions and reflections on what they do.

Following the synthesized strategies suggested by Kathy Charmaz (2014) in coding the interview data, we adopted a two-step process: first, we used open coding to identify major concepts and themes, and then we employed axial coding in both confirming previously found concepts and themes and building connections among them. We also followed the general guidelines offered by Joffe (2011) in detecting recurring thematic threads.

## IDENTITY NARRATIVES AND THEMATIC THREADS

The fifty-eight participants in our study were divided, quite unevenly, between fourteen studio managers and forty-four game players. We summarize our findings along the thematic streams based on our participants' revelations about their identification with the trade, what gravitates them to the job, their visions or plans for a possible career path in this field, and, above all, their perceptions of social stereotypes and biases toward them and their profession.

## THE FARMING BUSINESS

Studio managers and farming players (all male) are personally attached to the cause of gold farming, albeit for differing reasons. Studio managers are also investors and they maintain high stakes in the success of the business. Notably, most studio managers come from a white-collar background with previous career paths in fields such as banking, joint-venture corporate mid-level managers, and lucrative family businesses, and they all display an intimate and sophisticated understanding of the state of the trade of gold farming in China largely due to their personal encounters with online gaming and gold farming in their early years.

This runs counter to the conventional belief that people participating in gold farming have no other choices; that they are without a reputable or profitable path in an acceptable business. In Kunshan, which is located about an hour's drive from Shanghai, we visited a studio that occupies a whole floor in a luxurious four-star hotel, which the manager proudly told us is the gold standard of gold farming in China in its hardware, gaming environment, and player skills. Employees report to work every day via a biometric fingerprint reader, and each gold farmer carries a walkie-talkie for real-time coordination. Fringe benefits include two free meals each day for all staff. While its hotel locale incurs a heavy overhead cost, the studio also pays off nicely in profits: In the first two months of 2015, when business was at its height, the studio netted a profit of RMB¥1.2 million (US$189K) each month, while its average monthly income usually comes to about RMB¥400K (about US$64K). Its biggest bottleneck now, according to the manager, is not acquiring more lucrative contracts (it already has more than enough); rather, the challenge for them is in hiring enough qualified gold farmers.

Another exemplar enterprise is 5173 in Jinhua, one of the sites we visited in our research ("5173 in Jinhua: A Synoposis"). Specializing in online trading of virtual goods and assets, 5173 currently takes up about half of the market share in China (Hui 2014). With its own in-house studios, 5173 is one of the biggest employers in the area. As a matter of fact, most of the participants we interviewed in 5173 used its brand as justification against any doubts from friends or family about their involvement in gold farming—indeed, if a big, reputable company like 5173 is engaged in this, what is there to worry or be ashamed about?

## THE CALLING OF GOLD FARMING

Studio managers, as investors in the business, are also entrepreneurs. They build the studio by renting the space, purchasing computing equipment, paying utility bills, and, most important of all, hiring and managing staff. Thirteen out of the fourteen studios we studied are individually owned (and the remaining one is a partnership operation). It comes as no surprise that managers are the most sensitive about the legal status of the trade and express an obvious frustration over the lack of recognition for the profession of gold farming by government regulators. A few managers specifically made a point of highlighting this as a matter of importance to them. They mentioned their numerous attempts to get licensed at the local branch of the Administration of Industry and Commerce (AIC), the bureaucratic organization in charge of issuing business licenses, but to no avail.

> Many people are doing this [gold farming]. But AIC does not offer us any license, because they don't have this on their book. Regardless, gold farming is a fact of life, and they know that. It exists because there is the need for it in the marketplace. Also, current laws do not ban this. Taobao [China's leading e-commerce site], 5173, and many others are all doing this. This is a huge industry, but it is a gray area in reality. . . . There is nothing inglorious about this, because I make a living through my hard work. At this time, because the government does not know how to handle this, I cannot get a license, and therefore I can't pay tax to them. But don't blame me for this. (Studio Manager A, Shanghai)

A fellow manager in Kunshan echoed this sentiment:

> It is quite a nuisance to operate without a license. I went to AIC
> to apply for a license, but they didn't know how to deal with this.
> They said that they could offer me a license in the domain of cul-
> tural communication or something like that. But I declined since
> this has nothing to do with what I do. So I gave up. We have all
> intentions of operating like a normal business. However, the cur-
> rent regulatory regime does not serve us well; it is biased toward
> the gaming industry. (Studio Manager B, Kunshan)

It is logistically feasible to practice gold farming as a shadow business in
China, as is the case with a variety of other undertakings. In fact, it may
be more advantageous to operate it this way for the purposes of evading
taxation and official oversight. But repeated efforts of the studio managers—
and indeed, it may be called a fight—to obtain licensing means that they
intensely care about the (unrecognized) status of the field and would like
to elevate gold farming to the level of a government-approved profession. Nonetheless, not all studio managers are willing to join this fight.
The majority of them still care the most about making money, and whether
this is under the cloak of the online game industry in general or in the
name of a state-recognized vocation, it does not seem to bother them
much.

## VALUE MATTERS

One persistent theme we encountered in our conversations with both
studio managers and players is their frustration over the stigmatization
and social shaming of what they do and what they perceive as the inability
of family members and loved ones to understand their passion about
(and often the lack of family support for) doing this. The three Chinese
proverbs cited by most studio managers and players alike were "fool
arounders," "loafers," and "good-at-nothingers," all of which their family
members associated with them for what they do. Games are equated to
playthings in Chinese traditional culture, and the dominant value system
in society harbors no place for online gameplay as a worthy pursuit. In

this context, the conflict between gold farmers and their close ones is inevitable, as the following excerpts testify:

> A few years ago, when I told relatives and friends that I was doing gold farming, they would give me those weird looks. Now when I mention this, I get none of these looks any more. My family still does not understand why I do this. But they have finally come to terms with it. . . . I also remember an episode a few years ago— when I was in my second or third year at college—my brother and I came out of a Web café, an old, grey-haired man shouted "wastrels" at us. We were totally pissed off. (Studio Manager C, Zhengzhou)

> Subconsciously, most people associate playing online games with wasting time away. It does not matter how much money you make. Five thousand years of Confucianism has taught people this— nothing I can do to change it. My family was dead against me doing this at the beginning, including my wife and her parents. It was hard for them to understand that a graduate of Nanjing University [a prestigious university] decided to do this. When I started to make money, they became more receptive. (Studio Manager A, Shanghai)

One manager specifically cites the state support of the online game industry as justification for his involvement:

> Many people badmouth online games and despise game players. This is total bullshit. It shows their ignorance. If online games are so bad, why doesn't the state ban them? Why has online gaming evolved into a megabillion dollar industry? There is a demand for this in the marketplace. What we do serves a particular demand in the market. (Studio Manager D, Qingdao)

The wife of one studio manager shared with us how she feels:

> I don't really support his [my husband's] decision to make this his job. Why would one want to do online gaming when he could

pick a well-paying white-collar job? But he wouldn't listen to me, and there is not much I can do. However, there is one advantage to this position—he now does not have any business banquets like he used to in his old job. Frankly, I still don't like the idea of him doing online games. It's not something that he can do for the rest of his life. (Wife of a Studio Manager, Kunshan)

Players have a different level of involvement with gold farming, and they approach this differently too. They tend to be much younger, averaging in the early twenties, all male, and most of them are not long after finishing school (mostly high schools). They intimately share with managers the whole society-is-against-us perception. But unlike managers who make it known to the ones around them what they do, the majority of the players (about 80 percent) choose not to tell their parents and relatives that they are actually playing online games to make money. For the few who let their family know what they are doing, it is easy to note a lack of enthusiasm from family members. The typical responses we heard from the interviewees were that gold farming is the lesser of the evils from the viewpoints of the parents, such as "They don't object as long as I am happy doing it," "In so far as I stay out of trouble, they will let me do it," and "I have been playing games all along. Even if I don't do this as a job, I will play games anyway. My parents agree to let me do this on the condition that I tell them where I am all the time."

For the majority who decided not to disclose their work to their parents, all of them tactically found employment in studios that are in a city/region some distance away from home so that their families cannot find out what they do for a living. They typically tell their parents that they work in factories or other conventional jobs and keep in constant contact with family members via cell phone. The common fear from these players is that once their parents know what they do, it is likely that their parents will be upset and may yank them from the job. This trepidation is not unfounded, as we found out from two incidents in the process of our fieldwork. While we were visiting the studios, two players (associated with two different sites) were forced to return to their respective homes because their parents had recently learned that they were gold farmers. The parents were adamant, and the young men were obviously languishing and reluctant to leave. One studio manager, while speaking for his player, expressed his displeasure this way:

> There are many stubborn old folks who like to live in the remote past. They don't understand us at all. This young fellow is leaving us tomorrow. Why? Because his mother learned that he is gold farming, and she thinks this is shameful. So she demands him to go home right away. At moments like this, we can do nothing but obey the will of the parents. No matter how much money we make, there are people who think nothing of us. This is blatant misunderstanding. How is gold farming any different from delivering box lunches? We make a living through hard work! (Studio Manager E, Zhengzhou)

## THE RIGHT JOB FOR ME

Both studio managers and farming players display a palpable passion for the work they are doing. Most managers show varying levels of entrepreneurial spirit, and they are dedicated to the cause of gold farming because of the perceived prospect of the field. They mostly view themselves as a special type of entrepreneurs invested in a nascent but promising undertaking. Profit is the most obvious motive among them, as they have gambled a substantial amount of hard-earned money in the business. They all show a sophisticated understanding of online gaming and gold farming, and are optimistic about the prospects of return on investment down the road. These views are the most typical among them:

> I switched to this after years of doing e-commerce, because I feel confident about the future of the gold farming market. As long as online games exist, there will be the demand for it. Even if it is becoming more competitive in the field now, you will stand out above others if you are smart enough. (Studio Manager C, Zhengzhou)

> Our country is vigorously promoting cultural industry. Online games are part of this initiative. So I feel that the online gaming industry will thrive. And in order for that to happen, gold farming

will be needed. So I am optimistic that gold farming won't go away. (Studio Manager A, Shanghai)

Of course, it helps all the more that running a studio provides much-desired flexibility, as manifested in these statements: "I am totally on my own, no one bossing me around, and I don't have to take orders from anyone . . . I decide when to come to work, and what to wear"; "I cannot go back to the nine-to-five routine now, neither can I handle the complicated interpersonal relations found in corporate culture," and "I no longer have to attend lengthy, after-hours business banquets and can spend more time with my family." In particular, one manager revealed to us that he declined an offer for a corporate position with an enticing annual salary of half a million *yuan* (approximately US$80,000), because he is now so accustomed to the current "sandals and pajamas" work environment.

If managers are involved in the practice largely because of the perceived prospect of the business in the future, players are focused on the present. Regarding the biggest attraction of their job, an overarching theme we detected among almost all players is that they can play games and make money at the same time. The following excerpts summarize the gist well:

Compared with other jobs I have done, this one [gold farming] is relaxing and fun. I play games to make money. Cannot beat that.

I love gold farming, because I can play games with friends on the job. And it is a nice work environment—fast computers and air conditions. I also have the opportunity to play new games.

Of all the jobs I have done, this is the most worry-free. It's all about playing online games. I play games anyway whenever I have time, even if it is not for gold farming. Now I get paid for playing games. This is killing two birds with one stone. What more can I ask for?

A notable personality trait with many players is that they tend to be reticent and are mostly passive in reacting to our conversation cues. Most of them answered questions in very short sentence fragments and did not seem to be enthusiastic about talking to us. Most of the players have had other jobs in fields such as security, restaurants, factory assembly lines, delivery services, and construction. Their previous roles seemed to actually serve to consolidate their love for gold farming, because most of them used terms like "boring," "physically stressful," "tiring," "uninspiring," and "unsatisfactory work environment" while discussing past job experiences. At the same time, many players attributed their current passion for gold farming to their previous experience playing games during their middle and high school years. Many of them admitted that they often skipped school in order to play games in Internet cafés, and online gaming was also their most habitual pastime after school. So they considered gold farming to be a natural career choice that allowed them to revert to doing something they had always done in their juvenile years, a comfort zone that now allows them to make a living.

While it is popularly believed that long hours for low pay are typically associated with this profession, surprisingly, not a single player we interviewed lodged any complaint in regard to their pay or working hours. Most players typically work ten to twelve hours a day, and none perceived any pressure or burden in the workload. Instead, many of them considered the working hours an advantage, because they are flexible and can be easily adjusted to their personal preferences. At the same time, the compensation—which can go from a few thousand to over ten thousand *yuan* per month, according to our interviews—is better than alternative jobs in the market that are available to them. When asked about their plans for the future, interestingly, very few of them had given much thought to whether this should be a viable career path for the years to come. The prevalent attitude was, "I am happy at it now, and that is enough." A few players admitted that gold farming is not likely something they will be doing in the future, but they have no idea what they want to do or can do later. This is in contrast to the studio managers, most of whom seemed to have solid plans for expanding their business in the near future.


CONCLUSION

The age-old paradigm that views gameplay as unproductive has been under constant challenge. Because the boundaries between work and play and between consumption and production continue to blur in the game world, we are in urgent need of new perspectives to shed light on the evolving gameplay experience. The concepts of affective labor, playbour and prosumption have been employed to contextualize player production and creativity with regard to the participatory nature of online game culture. Our analysis of gold farming has introduced new dynamics to this theoretical stream on digital labor in the networked environment. While prevalent discussions of playbour pinpoint global capital and high-tech corporations as primary beneficiaries of playbour activities, we argue that gold farming is a type of transgressive play that allows gamers to negotiate possibilities and contest corporate monopoly in capitalizing on user participation. As a business practice, the evidence from our research shows that gold farming produces lucrative payoffs for both players and studio managers.

Both studio managers and farming players perceive a widespread presence of injustice and social shaming in Chinese society toward online games in general and gamers like themselves in particular. They perceive that their work fulfills a niche need in the marketplace and find solace in fondly branding their undertaking as meritorious because they earn a living through their hard work in the online game ecosystem. Deviant acts in online gaming communities are rather prevalent, as Kishonna Gray (2014) observes in her discussion of both racism and sexism. In a similar vein, gold farming can be considered a particular type of deviant gameplay—a transgressive act by a subsection of special-minded players who subvert the hegemony of play as defined by conventional game mechanics and player culture (Fron 2007) to turn playing into asset-looting and real-money trading.

For gold farmers, their upbringing and juvenile encounters with online games seem to play a pivotal role in their decision to pursue gold farming as a livelihood for the time being, yet what the future holds for them is very much an uncertainty. The trade of gold farming symbolizes eloquently the precarious conditions of the evolving labor market as a result of the de-standardization of employment in the digital economy (de Peuter 2011). As a marginal group that is still fighting for formal recognition by mainstream society, they may well get caught in the protracted woes of fast-paced social and industrial transformations in China for years to come.

## WORKS CITED

Bowman, N. D. 2016. "The Rise (and Refinement) of Moral Panic." In *The Video Game Debate: Unravelling the Physical, Social, and Psychological Effects of Video Games*, edited by R. Kowert and T. Quandt, 22–38. New York: Routledge.

Caillois, R. 1961. *Man, Play, and Games*. Urbana-Champaign: University of Illinois Press.

Charmaz, K. 2014. *Constructing Grounded Theory*. Thousand Oaks, CA: Sage.

de Peuter, G. 2011. "Creative Economy and Labor Precarity: A Contested Convergence." *Journal of Communication Inquiry* 35 (4): 417–25.

Dibbell, J. 2006. *Play Money: Or, How I Quit My Day Job and Made Millions Trading Virtual Loot*. New York: Basic Books.

Ernkvist, M., and Ström, P. 2008. "Enmeshed in Games with the Government: Governmental Policies and the Development of the Chinese Online Game Industry." *Games and Culture* 3 (1): 98–126.

Fron, J., Fullerton, T., Morie, J. F., and Pearce, C. 2007. "The Hegemony of Play." In *Situated Play: Proceedings of the 2007 DiGRA International Conference*, volume 4, edited by Akira Baba, 309–18. University of Tokyo, September 24–27.

Fuchs, C. 2014. *Digital Labour and Karl Marx*. New York: Routledge.

Golub, A. and Lingley, K. 2008. "'Just Like the Qing Empire': Internet Addiction, MMOGs, and Moral Crisis in Contemporary China." *Games and Culture* 3 (1): 59–75.

Gray, K. L. 2014. *Race, Gender, and Deviance in Xbox Live: Theoretical Perspectives from the Virtual Margins*. Waltham, MA: Anderson Publishing.

Hardt, M. and Negri, A. 2000. *Empire*. Cambridge, MA: Harvard University Press.

Huizinga, J. 1964. *Homo Ludens: A Study of the Play-Element in Culture*. Boston: Beacon Press.

Jin, G. 2006. "Chinese Gold Farmers in the Game World." *Consumers, Commodities, and Consumption: A Newsletter of the Consumer Studies Research Network* 7 (2). http://csrn.camden.rutgers.edu/newsletters/7-2/jin.htm.

Joffe, H. 2011. "Thematic Analysis." In *Qualitative Methods in Mental Health and Psychotherapy: A Guide for Students and Practitioners*, edited by D. Harper and A. R. Thompson, 209–23. Malden, MA: Wiley.

Nakamura, L. 2009. "Don't Hate the Player, Hate the Game: The Racialization of Labor in World of Warcraft." *Critical Studies in Media Communication* 26 (2): 138–41.

Newman, J. 2008. *Playing with Video Games*. New York: Routledge.

Pearce, C. 2006. "Productive Play Game Culture from the Bottom Up." *Games and Culture* 1 (1): 17–24.

Szablewicz, M. 2010. "The Ill Effects of 'Opium for the Spirit': A Critical Cultural Analysis of China's Internet Addiction Moral Panic." *Chinese Journal of Communication* 3 (4): 453–70.

Steinkuehler, C. 2006. "The Mangle of Play." *Games and Culture* 1 (3): 199–213.

Tai, Z. 2010. "Setting the Rules of Play: Network Video Game Policies and Regulations in China." *Iowa Journal of Communication* 42 (1): 45–72.

Taylor, T. L. 2009. *Play between Worlds: Exploring Online Game Culture*. Cambridge, MA: MIT Press.

Terranova, T. 2004. *Network Culture: Politics for the Information Age*. Ann Arbor, MI: Pluto Press.

Williams, D. 2003. "The Video Game Lightning Rod: Constructions of a New Media Technology, 1970–2000." *Information, Communication, and Society* 6 (4): 523–50.

Yee, N. 2006. "The Labor of Fun: How Video Games Blur the Boundaries of Work and Play." *Games and Culture* 1 (1): 68–71.

Zhang, L., and Fung, A. Y. H. 2014. "Working as Playing? Consumer Labor, Guild and the Secondary Industry of Online Gaming in China." *New Media and Society* 16 (1): 38–54.

# PART 3

# FEMINIST GAMING

CHAPTER 5

# THE SOBERING REALITY OF SEXISM IN THE VIDEO GAME INDUSTRY

STANISLAV VYSOTSKY AND JENNIFER HELEN ALLAWAY

T HROUGH A SERIES of interviews with employees in the video game industry and survey data analysis, this chapter argues that the gender dynamics of the industry discourage women from pursuing careers in gaming, inadvertently leading to games made from a distinctly male perspective that portray women in sexist stereotypes. This has adverse effects on the game playing community because the games that have problematic gender portrayals are also some of the most popular. Ultimately, these obstacles create a cycle that retains the masculinity of video game culture within the industry, the games themselves, and those who consume them.

While women in the game industry have been fighting sexism for decades, mainstream conversation about this issue began in 2012. The hashtag "#OneReasonWhy" developed as women throughout the game industry tweeted reasons why more women didn't work in games.[1] "My looks are often commented on long before the work I've done. #onereasonwhy," Tweeted Shanna Germain. "Because I get mistaken for the receptionist or day-hire marketing at trade shows. #1reasonwhy," wrote Kim Swift, lead designer of the iconic video game *Portal*. In 2013, articles like

"The Creepy Side of E3" discussed the misogynistic experiences of women who attended one of the industry's most important conventions.

These patterns coalesced in the work of game critic Anita Sarkeesian, who started a Kickstarter campaign in 2012 to fund an academic YouTube series focusing on the tropes and stereotypes women are portrayed as in games. While this campaign drew lots of media attention and financial support, it also drew thousands of rape and death threats from a misogynistic mob. This pattern of harassment, dubbed Gamergate in 2014, saw the threat of bombings and shootings against many women in the game industry, including Ms. Sarkeesian. #Gamergate also encompassed swatting[2] and doxxed[3] home addresses of several women who were outspoken against their attacks. Women who collected the personal information about their most severe attackers were largely ignored by law enforcement (Wu 2015).

While the examples above provide case evidence, there have been no attempts to empirically analyze the degree of sexism prevalent within the video game industry, its causes, and its impact on the content produced or the player base. This chapter explores the narratives of a diverse group of female game developers while highlighting their common experience with statistical evidence to support them.

## WORKPLACE DISCRIMINATION IN CONTEXT

While the video game industry is relatively new, gender-based workplace discrimination is not. Kollock, Blumstein, and Schwartz (1985) found that "power dynamics can create the conventional division of labor usually attributed to sex," especially in the relationship between power and masculinity in the workforce (45). The societal stereotypes of working men and women are "suited" to reinforce men's power in the workplace. The stereotypical traits of masculinity are often preferred for higher status positions in business and management while stereotypically female traits often relegate women to domestic or marginalized roles (Glick and Fiske 1997). This creates strain upon women who desire independent upward mobility in the workforce. Yoder (1991) found that women who work in traditionally male fields "experience performance pressures, isolation, and role encapsulation, but men do not" (183). Women experience harassment because men have "more to lose by the intrusion of women in great numbers" into male dominated fields, whereas a male intrusion to traditionally feminine fields leads to an increase in status (Yoder 1991). While gender has only recently become a topic of discussion in the video game industry, the conflicts associated with working in male-dominated fields have existed as long as patriarchal structures have been in place.

Contemporary research on workplace discrimination indicates that despite policy changes, everyday practices still encourage sexism and racism. Hiring processes often pay lip-service to "diversity" while not being able to articulate or follow through on hiring policies that develop gender and race equity (Embrick 2011). This attitude contributes to an environment in which harassment becomes acceptable, especially for women who assert their rights to be treated equally. Harassment is more common in male-dominated professions and those without sexual harassment policies or procedures. Statistically, women who engage in feminist activism tend to experience the greatest amount of harassment and sexism (Feather and Boeckmann 2007; Holland and Cortina 2013). Most men do not recognize sexist behavior or practices because they operate under the impression that since they are not infringing upon a woman's inalienable rights, their behavior is permissible. This belief denies the existence of overt sexism because it does not fit a definition created by men. Such behavioral patterns explain the current problems surrounding sexism in the modern workplace, including the game industry (Harris, Palazzolo, and Savage 2012). Furthermore, the structural environment of the gaming industry, with its focus on crunch time, and its reliance on passion as motivation for maintaining exploitative working conditions, privileges male laborers and masculine labor dynamics. This type of structural environment serves to reinforce an ideology that constructs game design as a masculine space and reinforces women's alienation in the industry (Consalvo 2008).

## GENDER REPRESENTATION IN VIDEO GAMES

While little scholarly research focuses on gender relations in the game industry, a plethora of scholarship has examined the lack of positive female representation in games themselves. According to Leonard (2006), "64% of platform game characters are male, 19% are nonhuman, and 17%

are female. More specifically, 73% of player-controlled characters are male, with less than 15% being female, of which 50% are props or bystanders" (84). Not only are there more nonhuman characters in games than female, but also 85.71% of female characters are dressed to show cleavage or other low necklines, emphasizing their sexuality (Beasely and Standley 2002).

Sexuality seems inextricable from female representation in games, and marketers ubiquitously brand video games as a heterosexual "boys only" medium. Not only are women underrepresented in video games and their advertisements, their hypersexuality emphasizes their helplessness and reinforces men as the more able gender (Christensen et al. 2008; Dill and Thill 2007; Ogletree and Drake 2007; Scharrer 2004). Research by Near (2012) found that Teen and Mature rated games' "sales are highest in games with box art depicting non-central, sexualized female characters" (263). Rather than rely on higher quality content or creative material, marketers continually use female sexuality to increase sales because it is convenient and cost effective. Not only do these high sales reinforce the sexualization of female characters, they also result in lasting impacts on beliefs about gender among male game players.

As male game players are exposed to hypersexualized and powerless representations of women, their attitudes toward gender become more conventional and their dominance in gaming culture is reinforced. The focus on the female character's exploited sexuality teaches the player that the male gaze defines a woman's most important traits (Dietz 1998). Behm-Morawitz and Mastro (2009) note that "exposure to sexualized female video game characters may promote more traditional, less egalitarian beliefs about women in the real world" (811). This has led to a series of problematic attitudes within the game playing community due to biased game content. Brenick and her colleagues (2007) state that male game players "are more likely than females to find stereotypes acceptable" (395). Additionally, by defining casual games as a feminine space and "hardcore" games as a masculine space, women experience increased marginalization and stigmatization in digital game cultures (Heeter et al. 2008; Salter and Blodgett 2012). The result is a common misconception that women do not enjoy hard-core games due to violence, competition, or other typically "masculine" game traits. However, "86% of girls responded that they didn't mind violence in games," which indicates that if women were marketed to, they would probably show interest in "masculine" games, which tend to carry more violent content (Ray 2004, 84). It has been noted that "gender and technology have a reciprocal relationship," which leads to the perpetuation of gender relations within games without any recent improvement (Undrahbuyan et al. 2007). Jansz and Martis (2007) believe that having more female game protagonists will help women take an interest in playing video games and pursuing careers in the game industry.

Ultimately, between games that feed binary gender constructions and a toxic and fragile masculinity (the necessity of proving one's hegemonic masculinity in the face of any momentary rupture) trained into men's behavior, creating gender equity within gaming has been challenging. Hard-core players are also not as likely to believe that game content has a negative impact on player behavior (Funk 2005). By playing video games with stereotypical gender depictions on a frequent basis, these men become desensitized to the games' content and have a harder time critiquing what they are playing. This dynamic contributes to the lack of women interested in video games and sets context for this study.

THE PYRAMID OF POWER

This study applies an analysis based on the conception of the pyramid of power, which classifies social hierarchy in Western societies with a tradition of patriarchal structures typical of the United States and many other developed countries that produce video games. Described by Sheri Graner Ray (2004), the concept operates thusly: the more power an individual has, the fewer peers they have; the less power an individual has, the more peers they have. This framework describes a dynamic wherein a small but powerful group of people has disproportionate social control. In an overwhelmingly male industry, the most powerful individuals are almost ubiquitously white cisgender men. Since very few women in the game industry possess organizational power, they are therefore powerless to intervene against the misogyny in the industry.

The pyramid of power "maintains that . . . if people are called to function at a level above them in the pyramid, their comfort level decreases" (Ray 2004, 97). Since the industry is overwhelmingly male, a woman who works in the video game industry is already functioning within a higher stratum of the pyramid. Women are placed lower in the pyramid by the industry because they have little to no representation in powerful positions. This can lead to discomfort from women who operate in a predominantly male space (Johnson 2013). However, men do not experience the same discomfort if they are required to move down the social strata; "They are comfortable with almost any role handed to them. Because they have always been in a position of power, it is difficult for them to relate to a position that is lower on the pyramid. They simply assume everyone feels as they do" (Ray 2004, 98). Because this dynamic is structural, a man may not believe that this privilege has been afforded to him, but it is something that exists outside of his control. As Consalvo (2008) notes, "While certain practices may not arise from sexist (or racist) ideologies, a sexist institution can arise, due to particular practices being valued and sustained, rather than alternate practices" (180). The pyramid of power serves as a useful framework for analyzing the game industry because it explains the social location of individuals from historically marginalized groups, including women. Since men inherently have more power in a patriarchal society (as well as games), they are ignorant of and defensive to the assertion that women and other marginalized groups struggle due to their identity. It also frames the discomfort women can experience being a part of the game industry. Since so few women are in positions of power in the industry, they must constantly operate in social strata above them in order to succeed by acquiescing to patriarchal norms.

METHODOLOGY

This study combines interview analysis with the results of a survey conducted over a two-week period.[4] The initial study consisted of thirty-four interviews with twenty-nine female and five male respondents using a snowball sampling method. In an industry as small and close as the game industry, it is virtually impossible to utilize a true random sampling method. All participants are designated with an interview participant number (e.g., Participant 12), with their gender identity noted as needed. In order to validate the interview data, a survey of 344 game industry professionals was conducted after the interview period. The survey used a non-random sampling procedure for similar reasons to the interview sampling methodology. A link to the survey was shared among game industry employees using email and Twitter, with 214 men and 130 women responding.

The interview questions were designed to gauge the extent of sexist experiences that the interview participants had discussed, as well as to understand attitudes toward current themes and controversies regarding gender relations in the video game industry. Additionally, many of the survey questions were designed to validate or otherwise provide elaboration for the interview data. Both interview and survey questions also focused on the possible link between video games and the gender dynamics of the industry to explore whether they exist in a reciprocal relationship.

## SEXISM WITHIN THE INDUSTRY

In this study *sexism* is defined as any discomfort or discrimination that a woman has experienced because of her gender. This is inclusive of *transmisogyny*, or the different types of sexism that non-cisgender women and the trans community experience, which may be as overt as pay gaps and sexual harassment, and as subtle as feeling uncomfortable because of being one woman on a team of twenty men (Boeckmann and Feather 2007, 32). However, it encompasses many discriminatory experiences, and applies to all women in the interviews. The majority of women interviewed (79%, n = 23) had experienced sexism to some degree within the video game industry. Ironically, while 7 of the 29 (24%) women studied initially said that they had never experienced sexism or discrimination at the beginning of the interview, they later detailed an experience in which they in fact had faced sexism. They themselves often expressed surprise once revealing this information. Additionally, 60% (n = 78) of women surveyed experienced sexism or harassment in the video game industry; 77% (n = 100) of women as well as 55% (n = 118) of men know a woman working in the video game industry who has experienced sexism. If we factor in the 61% (n = 90) of women who know a colleague who has acted in a way they found offensive on the basis of gender, it is safe to make the inference that there is an extensive amount of sexist behavior in game industry workplaces. Even a sizeable proportion of men surveyed appear to acknowledge this dynamic, as 44% (n = 95) of men also know a colleague who has acted in an offensive manner on the basis of gender. It may be reasonable to assume that these statistics indicate only a small portion of the total extent of sexism in the industry because some women have been conditioned to accept a certain amount of sexism into their daily lives. As there is a roughly 20% statistical gap between the women who were interviewed and the women who took the survey, it's possible that the remaining 20% of women who were surveyed are also victims of sexism that without an interviewer asking pointed questions, did not view their experiences as sexist. This learned tolerance of sexism could explain how sexist practices were able to persist in the game industry for so long before the recent boom in industry dialogue.

## Overt Sexism

The most common forms of overt sexism in the workplace involve pay disparities and discrimination in hiring and promotion. Such practices were common experiences for the women interviewed in this study. Women consistently experienced scenarios typical of a *glass ceiling*, or the point at which a woman will no longer advance in a company's hierarchy as a result of her gender. Practices such as pay discrepancies, denying women promotions, and blacklisting from future jobs any women who speak out about a sexist experience are indicative of this phenomenon. Many of these concepts were supported by the survey data. Almost a third (31%, n = 40) of women believe a glass ceiling exists in the video game industry, and 35% (n = 45) answered that co-workers discriminated against them to some degree. Additionally, 36.1% (n = 37) of women know of or suspect a pay discrepancy due to gender. Almost forty percent (n = 50) of women were not confident that their human resources department would be able to handle their disputes properly.

## Workplace Discrimination

Women in the industry experience discrimination in hiring and promotion solely as a result of their gender. Men are typically promoted ahead of women with similar, if not more advanced, skill sets and productivity. Below is a description of one such occurrence:

I was originally hired as a contractor . . . when I was hired, I was explicitly told, "We don't have a full-time position for you yet, but the first one that opens in design, we're going to put you in" . . . So, I . . . worked hard . . . I had clearly been doing an excellent job . . . Everyone said, "Holy crap, you're like the hardest worker we have, this was amazing . . . The week before Alpha, one of the designers left, so I'm sitting there going "Yes! Full Time position . . . !" The creative director came to me, and said, "So I know we told you we were going to give you a full-time position when one opened up; however, we've got this guy that we're trying to hire away from another company, and we can't offer him a contract position like we did you because you know, he's married, and he has a family he has to support, so he can't take a contract position, he has to have a full-time position available." I looked at him, and I was like, "I'm married. I have a family . . ." And he went . . . "I mean, you know, it seems kind of a waste to give you a full-time position when you're just prolly gonna end up having kids in a few years and leave anyway . . ." (Participant 12)

The experience described above demonstrates how the industry prioritizes male employees due to patriarchal assumptions regarding gender and work-life commitments, such as assuming that a woman would leave the industry entirely if she becomes a parent. Additionally, while it is common practice in the game industry to hire an employee from another company, this usually does not occur if there is already promising talent available for hire in house. In addition to the experience above, Participant 12 had difficulty entering the video game industry. She was the last member of her graduate school class to be hired into the industry, was paid half the salary of her male coworkers early in her career, and was turned away from an interview after an employer realized she was a woman. Such experiences were never discussed by any of the male study participants, which highlights the industry double standard in work practices.

Interview participants also consistently reported major disparities in pay compared to their male colleagues. Participant 25, a transgender woman, had an experience which indicates that such practices are in fact rooted in gender discrimination, "I didn't realize this until years and years later when I was looking at my tax cards next to each other . . . the year I transitioned [to a woman], and I had no other notice of anything—my salary actually went down by about 10%. . . ." The only evident explanation for the pay disparity was Participant 25's transition from male to female gender identity and presentation. When pressed for possible reasons for the pay disparity such as a lower performance at work or disputes with colleagues, she indicated that while some people socialized with her more than before, and others less than before, there had been no decline in performance nor outstanding disputes or issues that would have justified a decrease in pay.

COVERT SEXISM

Covert sexism, unlike the overt sexism mentioned above, is far subtler and involves everyday practices evident in conversation and the general culture of video game studios. The majority of women (70%, n = 91) and 51% (n = 110) of men agree that the video game industry has a "boys' club" culture. Interestingly, 70% (n = 91) of women and 54% (n = 116) of men also disagreed with the statement that "men in the industry are educated or informed on the issue of sexism." Most of the boys' club atmosphere that women cited as uncomfortable was rooted in unprofessional office conversations that men were comfortable engaging in, but most women were not, thereby ostracizing members of their community that do not fit the majority power structure.

By using language designed to exclude female participation, men are able to retain the status quo of masculinity in the video game industry. A male artist working on mobile and social games describes his firsthand experience with this dynamic:

On multiple occasions . . . , I have it documented personally . . . someone had posted an image, something someone did on DeviantArt, and I said, "boob armor makes no sense" And then another artist said, "It should probably not even be there." As in, the armor, right? She should just be naked. And then one of the other artists said, "Agreed, waiting for the Photoshop." (Participant 17)

Such gender dynamics create a sense of isolation, as a female sound designer explained:

> One [Title Game] Team, which was very male centered, very boy's club, I had a lot of a hard time fitting in with them. On that audio team, I was the only girl. They hung out together, the boys . . . and talk a lot and tell jokes to each other, and I was kind of just left out. And I don't think I was given a chance, and part of that was because I'm a girl, but I have a sharp wit and I like inappropriate humor . . . I don't mean inappropriate as in sexist, but just being fun and silly at work. I felt pretty lonely and outcast, really. (Participant 24)

This climate creates a set of work conditions that not only denigrate women, but also precludes any attempts to rectify the situation through official channels. As a result, women feel uncomfortable communicating to their coworkers and bosses why something is problematic. At the beginning of the development process, women are unable to socially connect with their male peers to the extent that they connect with one another (as evidenced by Participant 24's testimony), and without their feedback, the development team can turn into an echo chamber of masculine stereotypes (as demonstrated by Participant 17).

## BACKLASH FOR SPEAKING OUT

A common outcome for women employed in gaming who attempt to criticize this problem is ostracization. Participant 34, a female designer, discussed this in detail: "When females are pushed out, it feels a lot more abrasive, a lot more—it's very much like you're branded as a fire starter, but if you're male that just means you're a lot more forward and assertive." Ironically, when men in the industry stand up for the rights of women, they are often applauded for wishing to move the industry forward. However, women in the industry experience far more vitriol for the exact same practices. This contributes to and expands upon the frustration women experience when they stay silent in the industry. If women speak out in the industry, they risk open criticism of their behavior and fear losing jobs, and as a result remain silent. However, when a male counterpart speaks out on the very thing women experience, he does not receive the same negative reaction. This systematic silencing of women through ostracization perpetuates the "boys' club" culture and sexism within the game industry.

## THE SCOPE OF SEXISM IN THE GAMING INDUSTRY: A DISCUSSION AND CONCLUSION

### Overt Sexism's Structural Impact on the Industry

The results of the research presented in this chapter demonstrate a clear patriarchal gender dynamic in the game industry consistent with the pyramid of power (Ray 2008). The overt practices experienced by women in this study indicate the impact of male domination on the game industry. Interview respondents recounted incidents of limited upward mobility, pay discrepancies, and the ostracization of women who challenge the patriarchal structure of their workplaces. Participant 12's experience with her contract position discussed above is indicative of the pyramid structure in the practice of hiring and promotion. Traditionally, women operated in domestic and marginalized roles, which relegated them to the lower strata of the pyramid structure. However, Participant 12 clearly enjoys her work and strongly pursues it, despite the masculine environment; she is even praised for her exceptional work. Women who are perceived as engaging in non-traditional actions and roles have a greater chance of being harassed than women who are perceived as traditional, and Participant 12's active role in a male dominated field marked her as such (Holland and Cortina 2013). Another indication of the prevalence of the pyramid structure lies in Participant 12's supervisor's casual statement in regard to her fitness for a full-time position due to her gender and social expectations of eventual motherhood. In effect, he is asserting his superior position in the pyramid of power by deciding that stereotypically feminine life events will not only impact her career decisions, but also justify hiring a male designer with no experience with the company. Because of his position and power, he is able to deny Participant 12 a full-time position for which she is qualified simply because a man sought that position, which further prevented her from mobility into the higher echelons of the pyramid.

Women in the game industry also face clear discrepancies in pay compared to their male counterparts. In addition to experiencing hiring discrimination, Participant 12 received half the income of her male co-workers, with little resolution from the company. The gender dynamic in these types of discrepancies was made clear by Participant 25's experience with a change in pay scale when she transitioned to a female gender identity in her workplace. The incident above implies a policy of lower pay for female employees because she was able to compare salary differences before and after her transition. Study participants also reported ostracization from male coworkers and the fear that speaking out against sexist practices in the industry would negatively impact their careers. By keeping the social capital of women in the industry limited by masculine-oriented in-jokes and relationships, the industry creates a misogynistic bubble that women struggle to burst. In order to make an effort to gain power in the industry, women feel pressured to accept a toxic work culture, less pay, and less work stability than their male counterparts in order to "do what they love." Simultaneously, men are not required to make similar compromises. This unified culture prevents women from achieving positions of power in the industry and making structural and systematic changes.

## Office Sexism Leads to Biased Content

Female game characters, like many representations of women in media, are regularly relegated to sexual objects, which both game players and male industry workers consume. When Participant 20 expressed that she wanted game characters "to look more like Olympians and less like Playboy bunnies," it comes from the pervasive problem of hypersexualization of female game characters during development. This is partially the result of the terminology used to discuss and objectify female characters. As Participant 22 mentioned in her office's "code language" for female characters' body parts, the sexuality and nudity of females can only be referred to for the purpose of sex, on male terms (Schaare 2000). When designers hypersexualize their female characters at the expense of deeper character development, it becomes difficult for women to define characters by themselves. The industry discounts how masculine-oriented design choices could be costing it players who want to be represented. Despite the misconceptions about what girls and women like to play versus boys and men,

Yee (2008) found "the average gender overlap across all the listed motivations was actually 87 percent: the overwhelming majority of men and women like to do the same kinds of things in online games" (91). This relates to the experience Participant 32 detailed and their misinformed assumptions about who played their games. Yee's study on massively multiplayer online (MMO) games shows that women like the gameplay elements of traditionally "male" games. If more was done to improve the atmosphere, such as providing less sexualized body types and clothing for the avatars, it could lead to higher profits than those made by pandering to a small niche market that relies on hypermasculine content to play a game. For that to occur, the current structural paradigm needs to focus on creating a safe environment for women to voice their opinions on female characters without judgment.

The current power structures not only keep women from voicing their opinions on female characters, but potentially all other facets of design due to the ways men most often communicate. A study found that:

> Males tended to use . . . communication techniques to exert dominance . . . sometimes for a period of several days . . . female input into a discussion was stopped short by a male message . . . usually sexual or harsh in nature . . . it stopped all females from posting on any discussion for several days. In this way, males in the group 'silenced' the females. (Ray 2004, 78)

Men are able to assert their dominance from the pyramid structure onto the women and silence them. Using the pyramid structure, women must emulate men's communication methods in order to be heard at all, causing great strain and discomfort. The same study found that women only participated in the conversation when another woman commented, highlighting that when there are few women in the industry, women have less courage to speak out (Ray 2004). Men in the industry are therefore able to exploit their status in the higher pyramid strata as a means of ostracizing women from game development, which reasserts them as the gender with majority power.

When considering additional stresses associated with working in games, the few women who brave this industry must be resilient to endure every offense. Women are "a minority group in most development studios, they often express frustration at having to 'fit in' to a masculine culture, or worse, feel that they are being 'treated differently' simply because they are women" (Consalvo 2008, 188). In addition to the difficult and stressful working conditions of the video game industry, this feeling of different treatment can drive women away. As we saw in Participant 17's remarks about the chat room discussion he listened to about "boob armor," the single female artist in the studio did not say anything when the men asserted this conversation. The conversation was so hypermasculine in the language and content that the only way for any women to participate in the conversation was to accept demeaning language and participate in it.

*Impact of Masculinized Content on Players*

The pyramid of power structure in video games relies on a heavy relationship between the industry, game content, and how players perceive the content. When the tone of games is set as hypermasculine, or diminutive or sexualizing to women, men who play these games are not only far more likely to accept rape myths but also can cause men to view women for their sexuality above other traits (Beck et al. 2012; Mahood et al. 2010). It creates a vicious cycle of men who grow up playing misogynistic video games, who then enter the video game industry with the intent to make the games they like, which includes these tropes, and produce the same games for the next generation. This cycle maintains the current paradigm of power by preventing women from entering the video game industry due to the toxic effects these problems exert on women's physical and mental well-being. In order to improve the current condition, the game industry needs to acknowledge the current power structures and invest heavily in breaking them in order to allow diverse voices to feel safe enough to act.

Toxic attitudes towards women are not only held in the game industry, which makes combating the effect games have on players more difficult. Studies of evaluations of workplace performance based on gender indicate that men are more favorably reviewed even in controlled circumstances where all aspects of performance are identical except for gender (Abel and Meltzer 2007). In such circumstances, men are evaluated with greater favorability than their female colleagues. This is the result of the patriarchal social order; because greater social value is granted to men, more credence is given to men discussing social issues, despite women's greater experience with sexism and understanding its dynamics in western patriarchal society. Games predominantly made by men, therefore, perpetuate prioritizing men's voices in the medium, which not only impacts men's attitudes toward women in games, but the validity of women's voices in the greater world as well.

The pyramid of power reinforces the dynamics described in this chapter because men occupy the most powerful roles in the game industry, which results in women's systematic and habitual denial of power. Whether through direct harassment, pay cuts, or being silenced in a boardroom, the pyramid of power ensures that most women in the game industry stay in the same position—away from executive roles. These findings, unprecedented to a degree, reveal the sobering reality of sexism in the video game industry. Before the industry can move forward, it must accept that 60 percent of the women working in it admitted to feeling harassed because of their gender. The industry must acknowledge the creative potential and feats of women within it.

Much is left to be studied on this subject, including how female game players are treated, how motherhood is handled in the video game industry, and how men's attitudes about sexism in games shape the industry conversation overall. Ultimately, justice can be achieved within the structure of the existing video game industry through a revolution of the pyramid of power currently in place. Structural changes in recruitment and promotion are key measures for women to gain power in the industry. Women need to flock to this industry, until we have equal ranks of men and women creating games. We need women and male allies to lift one another up, so that the upper echelons of the industry begin to reflect the diversity of game players. It is only through supporting one another and refusing to stay silent that the boy's club of the industry will diminish.

NOTES

1   The campaign also included posts by men sharing stories of their female colleagues' experiences with discrimination and harassment.
2   *Swatting* is the practice of calling a SWAT team on someone's house in an attempt to cause the target physical and psychological harm.
3   *Doxxing* is when someone searches for and publishes private information about an individual with malicious intent.

4    The survey was released to the public September 9, 2013, and was closed at
      10 p.m. on September 23.

WORKS CITED

Abel, M. and Meltzer, A. 2007. "Student Ratings of a Male and Female Professors'
    Lecture on Sex Discrimination in the Workplace." *Sex Roles* 57 (3–4): 173–80.
Beasley, B., and Standley, T. C. 2002. "Shirts vs. Skins: Clothing as an Indicator of
    Gender Role Stereotyping in Video Games." *Mass Communication and Society* 5 (3):
    279–93.
Beck, V.S., Boys, S., Rose, C., and Beck, E. 2012. "Violence against Women in Video
    Games: A Prequel or Sequel to Rape Myth Acceptance?" *Journal of Interpersonal
    Violence* 27 (15): 3016–31.
Behm-Morawitz, E., and Mastro, D. 2009. "The Effects of the Sexualization of
    Female Video Game Characters on Gender Stereotyping and Female Self-
    Concept." *Sex Roles* 61 (11–12): 808–23.
Brenick, A., Henning, A. Killen, M. O'Connor, A., and Collins, M. 2007. "Social
    Evaluations of Stereotypic Images in Video Games: Unfair, Legitimate, or 'Just
    Entertainment?'" *Youth and Society* 38 (4): 395–419.
Christensen, J., Dickerman, C., and Kerl-McClain, S. B. 2008. "Big Breasts and Bad
    Guys: Depictions of Gender and Race in Video Games." *Journal of Creativity and
    Mental Health* 3 (1): 20–29.
Consalvo, M. 2008. "Crunched by Passion: Women Game Developers and Workplace
    Challenges." In *Beyond Barbie to Mortal Kombat: New Perspectives on Gender and Gam-
    ing*, edited by Y. B. Kafai, C. Heeter, J. Denner, and J. Y. Sun, 177–92. Cambridge,
    MA: MIT Press.
Dietz, T. L. 1998. "An Examination of Violence and Gender Role Portrayals in Video
    Games: Implications for Gender Socialization and Aggressive Behavior." *Sex
    Roles* 38: 425–42.
Dill, K. E., and Thill, K. P. 2007. "Video Game Characters and the Socialization of
    Gender Roles: Young People's Perceptions Mirror Sexist Media Depictions." *Sex
    Roles* 57: 851–64.
Embrick, D. G. 2011. "The Diversity Ideology in the Business World: A New Oppres-
    sion for a New Age." *Critical Sociology* 37 (5): 541–56.
Feather, N. T., and Boeckmann, R. J. 2007. "Beliefs about Gender Discrimination
    in the Workplace in the Context of Affirmative Action: Effects of Gender and
    Ambivalent Attitudes in an Australian Sample." *Sex Roles* 57: 31–42.
Funk, J. B. 2005. "Children's Exposure to Violent Video Games and Desensitization
    to Violence." *Child and Adolescent Clinics of North America* 14: 387–404.
Glick, P., and Fiske, S. T. 1997. "Hostile and Benevolent Sexism: Measuring Ambiva-
    lent Sexist Attitudes toward Women." *Psychology of Women Quarterly* 21: 119–35.
Harris, K. L., Palazzolo, K. E., and Savage, M. W. 2012. "'I'm Not Sexist, but . . .':
    How Ideological Dilemmas Reinforce Sexism in Talk about Intimate Partner
    Violence. *Discourse and Society* 23 (6): 643–56.

Heeter, C., Egidio, R., Mishra, P., Winn, B., and Winn, J. 2008. "Alien Games: Do Girls Prefer Games Designed by Girls?" *Games and Culture* 4 (1): 74–100.

Holland, K. J., and Cortina, L. M. 2013. "When Sexism and Feminism Collide: The Sexual Harassment of Feminist Working Women." *Psychology of Women Quarterly* 37 (2): 192–208.

Jansz, J., and Martis, R. G. 2007. "The Lara Phenomenon: Powerful Female Characters in Video Games." *Sex Roles* 56: 141–48.

Johnson, R. 2013. "Toward Greater Production Diversity: Examining Social Boundaries at a Video Game Studio." *Games and Culture* 8 (3): 136–60.

Kollock, P., Blumstein, P., and Schwartz, P. 1985. "Sex and Power in Interaction: Conversational Privileges and Duties." *American Sociological Review* 50 (1): 34–46.

Leonard, D. J. 2006. "Not a Hater, Just Keepin' It Real: The Importance of Race- and Gender- Based Game Studies." *Games and Culture* 1 (1): 83–88.

Mahood, C., Yao, M., and Linz, D. 2010. "Sexual Priming, Gender Priming, and the Likelihood to Sexually Harass: Examining the Cognitive Effects of Playing a Sexually-Explicit Video Game." *Sex Roles*, 62 (1-2): 77–88.

Near, C. E. 2012. "Selling Gender: Associations of Box Art Representation of Female Characters with Sales for Teen- and Mature-Rated Video Games." *Sex Roles* 68: 252–69.

Ogletree, S. M., and Drake, R. 2007. "College Students' Video Game Participation and Perceptions: Gender Differences and Implications." *Sex Roles* 56: 537–42.

Ray, S. G. 2004. *Gender Inclusive Game Design: Expanding the Market.* Hingham, MA: Charles River Media.

Salter, A., and Blodgett, B. 2012. "Hypermasculinity and Dickwolves: The Contentious Role of Women in the New Gaming Public." *Journal of Broadcasting and Electronic Media* 56 (3): 401–16.

Schaare, P. 2000. "Here's Looking at You: Deconstructing the Male Gaze." *Social Alternatives* 19 (3): 45–47.

Scharrer, E. 2004. "Virtual Violence: Gender and Aggression in Video Game Advertisements." *Mass Communication and Society* 7 (4): 393–412.

Undrahbuyan, B., Royse, P., and Lee, J. 2007. "Women and Games: Technologies of the Gendered Self." *New Media and Society* 9 (4): 555–76.

Wu, B. 2015. "Gamergate Death Threat Is a Slam Dunk for Prosecutors: Will They Act?" www.themarysue.com/will-prosecutors-act-on-gamergate-death-threat.

Yee, N. 2008. "Maps of Digital Desires: Exploring the Topography of Gender and Play in Online Games." In *Beyond Barbie to Mortal Kombat: New Perspectives on Gender and Gaming,* edited by Y. B. Kafai, C. Heeter, J. Denner, and J. Y. Sun, 83–96. Cambridge, MA: MIT Press.

Yoder, J. D. 1991. "Rethinking Tokenism: Looking beyond Numbers." *Gender and Society* 5 (2): 178–92.

# CHAPTER 6

# THE PERPETUAL CRUSADE

*Rise of the Tomb Raider, Religious Extremism,
and the Problem of Empire*

KRISTIN BEZIO

ALTHOUGH INCIDENTS OF anti-Islamic and Islamophobic attacks were already more frequent in the United States following September 11, 2001, they have increased almost exponentially since the American presidential campaign of 2015–2016, having risen "by 57 percent in 2016" alone (Buncombe 2017). A report by the Council on American-Islamic Relations (CAIR) issued in 2017 explains that, "From 2014 to 2016, anti-Muslim bias incidents jumped 65 percent. In that two-year period, CAIR finds that hate crimes targeting Muslims surged 584 percent" (2). Under the influence of the increasingly prominent "alt-right," the American media response to these acts of Islamophobia has been as similarly "weak and over conciliatory" as its reaction to the harassment of women in gaming and to white supremacist pressure to reclaim the United States by closing its borders (Lees 2016). The conjunction of rising Islamophobia and alt-right Internet culture means that video game critics and developers alike should pay increased attention to the way people of color—especially Blacks and Arabs—are represented in games in order to mitigate or even improve not only cross-cultural tolerance and understanding (Šisler 2008, 204) but justice. At the end of 2015, in the midst of this upswing in

American Islamophobia, Core Dynamics released the second game in the rebooted *Tomb Raider* franchise: *Rise of the Tomb Raider* (*RotTR*).[1] Like its 2013 predecessor (*Tomb Raider*), *RotTR* employs narrative elements that encourage its players to consider their own complicity in Western imperialism and bias, specifically, in *RotTR*, in relation to contemporary concerns about Islamic refugees.

In the narrative of *RotTR*, the Crusades went underground after the 1453 fall of Constantinople, perpetuated in secret by a Vatican-sponsored organization known as Trinity in pursuit of a holy artifact—the Divine Source—capable of granting immortality. Trinity is opposed by the Remnants, descendants of a Byzantine religious sect who fled the Middle East in 972 before being driven into Siberia (Crystal Dynamics 2015). The deliberate choice in *RotTR* to reconstruct a narrative of the Crusades from the perspective of the Remnants acts in the game as implicit criticism of contemporary religious extremism and intolerance by forcing the player, as Lara Croft, to place herself in direct opposition to the traditionally dominant Western religious paradigm.[2]

Despite the prominence of this narrative message of tolerance, the game frequently struggles to maintain its own ideology of moderation and acceptance.[3] Educated, white, wealthy, and English, Lara embodies multiple characteristics of imperial Western oppression. In *RotTR*, she asks for assistance from the Remnants—who are economically impoverished, uneducated by Western standards, technologically un-advanced, and culturally isolated from the modern world. She demands both their resources and their lives in her search for the Divine Source, a traditional narrative of Western pursuit of intellectual capital leading to the exploitation of native populations. As such, the game partially undermines its own attempt to advocate for diversity and tolerance by unintentionally devaluing a migrant population in the service of imperialist expansionism, problematically situating Lara Croft as its (white) savior, despite her culpability in its near destruction.

## ORIENTALISM AND OPPRESSION

At its center, the *Tomb Raider* franchise, premised upon the archetypal Western explorer-archaeologist, "relies upon a set of Western cultural assumptions of superiority which manifest in ways categorized by cultural theorist Edward Said as 'Orientalist'" (Bezio 2016, 189). Said ([1979] 1994) defines Orientalism as "a way of coming to terms with the Orient that is" (1) predicated on the West's imperial relationship to many lands and peoples of the East: "the Orient has helped to define Europe (or the West) as its contrasting image, idea, personality, experience" (1–2). The Orientalist perspective, explains Said ([1979] 1994), defines, delineates, and catalogues the peoples, practices, and artifacts of the East (broadly speaking) in contrast to the presumed superior traditions of the Christian West.

Western archaeological exploration—particularly as practiced extensively in the nineteenth and early twentieth centuries—is an Orientalist praxis, which reduces entire cultures to catalogues of artifacts on display (and in storage) at Western museums. Although modern archaeology has adapted its practices to be significantly less imperialist than in the past, Orientalism continues to manifest in modern, twenty-first century acts of misrepresentation, cultural appropriation, and popular culture depictions of Western archaeologists and explorers. These texts and images situate "the Westerner in a whole series of possible relationships with the Orient without ever losing him the relative upper hand" (Said [1979] 1994, 7), perpetuating imperial and Orientalist attitudes which often exacerbate extant cultural and ideological tensions and stereotypes.

A central figure in this narrative is the "white savior," a Western, white (typically male), and educated individual whose role is to save (often, to convert, in religious or political terms) the primitive "natives" from their own ignorance and superstitions, a trope commonly known as "White Man's Burden." Early European travel accounts frequently situate missionaries and explorers as heroic combatants against barbarity, a theme adopted in fictional works from Shakespeare's *The Tempest* to Burrough's *Tarzan of the Apes* to Spielberg's *Indiana Jones and the Temple of Doom* and Crystal Dynamics' reboot of the *Tomb Raider* series.

The most recent of these further engages in hegemonic imperialism by virtue of its genre; video games, Dyer-Witheford and de Peuter (2009) explain, "are a paradigmatic media of Empire—planetary, militarized hypercapitalism—and of some of the forces presently challenging it" (xv). Gray (2014) similarly argues that games and gaming culture "not only reflect entrenched inequality and lived male/white privilege" as a product of imperialism, "but serve as an important instrument in the reproduction of hegemony" (xiv). This hegemony is specifically explained by Fron et al. (2007), who situate digital games as the products of an industry that "has influenced the global culture of play in much the same way that hegemonic nations, such as the British Empire or post-WWII America, have, in their times of influence, dominated global culture" (1). In large part, this hegemonic masculine, Western whiteness is the consequence of an industry populated primarily by Western white men who "construct realities from their perspective of the world," a perspective that "is far too often stereotypical and not truly representative of women or people of color" (Gray 2014, 7). Video games thus function both as and within an imperialist paradigm in which the oppressive forces of white, Western, masculine hegemony take precedence (Bezio 2016; Mukherjee 2016; Šisler 2008; Leonard 2006).

In particular, Newman (2013) explains how the purpose of digital gameplay often aligns with imperial colonial praxis: "What is really important to the player is staying alive . . . long enough to explore, conquer and colonize the space of the gameworld" (110). Violent gameplay, especially, participates in Orientalist praxis. *RotTR* is not a first-person military shooter. Höglund (2008) observes that "Orientalism both then and now is intimately connected with economic and military practice" through the commodification of violence as a game and within the game, both narratively and (qua loot and experience points) mechanically. As I have explained elsewhere, "The vast majority of procedural mechanics focuses on actions of empire and archaeology: exploring unknown space, claiming territory, collecting loot and resources, killing enemies (usually alien or Otherized). Often, game spaces are explicitly colonial, unsettled" or abandoned "territory (tropical islands, unpopulated medieval or fantasy landscapes, deep space), and the challenges faced by players are directly related to taming the game space's 'wildness'" (Bezio 2016, 195). As such, adventure games like *RotTR* engage with the dominant ideological strictures of the West, placing them in opposition to and as superior over the cultural practices and beliefs of the non-West.

## FROM TREASURE-HUNTER TO ARCHAEOLOGIST: LARA CROFT

The *Tomb Raider* franchise first appeared in 1996, seeking to capitalize on the success of Spielberg's *Indiana Jones* series (Anderson and Levene 2012, 239). The original Lara Croft, the game's amply-endowed protagonist, was aristocratic and English, a mixture of titillation and imperial exploitation (Core Design 1996b). Lara, explains Breger (2008), explores "mostly 'exotic' environments, with the explicit purpose of collecting the cultural treasures of past civilizations hidden in them" (42). In short, the original Lara embodied white, imperialist, heteronormative male fantasies of conquest and acquisition.

In the 2013 Crystal Dynamics re-envisioning of the franchise, Lara's physiology and background are altered: her physical proportions are more average, her clothing far less revealing, and her occupation changed from wealthy aristocratic treasure-hunter to working (although still aristocratic) archaeologist, likely at least in part due to the influence of *RotTR*'s lead writer, Rhianna Pratchett.[4] Yet, despite these changes, she nevertheless still fits into the archetype of the Orientalist hero: "The modern Orientalist was, in his view," explains Said ([1979] 1994), "a hero rescuing the Orient from the obscurity, alienation, and strangeness which he himself had properly distinguished" (121). In the 2015 *RotTR*, Lara is a seasoned archaeologist, having survived the adventures of the 2013 game. Given all this, any player who assumes the digital guise of Lara Croft is "constrain[ed] . . . to follow certain assumptions about his or her culture" (Mukherjee 2016, 8) which are situated within an existing imperialist framework.

The narrative of *RotTR* follows Lara and Jonah Maiava (from *TR2013*) into Siberia on their quest to find the lost city of Kitezh using her father's research notes. They are pursued throughout the game by Trinity and join forces with the Remnants, descendants of religious schismatics from the tenth century who fled to Siberia to protect a relic known as the Divine Source. The game's narrative thus attempts to situate itself in opposition to imperial and established authority (the Vatican), yet ultimately struggles against its own Orientalist paradigm which positions Lara as a benevolent Western savior.

In *RotTR* and its 2013 predecessor, the procedural rules of gameplay actively participate in Orientalist praxis by means of Lara's archaeological exploration. In addition to its standard adventure-genre gameplay—puzzle solving, combat, and exploration—the rebooted *Tomb Raider* franchise has added a series of artifacts: resources used for crafting weapons upgrades or improving health; quest objects that must be found or destroyed; maps that reveal the locations of these items; relics, which are historical material objects of art or everyday use; and journals (text and audio) that reveal background and narrative clues. Whenever Lara finds a relic or journal, the game moves to the catalogue entry for that artifact; Lara's voice then explains the cultural significance of the relic or the journal author's voice narrates the text. Just as imperial Western archaeologists reconstructed historical narrative through excavation and collection, so, too, Lara constructs portions of the game's narrative through the collection of these artifacts.

However, *RotTR* attempts to invert the standard Western Orientalist narrative, vilifying instead of valorizing the imperial power (Trinity) in an attempt to interrogate the paradigm of hegemonic empire. In the process, *RotTR* makes a claim for the ability of games (more broadly) to engage in critical discourse with contemporary issues of politics and social justice. In its narrative foregrounding of the negative impact of war and prejudice on refugee populations, the game clearly hopes to encourage an attitudinal shift toward acceptance of others, particularly Muslims and refugees. As such, *RotTR* is one of many post-2005 games intentionally attempting to engage with contemporary problems of social justice.[5]

In their chapter "Shifting Implicit Biases with Games Using Psychology," Flanagan and Kaufman (2016) describe the best practices for what they term "Embedded Design," a set of game-design principles that encourages players to overcome implicit biases (226).[6] Among these principles, Flanagan and Kaufman (2016) explain, are the following:

- **Combine on-topic and off-topic content**. Interweave playful content with serious, educational, or 'message-related' content . . .
- **Avoid imbalanced representations**. Avoiding an imbalance or overrepresentation of counter-stereotypical examples . . .

- **Design for repetition** . . . repetition is a particularly key ingredient to psychological change when it comes to reversing well-ingrained implicit attitudes or associations . . .
- **Be less obvious.** In general, we have found that simply making the purpose or aim of a "device" less explicit or obvious increases a player's pleasure, interest in repeat play, and openness to change. (226–27)

For the most part, *RotTR* follows the first and fourth principles, mingling its narrative about rescuing the Divine Source from Trinity with repeated messages about the difficulties and oppression faced by religious minorities and refugees in such a way that the player does not immediately associate the Remnant with Syrian refugees or Trinity with the American religious right. However, *RotTR* fails narratively at the second and mechanically with the third principle, for opposite reasons.

The majority of *RotTR*'s attempts to engage in social criticism are narrative (and, as such, the majority of this analysis focuses on narrative elements), yet the game falls short of successfully "avoid[ing] imbalanced representations." Although *RotTR* does not contain characters who are explicit racial stereotypes (such as Lara Croft's original "Incan Guide," who wore a sombrero and poncho, in the 1996 *Tomb Raider*), it does employ stereotypical racial and cultural assumptions in its depiction of the Remnants as third-world refugees (to be discussed more later). As Leonard (2006) explains, the practice of reducing "Others" to racial, religious, or ethnic stereotypes—such as, for instance, "the Arab as terrorist" (85)—"elicit pleasure, and play on white fantasies while simultaneously affirming white privilege through virtual play" (86).

Mechanically, *RotTR* seems to engage in "Design[ing] for repetition," but the specific mechanics used in the game problematically reinforce the player's (presumably) Western assumptions of superiority and control. The mechanics of exploration, acquisition, and combat replicate the praxis of empire and emulate the process of imperial conquest for the player. This set of mechanics runs counter to *RotTR*'s narrative of acceptance and protection, and is a not insignificant reason why the game's attempt to countermand imperialism falls short. Throughout the game, the player is expected to collect artifacts and journals; to destroy other objects or artifacts; and to kill enemies of both the human (Trinity) and animal variety in order to increase Lara's experience and unlock additional skills. As Höglund (2008) explains, the continuous and positively reinforced use of imperialist violence "effectively conveys to the gamer that continuous [imperialist] warfare lends safety and cohesion to society rather than destabilizing the world," a false narrative clearly evident in *RotTR* through Lara's interactions with the Remnants. Although the specifics of these objects and enemies change as the game progresses, *RotTR* nevertheless reinforces the actions being taken through repetition, replicating imperialist praxis rather than encouraging more socially and culturally conscious behaviors. Thus, although *RotTR* is "Design[ed] for repetition," that very repetition also undermines the game's narrative attempts to encourage increased acceptance and social consciousness.

## THE LEGACY OF THE CRUSADES

The legacy of the Crusades pervades the core narrative of *RotTR*, centered around the struggle between Trinity and the Remnants. As Lyons (2012) observes, "For almost ten centuries, attempts at understanding have been held hostage to a grand, totalizing Western narrative that shapes what can and, more important, what cannot be said and thought about Islam and the Muslims," relying on a stereotype that "remains very much rooted in its medieval beginnings" (1, 26). Although the specific history of the Crusades is largely irrelevant to *RotTR*'s narrative and gameplay, the conflict between established institutional Western religion and ostensible heresy cannot be ignored, as it provides the backbone of *RotTR*'s argument against religious extremism.

The inclusion of religious violence—particularly that modelled after the Crusades—has been minimized by scholars such as Perreault, who argues that "It doesn't appear that game developers are trying to purposefully bash organized religion," instead dismissing the thematic frequency as nothing more than "using religion to create stimulating plot points" ("Video Games Depict . . ." 2012). Perreault's conclusion ignores the essential point of narrative analysis; while it may be true that religious violence makes for a compelling narrative ("Video Games Depict . . ." 2012), the plethora of non-religiously motivated violence in games (and other media) nevertheless suggests that religion is a deliberate focus, one that need not necessarily be to "bash organized religion." There is also the perhaps obvious counterpoint that the reason religious violence is "compelling" is that it is a relevant topic to players due to its cultural immediacy. Furthermore, the way in which a game—such as *RotTR*—depicts religion necessarily enters that game into the public discourse surrounding it, meaning that the choice is both intentional and worth analysis.

For instance, by paralleling the Remnant–Trinity conflict in the game with the Crusades, *RotTR* directly addresses the twenty-first century rise in Islamophobia, a historical legacy inherited from the Crusades reignited by the terrorist attacks on 9/11 in the United States and exacerbated by the Syrian Civil War (2011–present) and the expansion of extremist Islamic groups such as Al Qaeda and the Islamic State (ISIS/ISIL/Daesh). Popular Western demonization of Muslims draws from stereotypes established during the Crusades, which valorize a Christian discourse of military dominance as virtue and vilify Muslims as technologically primitive, violent, and barbaric.[7] More recently, this Islamophobia has manifested in protests throughout the West against the construction or restoration of mosques, the right of Muslim women to wear a burqa or hajib, and attempts to refuse Syrian refugees asylum (Lyons 2012, 10).[8] In reconstructing a Crusade narrative that draws on these twenty-first century misconceptions, *RotTR* encourages its players to develop empathy for those targeted by Islamophobia and ethno-religious oppression, particularly since Lara's targets are Christian (mostly white) men rather than the harmful stereotype of the Islamic terrorist (Šisler 2008, 205).

The game begins in Siberia as Lara and Jonah scale a remote mountain in search of the lost city of Kitezh. Within about fifteen minutes of gameplay, Lara is swept away by an avalanche and loses consciousness, causing a series of flashbacks (Crystal Dynamics 2015). The first of these takes the player to Lara's office in London two weeks earlier, where there is a depiction of the Crusades with a hand-drawn red circle and the hand-written word "Trinity?" alongside a sticky note, which reads "Important!" (Crystal Dynamics 2015). A voice recording from Richard Croft (Lara's father) explains that Trinity is "an ancient sect with designs on controlling the future of humanity" (Crystal Dynamics 2015). The origin of the followers of the Prophet in the Byzantine Empire and the inclusion of the Mongols through artifacts and journals of an unnamed Trinity "Tracker" further solidify the link between Trinity and the Crusades. Phillips (2015) notes that over their four-century span, the Crusades targeted not only Muslims, but also "the pagan peoples of the Baltic region, the Mongols" and "political opponents of the Papacy and heretics (such as the Cathars or Hussites)" (27). In *RotTR*, a journal from Decius (a tenth-century schismatic) explains that Trinity's motive for pursuing the Prophet is similar: "the Knights of the Order of Trinity . . . have come to silence the Prophet—to quell his blasphemy and eradicate our movement" (Crystal Dynamics 2015). By making this connection explicit, *RotTR* intentionally draws upon the history of the Crusades and the associated pattern of Western religious oppression.

The second flashback takes Lara to the northwest border of Syria. After being chased by Trinity, Lara scrambles down the side of a ledge overlooking a city in the valley below. Explosions periodically disrupt the cityscape, as though the city is in the midst of shelling. By thus calling specific attention to the Syrian conflict, the game provides an indirect link between its content—religious extremism, Western imperialism, and oppression—and contemporary political discussions of terrorism, drone strikes, and violence in the Middle East. By linking Syria with both the followers of the Prophet and Trinity, *RotTR* all but forces players to map the historical trajectory of oppression founded in the Crusades onto the modern conflict between Western powers and religious extremist groups in the Middle East early in the game, providing context for the remainder of gameplay.

Outside the game, twenty-first century rhetoric frequently makes use of the language and ideology of the Crusades as a means of promoting Western authority in areas of the Middle East. Particularly given George W. Bush's "disastrous use of the word 'crusade' to describe the 'war on terror'" (Phillips 2015, 27), on September 16, 2001, it is clear that the historical legacy of religious persecution begun by Urban II in 1095 continues to prioritize military engagement as an appropriate and even virtuous response to the presence of religious difference. Lyons (2012) observes that

Since September 11, 2001, the West has launched two major wars against Islamic countries; contributed directly through conflict to the deaths of tens of thousands of Muslims in Iraq and Afghanistan and indirectly to the loss of many tens of thousands more lives through disruptions to health and other basic services. (3)

Each of the components Lyons mentions resonates in *RotTR* in the mistreatment of the Remnant population. In one of the Optional Challenge Tombs—Whirlpool Sanctuary—Lara finds a journal from the early Remnants that illustrates the depth of despair to which war with Trinity has driven them: "The dead choke the rivers. Our children's blood is spilled on the valley floor. We live, but with what? Our city entombed? Our sons and daughters murdered?" (Crystal Dynamics 2015). In another Challenge Tomb—the House of the Afflicted—a journal entry from a Byzantine physician laments the lack of basic medical supplies: "We are crippled by our isolation. We have with us the combined medical knowledge of the Empire, a millennia of learning that tells us how to treat every ailment. But here, on the edge of the world, the lack of one simple flower leaves us helpless" (Crystal Dynamics 2015). These historical accounts situate the Prophet's followers as war-time refugees driven from their own native country due to religious persecution; in *RotTR*, their descendants provide a similar parallel, but from the perspective of those who have already migrated and settled in a new country yet remain targets of Western hostility.

However, this is as far as the parallel in *RotTR* takes us before it inverts the comparison; in the game's narrative, Christians are depicted as hyperviolent radicals while the Remnants prioritize freedom, virtue, and harmony with the natural world. This deliberate inversion of the Crusade paradigm forces players to recognize the false dichotomy established in the contemporary world between the Christian West and Muslim Near East; from another perspective, it suggests, the West are the aggressors, as potentially fanatical and violent as those we have labeled heretics. *RotTR* thus uses this narrative comparison to condemn religious extremism on both sides, encouraging players to accept differences of faith and culture.

# THE (UN)HOLY TRINITY

Within the paradigmatic oppression and persecution of Muslims produced by the legacy of the Crusades is the corresponding valorization of militaristic action taken in response to—or, as in the case of George W. Bush's search for weapons of mass destruction in Iraq, in anticipation of—the threat of radical Islamic terrorism. As Lyons (2012) observes, the West has "arrogated to itself a monopoly over the legitimate use of force in conflicts involving the Muslim world. . . . The result is an unchallenged discourse that affords the West the power to determine which tactics, weaponry, and targets are legitimate and which are not" (111). In *RotTR*, Trinity stands in for these contemporary military forces.

Trinity inherited both religious zealotry and ideological valorization of violence from their Crusading predecessors, as many of the contemporary journals and artifacts that Lara finds emphasize violence as "God's work." For example, in the Soviet weather station there is a rifle shell with the phrase "Kill them all, God will know his own" (Crystal Dynamics 2015) engraved on the bottom in Latin. A series of journals from one Trinity soldier focuses on the alignment of violence and religious extremism, including one aligning homicide with divine purpose: "Konstantin," the leader of Trinity's forces, "keeps telling us that we're doing God's work" (Crystal Dynamics 2015). These journals emphasize the danger of religious extremism, but deliberately focus on a Westernized, white, Christian perspective in order to demonstrate the danger of extremism in any (not just Islamic) ideology. Interestingly, *RotTR* also includes a set of journals from the Trinity supply technician, who serves as an outsider proxy for the player's perspective, describing the operation as "fucking Jonestown out here," and stating his sense that "I'm on the wrong side of history" (Crystal Dynamics 2015). This suggests that he understands that Trinity's role in the narrative is that of the oppressor and is also aware of his own complicity—perhaps analogous to that of the player—in oppressive praxis.

However, despite the narrative condemnation of violence, *RotTR*'s gameplay demands that the player engage in violence of her own. While the collection of journals and artifacts does give the player additional experience, combat is the game's primary mechanic: Lara spends more time engaged in killing than she does in collecting artifacts or conversing with Remnants. Thus, although the narrative suggests that violence and religious extremism are worthy of condemnation, the game's combat mechanics—including melee, range weapons (bow and guns), dodging mechanics, and quick-time events—reward the player for violent actions with achievements, experience points, brief cut-scenes featuring gore and blood-spatter, and resources. So although the game linguistically appears to condemn the violence inherent in Western imperialism and religious radicalism, the player-qua-Lara is arguably the most violent figure in the game, undermining its narrative message of peaceful acceptance.

## REFUGEES FROM RELIGION

Juxtaposed against Trinity are the Remnants, the descendants of the original followers of the Prophet. The supply technician explains that the Remnants are "lost in time. We're talking furs, skins, and iron arrowheads" (Crystal Dynamics 2015). Here we see one of the stereotypical and paternalistic assumptions associated with refugees: that they are primitive and unable to care for themselves, instead having to rely on Western "rescuers" (like Lara). In *RotTR*, the Remnants' primary purpose is to protect the Divine Source, which legend claims contains a piece of the soul of God and has the power to confer immortality (Crystal Dynamics 2015). The Remnants are led by Jacob, the Prophet, who encourages his followers "to become stewards, not conquerors" (Crystal Dynamics 2015) of the land. One of Decius's journals describes the Prophet's teachings as charismatic, but his account is vague: "Heard the liquid truth of his words roll across the Forum of Constantine. He claimed not to speak for God, claimed that no man could. But his wisdom was plain, and not a one of us in that Forum could deny that he spoke the truth" (Crystal Dynamics 2015). Aside from this, *RotTR* does not describe the Remnants' beliefs, obfuscating doctrine in order to make them as sympathetic as possible to a wide range of players.

Despite the intentional vagueness of the Remnants' doctrine, they are meant as an analogue to non-extremist Muslims, both those who faced historical persecution during the Crusades and modern Muslims targeted by Western Islamophobia. Lyons (2012) notes that "Muhammad was also denounced as a false prophet and a heresiarch" (55–56), a label that, Decius's journals explain, also applies to *RotTR*'s Prophet, who was driven from the Byzantine Empire by the Church for heresy (Crystal Dynamics 2015). Further cementing the link between medieval Islam and the followers of the Prophet in *RotTR* is their geographic similarity; apocalypticism had "a long history in the increasingly isolated Byzantine lands that directly bordered the dynamic and expansive empire of Islam" (Lyons 2012, 56), a coincidence in origins that marks the followers of the Prophet in *RotTR* as symbolic representatives for contemporary Muslims (particularly refugees).

Interestingly, *RotTR* also includes examples of radicalism among the Prophet's followers in its portrayal of the Deathless, the Prophet's ancient undying army. Jacob explains that, "I once used the Source to grant my armies their long lives. But it was a terrible mistake. When enemies attacked Kitezh, the Deathless Ones brought the ice from the mountains down upon the city. Thousands were killed. They committed an atrocity to keep the power" (Crystal Dynamics 2015). His example is meant to explain why the Divine Source must be kept away from Trinity, but the entry also recognizes the potential for extremism in any religion, and a warning that all forms of extremism pose a threat to civilization, irrespective of the doctrine from which they spring.

## LARA CROFT, EXCEPTIONAL ORIENTALIST

Through its representations of both Trinity and the Remnants, *RotTR* narratively argues for a more tolerant—less oppressive—global community. However, despite these positive intentions, *RotTR* suffers from an imperialist framework that problematizes its otherwise progressive argument. In *RotTR*, Lara takes it upon herself to protect the Remnants not only from Trinity, but also from their duty to safeguard the Divine Source, exploiting them in order to secure it for herself. As the conflict with Trinity intensifies, Lara begins to coerce Jacob and his daughter Sofia into helping her. In one conversation with Sofia, Lara tells her that, "Your people are already dying. You can't protect it forever" (Crystal Dynamics 2015), intimating that the Remnants will only be safe if they reveal the Divine Source's location to her. The problem with Lara's justification is that it smacks strongly of the paternalistic "White Man's Burden;" her belief that the Remnants would be able "to live in peace" (Crystal Dynamics 2015) if only she (Lara) were to remove the Divine Source is ultimately only a convoluted argument for why Lara is superior (in an Orientalist sense).

The way *RotTR* frames the final confrontation and destruction of the Divine Source (which takes place primarily during a cut-scene and out of the player's control) situates Lara as an imperial savior not just of the Remnants, but also of all humanity. Standing in the Chamber of Souls in the center of Kitezh, Lara confronts Ana, Konstantin's sister, over the Divine Source:

> ANA: Think of the millions suffering and dying. We can save them. We can change the world. Together.
>
> LARA: The cost is too high, Ana. We aren't meant to live forever. Death is a part of life.
>
> ANA: That's easy for you to say. You aren't the one who's dying.
>
> LARA: But this isn't about you. This is about humanity. About protecting what it means to be human. (Crystal Dynamics 2015)

Ana pulls a gun on Lara, telling her that she "doesn't have to die for this," to which Lara replies, "But I'm willing to" (Crystal Dynamics 2015). Of course, Lara is not the one who dies "for this;" Jacob is, as when Lara smashes the Divine Source, he dies, although not before confirming Lara's heroic status by telling her, "In all my years, I've met few as extraordinary as you," assuring her that she has "ma[d]e a difference" (Crystal Dynamics 2015). Although Jacob sacrifices his immortal life to ensure peace for his people, Lara is the game's hero—the educated, white, imperial savior who makes the decision to sacrifice both Jacob and the Divine Source (albeit with Jacob's permission).[9]

The game concludes with Lara's return to Western civilized space—her father's office on the Croft estate—where Jonah confirms that she made the right choice and that her father would be proud. Interestingly, at this point *RotTR* turns Lara away from the patriarchal framework that has structured both *RotTR* and *TR2013*'s narratives, as she says, "It doesn't matter what choices he would have made. I have to make my own" (Crystal Dynamics 2015). She follows this assertion of individuality with a reassertion of her role as (imperial) hero: there are, she says, "secrets out there that can change the world. I need to find them. Not for my father, not for anyone else . . . I can make a difference. I can make the right difference" (Crystal Dynamics 2015). Although this concluding proclamation declares Lara's independence from her father's legacy, it nevertheless remains inscribed by imperial praxis in which Lara represents "good" imperial power. Weaver-Hightower (2014) explains this trope:

> These archaeological raiders [like Lara Croft and Indiana Jones], in the name of benevolent empire, always prevail over evil empire, a neoimperial fantasy in itself since the vaguely Anglo-American "benevolent" empire induces control indirectly (in neo-imperial fashion) while the Nazi/Indian/Egyptian/communist "evil" empire forces its authority over people, as backed up by violence and exploitation. (114)

Lara, despite her good intentions, stands as an icon of benevolent empire, seeking to defend both peoples (like the Remnants) and artefacts (like the Divine Source) from violent oppression.

Crystal Dynamics clearly sought to make Lara a hero, independent, a defender of justice, and a figure of cultural acceptance. However, Lara's (and Crystal Dynamics') intentions ultimately cannot escape the paternalism of benevolent empire, and, despite their efforts to the contrary, Lara's actions—particularly those circumscribed by the game's violent and acquisitive mechanics—remain exploitative. She, as Mikula (2010) argues, "brings together the aspirations of modernism—the imperialist pursuit of power and global prestige—and their postmodern problematization and fragmentation. Paradoxically," Mikula concludes, "she critiques neo-imperialism by enacting her own complicity with it" (83). She is both an icon of (benevolent) empire and a rebel against systematic (evil) imperial oppression, both heroic savior and agent of destruction.

## CONCLUSION

How, then, are we to evaluate *RotTR* in terms of social justice? Despite its failure to escape the constraints of (benevolent) empire, *RotTR* nevertheless narratively advocates for its players to take a more conscientious stance regarding tolerance and acceptance. Players are encouraged to empathize with the Remnants, to feel protective toward them and, ultimately, to make the choice to save them from Trinity's imperial religious radicalism. The alignment of this radicalism with Western empire intentionally inverts the long-standing popular culture paradigm in which the West saves the East from superstition and barbarism. In *RotTR*, Trinity represents Western institutional oppression and racism, and players are intended—through Lara—to condemn (or, at least, to question) the ideological suppositions that produce Orientalist praxis. As the victims of this oppression, the Remnants assume the position of subjected "native" populations, yet their characterization mitigates their Otherness relative to a Western audience, both rendering them more "worthy" of empathy and undermining the very argument for tolerance they were designed to fulfill.

Nevertheless, by calling attention to the long history of Western Islamophobia and religious extremism, *RotTR* engages critically with one of the most significant global issues of contemporary social justice. The game's struggle to balance its desire to foster tolerance and acceptance— particularly of immigrants, refugees, and those of non-Christian faiths— with centuries of Orientalist, Islamophobic, and xenophobic Western culture is a symptom of the bias against which the game's narrative positions itself; as an artifact of Western imperialist popular culture, *RotTR* is always already contained within the paradigm it wishes to explode. Yet in spite of this, *RotTR* continues to insist on aligning Lara (and, through her, the player) with the Remnants rather than with Trinity, encouraging its players to recognize in the journals and artifacts of Remnant history stories from their own contemporary sociopolitical context and, by extension, to use that parallel as a catalyst for empathy and even intervention.

In fact, the conflict between *RotTR*'s Western imperial perspective and its desire to foster empathy with the oppressed enables it to better bridge the cultural gap between its Western audience and its political intentions. Because Lara herself is white, Western, and imperialist, she is more accessible to players who share her paradigmatic context; if Lara can become a champion for the protection and rights of minority and religious refugees, then so, too—argues *RotTR*—can the player. Thus, although *RotTR*, as a product of the still predominantly white, imperial, and patriarchal game industry, remains constrained by its own (benevolent) paternalism, it—like Lara—nevertheless does try to "make the right difference."

Perhaps as our society and our games mature, we will see more developers take on the challenge to end the imperialism of hegemonic play, "to critique rather than adopt and perpetuate the rhetoric of the hegemony of play, and to explore new avenues of inclusiveness and diversity" (Fron et al. 2007, 2) by hiring developers of color and from diverse ethnic, social, and religious backgrounds, as well as creating games that leave behind violence and exploitation, or at least work harder to problematize them in a mechanical as well as narrative context, in order to better serve cultural and social progress.

## NOTES

1   Subsequent references to the game will use the abbreviation "*RotTR*." *RotTR* was released in 2015 limited to Xbox 360 and Xbox One consoles, with a later release date of 2016 for PC and PlayStation 3 and PlayStation 4 consoles.

2   Because Lara is a female character, for the sake of simplicity I will use female pronouns for the player.

3   This chapter takes for granted the presumption that, as Ian Bogost (2010) has argued, games can and do intentionally "facilitate the player's understanding of contemporary political processes and issues" (134), and that the commentary in *RotTR* is therefore intentional critique of our current sociopolitical context.

4   Subsequent references to Crystal Dynamics' 2013 *Tomb Raider* will use the abbreviation "*TR2013*."

5   There was a noticeable shift following 2005 toward games that attempt to engage their players with ethical questions concerning race, religion, and gender (with varying degrees of success), including *Portal* (2007), *BioShock* (2007), *BioShock Infinite* (2013), *Gone Home* (2013), the *Mass Effect* series (2007–2017), among others.

6   The term *implicit bias* "refers to the attitudes or stereotypes that affect our understanding, actions, and decisions in an unconscious manner. These biases, which encompass both favorable and unfavorable assessments, are activated involuntarily and without an individual's awareness or intentional control" (Kirwan Institute 2017).

7   Particularly during the Crusades, this characterization is antithetical to the technological and scholarly advancement that took place during the period from the eighth to thirteenth centuries known as the Islamic Golden Age (Hassan n.d.).

8   These reactionary protests increased significantly following the terrorist attacks in Paris on November 13, 2015. *RotTR* was released on November 10, 2015,

responding to both anti-Muslim sentiment and the reaction against it, which
have been part of long-standing discussions of Islamic terrorism since 2001.

9   As it is a *Tomb Raider* game, it is natural for Lara to be its hero. The significant
component here is that Lara makes the decision *for* Jacob that he will sacrifice
his life, just as she was willing to exploit the Remnants in her quest for the
Divine Source.

## WORKS CITED

Anderson, M., and Levene, R. 2012. *Grand Thieves and Tomb Raiders: How British Video Games Conquered the World*. London: Aurum Press Ltd.

Bezio, K. M. S. 2016. "Artifacts of Empire: Orientalism and Inner-Texts in *Tomb Raider* (2013)." In *Contemporary Research on Intertextuality in Video Games*, edited by C. Duret and C.M. Pons, 189–208. Advances in Multimedia and Interactive (AMIT) Book Series. Hershey: IGI Global.

Bogost, I. 2010. *Persuasive Games: The Expressive Power of Videogames*. Cambridge, MA: MIT Press.

Breger, C. 2008. "Digital Digs, or Lara Croft Replaying Indiana Jones: Archaeological Tropes and 'Colonial Loops' in New Media Narrative." *Aether: The Journal of Media Geography* 2: 41–60.

Buncombe, A. 2017. "Muslim Hate Crimes: Reports of Islamophobic Incidents in the US Soared Again in 2016." *The Independent*, May 14.

Champion, E. 2004. "Indiana Jones and the Joystick of Doom: Understanding the Past via Computer Games." *Traffic* 5: 47–65.

"Civil Rights Report 2017: The Empowerment of Hate." 2017. Washington DC: Council on American-Islamic Relations. www.islamophobia.org/images/2017 CivilRightsReport/2017-Empowerment-of-Fear-Final.pdf.

Core Design. 1996a. *Tomb Raider*. PC. London: Eidos Interactive, Square Enix.

———. 1996b. *Tomb Raider: PC Manual*. London: Eidos Interactive.

Crystal Dynamics. 2013. *Tomb Raider*. XBox 360. Tomb Raider. San Francisco: Square Enix.

———. 2015. *Rise of the Tomb Raider*. XBox 360. Tomb Raider. San Francisco: Square Enix.

Dyer-Witheford, N., and de Peuter, G. 2009. *Games of Empire: Global Capitalism and Video Games*. Electronic Mediations 29. Minneapolis: University of Minnesota Press.

Flanagan, M., and Kaufman, G. 2016. "Shifting Implicit Biases with Games Using Psychology: The Embedded Design Approach." In *Diversifying Barbie and Mortal Kombat: Intersectional Perspectives and Inclusive Designs in Gaming*, edited by Y. B. Kafai, G. T. Richard, and B. M. Tynes, 219–33. Pittsburgh: ETC Press.

Fron, J., Fullerton, T., Morie, J. F., and Pearce, C. 2007. "The Hegemony of Play." In *Situated Play: Proceedings of the 2007 DiGRA International Conference*, volume 4, edited by Akira Baba, 309–18. University of Tokyo, September 24–27.

Gray, K. L. 2014. *Race, Gender, and Deviance in Xbox Live: Theoretical Perspectives from the Virtual Margins*. Theoretical Criminology Series. Amsterdam: Elsevier.

Hassan, A. Y., al-. 2015. "History of Science and Technology in Islam." *History of Science and Technology in Islam*. www.history-science-technology.com/articles/articles%208.html.

Höglund, J. 2008. "Electronic Empire: Orientalism Revisited in the Military Shooter." *Game Studies* 8 (1). http://gamestudies.org/0801/articles/hoeglund.

Kirwan Institute. 2017. "Understanding Implicit Bias." Kirwan Institute at the Ohio State University. http://kirwaninstitute.osu.edu/research/understanding-implicit-bias.

Lees, M. 2016. "What Gamergate Should Have Taught Us about the 'Alt-right.'" *Guardian*, December 1.

Leonard, D. J. 2006. "Not a Hater, Just Keepin' It Real: The Importance of Race- and Gender-Based Game Studies." *Games and Culture* 1 (1): 83–88.

Lock, P. 2006. *Routledge Companion to the Crusades*. London: Routledge.

Lyons, J. 2012. *Islam through Western Eyes: From the Crusades to the War on Terrorism*. New York: Columbia University Press.

Mikula, M. 2010. "Gender and Videogames: The Political Valency of Lara Croft." *Continuum: Journal of Media and Cultural Studies* 17 (1): 79–87.

Mukherjee, S. 2016. "Playing Subaltern: Video Games and Postcolonialism." *Games and Culture* 1–17.

Newman, J. 2013. *Videogames*. 2nd ed. London: Routledge.

Phillips, J. 2015. "The Crusades." *History Today* 65 (5): 26–34.

Said, E. W. [1979] 1994. *Orientalism*. New York: Vintage.

Šisler, V. 2008. "Digital Arabs: Representation in Video Games." *European Journal of Cultural Studies* 11 (2): 203–20.

"Video Games Depict Religion as Violent, Problematized, Study Shows." 2012. *PHYS. ORG*. https://phys.org/news/2012-02-video-games-depict-religion-violent.html.

Weaver-Hightower, R. 2014. "Tomb Raider Archeologists and the Exhumation of the US Neoimperial Cinematic Fantasy." *Journal of Popular Culture* 47 (1): 109–28.

CHAPTER 7

# NANCY DREW AND THE CASE OF GIRL GAMES

ANDREA BRAITHWAITE

CONVERSATIONS ABOUT GENDER and gaming are seemingly end-less. Recent debates about women and video games have drawn our attention to what it's like for women in gaming communities: women frequently face a lot of pushback as they are often considered to be unwel-come visitors in spaces stereotyped as "for the guys." Concerns about women and games—or, more specifically, about what happens to games when women play them—have long animated discussions within and about the gaming industry and its communities. In the late 1990s, these concerns coalesced into the "girls' games movement," with a handful of companies explicitly targeting girls as a demographic deserving distinct "girl"-games.

Her Interactive is one of the most successful companies to come out of the girls' games movement. In 1998, Her Interactive released *Secrets Can Kill*, the start of a long line of mystery adventure games featuring iconic young female sleuth Nancy Drew. Like other girls' games companies, Her Interactive positioned itself as an intervention into popular ideas about gender and games. By examining the development of these games, we can see how "girls' games" operated as a discourse, an industrial practice, and a marketing strategy. Her Interactive launched in 1995, with the goal of "turn[ing] today's teenage girls into serious gamers" (Cook 1999). To date, Her Interactive has sold more than nine million games, received more than thirty awards ("Her Interactive Releases"), and has received consistently strong reviews on game review sites like metacritic.com. The Her Interactive archives, housed at the Strong Museum of Play in Rochester NY (United States), offer one specific entry point into girls' games. Documenting the aims and practices of a company deeply embedded in the movement, these archives also help illustrate the ideological and industrial contours of this historical moment in gaming.

Her Interactive and the Nancy Drew games are important contributions to such a picture. The company's longevity; its approach to design, development, and marketing; and the ongoing popular resonance of Nancy Drew as a pop culture figure show how gender is entrenched as a cultural and consumer imperative, as well as how to creatively negotiate these conditions. Gaming's history as a largely insular culture has helped incubate intolerance toward gender, sexual, and racial differences (Kirkpatrick 2016; Lees 2016; Shaw 2013; Leonard 2006; Kline, Dyer-Witheford, and de Peuter 2003), which has notably bubbled over in high-profile hate and harassment campaigns (Braithwaite 2016; Consalvo 2012; Salter and Blodgett 2012), and informed broader social movements such as the rise of the ultra-conservative alt-right in the United States (Nagle 2017; Lees 2016). The "refusal to engage critically such 'kid stuff' has dire consequences" beyond the success or failure of any given game studio, and so attending to Her Interactive and the Nancy Drew games is an opportunity to identify strategies that challenge the attitudes in and around games (Leonard 2006, 87).

## NANCY DREW AND THE GIRLS' GAMES MOVEMENT

A close look at the origins of the Nancy Drew games illustrates the cultural and economic dynamics of gaming in the 1990s. Upon their release in 1930, the Nancy Drew novels were an immediate hit. In these stories, clever teenaged girl Nancy Drew solves various complex crimes and earns the acclaim of her friends and neighbors. She dives headlong—and often solo—into mysterious situations, always emerging triumphant. Unlike other young female heroines at the time, Nancy was unfettered by gender roles that kept girls away from the action. She "not only demands equal rights, she demands equal danger" (Zacharias 1976, 1036; see also Jenkins 1998). Ilana Nash argues that this autonomy and mastery are key components of Nancy Drew's ongoing success, "constitut[ing] nothing less than one's ability to imagine herself as a competent and important presence in the world" (2006, 49).

Yet female characters like Nancy Drew were largely absent from the 1990s game landscape, which was dominated by action-adventure and combat games. Marketed to young males, these types of games were widely assumed to be played by young males as well (Kirkpatrick 2016; Cote 2015; Kline, Dyer-Witheford, and de Peuter 2003). Still reeling from the North American game industry's spectacular crash in 1984 (Donovan 2010), the few large companies rebuilding the market (like Sony and Microsoft) were reluctant to stray from familiar genres and audiences. Potential financial losses provided a "powerful incentive to stick with the tried and true and ride on the coattails of proven success" (Kline, Dyer-Witheford, and de Peuter 2003, 251; see also Donovan 2010; Pearce 1998). Most games followed the formula established by titles like *Duke Nukem* (1991), *Resident Evil* (1996), and *Quake* (1996)—powerful protagonists enacting mass destruction. These trends intensified in the late 1990s and into the 2000s: when "73% of player-controlled characters are male," players—both actual and potential—could presume "video games are a space about and for males" (Leonard 2006, 84).

The girls' games movement was determined to push at these boundaries. For many, getting more girls into games was also key to getting more girls comfortable with technology. Girls' apparent indifference to games, many worried, could generate a general dislike of technology and negatively impact their future: "It is not just that girls seem to like today's computer games less than boys do, but that these differential preferences are associated with differential access to technological fields as the children grow older, and this differential access threatens to worsen as technological literacy becomes a precondition for employment" (Cassell and Jenkins 1998, 11; see also Huntemann 2013; Taylor 2006). Girls' interest in and access to games was more than an issue of unequal participation. It was also framed in terms of the utopian promise of digital technologies; to ensure girls would be part of this technology-driven future and its "new economic reality: training and education for high-skilled, weightless work" was a priority (Huntemann 2013, 43). The girls' games movement was thus a form of critique. Fraught with arguments about technology, gender, equality, and access, it suggested that the games industry poorly served what were understood to be girls' interests.

But what are girls' interests? Uncertainty about girls and games pervades the news clippings archived by Her Interactive, showing how the media constructed "games for girls" as a social and technological problem. For instance, many articles saw girls' relationships with computers and games as confusing and mysterious. With headlines noting "girls' special interests" (Oshiro 1997) or looking at "solving the girl mystery" (Newson 1997), girls' interests in technology were presumed to be "undiscovered territory" (Gamboa 1997)—an anxiety-generating unknown. Such discourses are part of what Fron et al. call the hegemony of play:

> [The] game industry has infused both individuals' and societies' experiences of games with values and norms that reinforce that industry's technological, commercial and cultural investments in a particular definition of games and play, creating a cyclical system of supply and demand in which alternate products of play are marginalized and devalued. (2007, 1)

Past beliefs about gender-appropriate entertainment also informed expectations for video games in the 1990s. Children's play is often construed as productive, an activity that helps shape them for their future, properly gendered selves. The issue of girls' games was thus also a matter of defining "girls." The games that dominated the market in the late 1990s, Henry Jenkins (1998) argues, built upon historical gendered ideals of play. Boys' culture, rooted in outdoor adventure and exploration, emphasized autonomy, mastery, aggression, and individualism to produce young men ready to tackle the public sphere. Girls' culture, meanwhile, relegated girls to domesticity—indoor spaces in which girls were encouraged to hone skills that would help them help others. Such goals were at odds with the games most widely available in the 1990s, and concerns about the levels of aggression and action in video games were, more accurately, concerns about girls potentially performing "boy" traits, and thus not being "girls" (Walkerdine 2006).

By turning the Nancy Drew books into video games, Her Interactive intervened in popular narratives about gendered play preferences. Nancy Drew had already reclaimed the boys' space of action-adventure stories, "envisioning alternative definitions of girlhood" even before her transition to video games (Nash 2006, 27; Jenkins 1998). She is the kind of protagonist commonly found in video games at the time: agentive, active, and able. Her Interactive's young female focus group participants thought so as well, describing her as smart, confident, adventurous, and assertive (Focus Group 1997). Yet translating Nancy Drew's narratives into video games meant rethinking game design. The girls' game movement effectively problematized the "production process and environment for the creation of digital games," as well as what counts as a game (Fron et al. 2007, 2). Given that girls' interest in technology was "undiscovered territory" (Gamboa 1997) and that existing approaches to video game development did not actively address girls, girls' games would need to be created differently in order to uphold the presumed gap between girls' and boys' play. Girls' games were not just an ideological and discursive construct, but also an industrial practice.

## CREATING GIRLS' GAMES

The girls' games movement distinguished itself in part by its array of participants: "female high-technology entrepreneurs and feminist researchers and activists interested in making better opportunities for girls and women in cyberspace, and various industry leaders and venture capitalists who were keen to crack the female market" (Kline, Dyer-Witheford, and de Peuter 2007, 260). For instance, Her Interactive's Megan Gaiser was originally a documentary filmmaker; Purple Moon's Brenda Laurel started out with an MFA in theatre; Mattel's Nancy Martin had an English degree; Sega's then-vice president of corporate and consumer communications Lee McEnany Caraher specialized in medieval studies. Many entered the industry with a "political commitment to female empowerment, one consistent with their own non-traditional career choices," and their approach to game design reflected this broader goal (Cassell and Jenkins 1998, 17).

Two of the most prominent girls' games companies, Mattel and Purple Moon, relied heavily on academic and observational research in order to construct a particular combination of gameplay and environments as "for girls." Typical activities included fostering emotional connections with non-player characters (NPCs). Purple Moon's *Secret Paths in the Forest* (1997) encouraged players to recognize and manage the feelings of others, what Laurel describes as a "complex emotional navigation of social space . . . [an] emotional rehearsal for social navigation" (1998, 123–24). Its serene meadow environment created a quiet and private space for these emotions to be articulated and accommodated. Girls' games frequently had a second-person perspective, in which the player's role was to help the game's NPCs; Mattel's *Barbie Fashion Designer* (1996) asks players to create outfits not for themselves, but for Barbie.

Her Interactive also involved girls in various aspects of the production process via its Teen Advisory Panel. Comprised of nearly seventy girls between the ages of eight and seventeen, this panel was a core component in the development of the early Nancy Drew games. Girls seemed thrilled at the prospect of contributing to the development of a video game, and answers to the enrollment questionnaire (1998–1999) painted a more nuanced picture of girls' relationships to technology and games than press coverage has suggested. For instance, some wrote that they wanted to be involved *because* of their love of technology: "I am interested in the newest and best things in the computer world;" "Because computers and computer games are my life. Why not do it for more than fun! Whenever I play games I always think that this should be better or different, and that should be better! I really think I could help you." Many girls were already avid players; they reported playing games such as *Doom* (1993), *Quake* (1996), *SimCity* (1989), *Myst* (1993), and *Need for Speed* (1994). Others were clearly disappointed with available games and were eager to help change this landscape: one was "tired of boy games where the girl is rescued and almost always has big boobs. Would like brave and smart girls. And athletic girls. Would like to see a girl save a boy."

The Teen Advisory Panel was an integral part of the game development and production process. Her Interactive's archives detail the girls' involvement in character and storyline development, as well as interface and environment design. Their feedback was incorporated directly into the final product, and Her Interactive's game production binder (1999) notes the extent of changes made to *Stay Tuned for Danger* based on the panel's experiences:

> One of the most valuable experiences during art development was the opportunity to witness focus groups firsthand . . . Reading facial expressions was also a big part of learning what did and didn't work in terms of graphics, design, and functionality . . . The focus group summaries that were distributed to the team were extremely helpful. These documents should reside on the server as permanent team reference.

While "trying to design from gauging existing tastes or play preferences is one of the most conservative approaches and rarely results in innovation" (Taylor 2006, 102), the Teen Advisory Panel pushed Her Interactive to create a girls' game that challenged the accepted narratives of what and how girls play. It is no wonder the Teen Advisory Panel was also thanked explicitly in the game itself: *Secrets Can Kill*'s production credits list all of the panel's members.

## PLAYING GIRLS' GAMES

While the Nancy Drew games developed in the same context and with similar cultural and entrepreneurial goals, games like *Secrets Can Kill* and *Stay Tuned for Danger* offered different play experiences than Purple Moon's *Secret Paths* series or Mattel's *Barbie Fashion Designer*. For instance, Nancy's friends George and Bess and boyfriend Ned only become part of the game at the player's request; they can be called upon for tips or advice ("Would like option to get the answer through a friend in the context of the game") but are otherwise irrelevant to the storyline. As Her Interactive's focus group notes (1997) show, the Teen Advisory Panel suggested minimizing social interactions so that the player remained at the center of the narrative and gameplay.

As murder mysteries, potential suspects populate the Nancy Drew games; NPCs should be interrogated rather than befriended. The Teen Advisory Panel helped determine the tone of these characters—how to make them seem more or less suspicious, depending on their role—by suggesting changes to dialogue, appearance, and behavior. These adjustments demonstrate how these girls were less concerned with being social and more interested in mastering the material; their changes focused on how to become the one who knows all the answers and not the one who makes all the friends—a clear divergence from what other girls' game products provided.

The Nancy Drew games also create a series of spaces to explore. Like Purple Moon's *Secret Paths*, these environments are full of hidden items uncovered by interacting with all possible nooks and crannies. However, these places are anything but peaceful. With the culprit always lurking, high school hallways and local diners are not solely spaces of discovery but also of potential threat—one wrong move in *Stay Tuned for Danger*, for instance, traps the player in a locked TV studio with the murderer. As befits a super-sleuth, the Nancy Drew games are set in a variety of public places: a haunted hotel in Germany, a museum in Washington, D.C., a soap opera set in New York City. Richly detailed and immersive, these places are primarily there to be conquered, to serve the player's ultimate purpose of solving the crime.

The games also highlight player agency and expertise. While other games situate girls as helpers, Her Interactive positions players as Nancy, "so the player gets to experience what it is to be brilliant" ("Her Interactive CEO" 2011). The Teen Advisory Panel's game evaluation forms (1998–1999) show that *being* Nancy was a key part of the games' appeal "because you feel like you are her." This sentiment was reiterated by early customers as well: "I have tried other adventure games but keep coming back because I love the format of the Nancy Drew Game, It generates the feeling that you are part of the story and that is why I think Nancy drew [sic] is superior to many other games on the market" (Her Interactive Selected 2008). Yet being Nancy was also one of the games' more daunting prospects initially. Nancy Drew's storied history made some girls anxious; focus group notes (1997) suggest she was "too serious and too perfect" and many requested adjustments before they stepped into that role themselves, such as "have something wrong with her," "she should have some body fat," and "have a scar, blemish." These revisions were central to the production process. Her Interactive's debrief for *Message in a Haunted Mansion* (ca. 2000) lists "More opportunities for Nancy to actually mess up rather than just get stuck" in its successful development strategies.

Her Interactive's Teen Advisory Panel helped situate the early Nancy Drew games both within and against the girls' games movement of the late 1990s. Like other companies attempting to address a female audience, Her Interactive relied heavily on girls themselves as they created their products. In contrast to their competitors, however, Her Interactive designed distinct environments and experiences. Negotiation about the places for and pleasures of being Nancy Drew "narrates a particular story of certain bodies within a larger social structure" (Gray 2014, 16). For a young female sleuth in a field and format otherwise dominated by men, emotional connections, safe spaces, and second-person storytelling were ignored in favor of elements more closely aligned with boys' culture: expertise and mastery, danger, and narrative agency and control.

## HAILING THE GIRL GAMER

Despite these differences, Her Interactive's initial promotional material propagated a perception of games and gaming as gendered. This strategy can be seen as an effort to intervene in another aspect of the hegemony of play: "the cultural positioning of games and 'gamers'" (Fron et al. 2007, 2). As Adrienne Shaw (2013) explains, "Being a gamer is defined in relation to dominant discourses about who plays games, the deployment of subcultural capital, the context in which players find themselves, and who are the subjects of game texts." By attempting to redefine these factors, the girls' games movement helps us see why many girls in the 1990s may have been reluctant to identify as gamers. By creating games with female protagonists and alternative play styles, these companies were also trying to change the conversations around gender, gaming, and technology.

Her Interactive tried to shift these perceptions by addressing young girls as gamers. Shaw (2013) argues video games "hail" players, impacting "how and if people who play video games turn to the hail 'hey gamer,' and the implications this has for diversity of in-game representation if they do not believe that they are the ones being hailed." Most video game companies in the 1990s targeted young males, effectively leaving girls and women out of the picture (Kirkpatrick 2016; Cote 2015; Pearce 1998). As Sega's Caraher notes, these companies didn't consider a female market to be worth the cost: "Maybe we should spend time marketing to girls. We just haven't chosen to, because the bigger part of the market is boys. The girls are secondary. They come after" (1998, 197). Girls were rarely hailed as gamers. Mattel and Purple Moon stepped into this gap with girl-centric marketing, what Janelle Brown (1996) calls the "cootie" approach—"producing titles that will actually deter boys." *Barbie Fashion Designer*, for instance, was pitched to the public not just as "for girls," but also explicitly "not for boys," to encourage girls' perceptions of themselves as *the* audience rather than merely a residual one.

Her Interactive's early marketing modified this "cootie" approach while still situating the Nancy Drew games as girls' games. Eschewing the typical pink and purple palette, the packaging for these first few Nancy Drew games prominently featured the tagline "For girls who aren't afraid of a mouse!"— an explicit call to young female players who saw themselves as already (or potentially) tech-savvy. This echoed the girls' games movement's hope of familiarizing girls with computers and technology, and Her Interactive's sample reel (2000) wove this aspect into the games' predicted appeal. This short video frames girls, often in pairs, in front of a computer as they talk to each other about what steps to take next. The camera regularly zoomed in on the girls' hands on the mouse, visually reminding viewers that these games are both entertaining and technologically educational. Such use of these girls, and their bodies, contrasts sharply with the trade show promotional model, one of the few visible articulations of women and technology at the time. While the "sexualized presentation and treatment of promotional models underscores the spectacle of the booth babe, whose presence is designed to amuse the (assumed) heterosexual male trade show audience," Her Interactive's participants aim instead at an assumed female (and/or parental) audience by emphasizing the young women's bodily autonomy in their capacity to use technology (Huntemann 2013, 52).

Her Interactive frequently positioned the Nancy Drew games as collective female endeavors. Box copy for *Stay Tuned for Danger* encouraged potential players to share the experience with other women: "Great opportunities for collaborative sleuthing with Mom, sis and friends!" An ad from the September 2004 issue of *Elle Girl* magazine suggested that *The Secret of Shadow Ranch* (2004) would be a great group activity and a chance to take technology back: "What's the coolest way to spend a night with your girlfriends? Invite them over for a sleepover to play the new interactive PC game, Nancy Drew: The Secret of Shadow Ranch . . . Add some popcorn, kick your brother off the computer, and get ready to stay up all night!" Even without the stereotypical colors of "girl technology," Her Interactive's initial marketing strategies still upheld presumed gender variations in gameplay styles and preferences. This is underscored by other archival promotional documents, such as the reviewer's guide (1998) for *Secrets Can Kill*, which encourages popular critics to consider "both blatant and subtle differences in gameplay preferences. Girls like adventures where they can collect experiences, forge relationships and manage complex social interactions."

This material suggests that Her Interactive considered the rhetorical power of gender differences to be the most promising way to break into the market, even when their Teen Advisory Panel noted otherwise—pinning girls in what Gray calls "an invisible prison of intersecting gazes" (2014, 7). While numerous girls reported playing—and loving—games like *Doom* and *Quake*, and most girls most often played games by themselves, the public presentation of early Nancy Drew games fit easily alongside the "cootie" approach used by companies like Mattel and Purple Moon. This disjuncture between the lived experiences of the girls on the Teen Advisory Panel and the idealized play of girl gamers indicates the stranglehold of the hegemony of play as it existed in the 1990s. Girls' game companies found themselves trying to negotiate between what actual girls found enjoyable, and what popular discourse found acceptable. Direct challenges to gender stereotypes were perceived as too risky when companies were still fighting to establish financial security. For many, games that could revolutionize the industry could also bankrupt their fledgling companies: "People who push the envelope so far have to wait for the market to catch up to them" (Caraher 1998, 211; Pearce 1998). Girls' game companies figured compromise was the best route to more diverse products in the future; the challenge lay in "figur[ing] out how to insert new genetic material into the culture without activating its immune system. That's the hardest thing in the world" (Laurel 1998, 131).

Nancy Drew's eighteen years as a video game heroine indicate that Her Interactive's hailing strategies were ultimately successful, though not necessarily by addressing their intended audience. Her Interactive's selected press coverage and customer feedback (2008) reveals that the game's success was not driven solely by young female players. Many reviewers were quick to disclose that they did not fall into the game's target market, yet loved the games nonetheless:

> Hello! I would definatly [sic] not fit in to your tipical [sic] demographic but I just finished 'The Last Train to Blue Moon Canyon' and had to write to tell you how much I enjoyed it. First off my name is [redacted] and I am a 44 year old gay male who loved to read Nancy Drew books when I was a kid . . . driving that car was a hoot and the mining car ride in 'Canyon' was great fun . . . the cheeky dialogue options had me laughing out loud.

For many, Nancy Drew's appeal rests less on her gender and more on exploring, investigating, and eventually unmasking the murderer.

Players thus saw the Nancy Drew games as offering alternative, rather than feminine, gameplay. Some even challenged Her Interactive's explicitly gendered marketing; one letter-writer tells the company:

> I am a 15 year old who very much enjoys Nancy Drew Games. However, I was very, very offended when Nancy said 'Girls can blow things up! At least they can help.' That, in my opinion, was a very sexist comment. I always thought of Nancy as a role model, but I was hurt at this. She frequently acts docile around Ned and can make snap judgements too . . . I found this very offensive and stereotypical . . . Thank you for reading. I will continue playing the games until something crosses the line. (Correspondence 2005)

From this vantage point, pitching Nancy Drew games as empowering felt inconsistent with what the games offered, a marketing ploy that some young female players found disingenuous.

Many critics shared this perspective, "argu[ing] that the call for girls' games should be an invitation to explore new formats, to develop alternative models of software rather than simply to conform assumptions about gender that are created and reinforced by existing market pressures" (Cassell and Jenkins 1998, 24; see also Taylor 2006). Some game designers were equally skeptical. As Theresa Duncan, part of the production team behind the quirky *Chop Suey* (1995), opined: "I find some of the attention paid to girls recently patronizing, and I think that has a lot to do with girls' pocketbooks" (1998, 174).

Struggles over the meaning, use, and relevance of girls' games speak more broadly to the confluence of cultural and consumer forces that characterize the hegemony of play. Purple Moon—absorbed by Mattel in 1999—was, for Fron et al. an example of this hegemony in action: "Purple Moon was, in short, gobbled up by the Hegemony of Play" (2007, 3). In hindsight, it is relatively easy to attribute Purple Moon's demise to the company's clear gendering of its games. Yet, as the company's former CEO Brenda Laurel reminds us, today's gaming environment is different: "I get a lot of crap from both women and men who don't understand the social context in which Purple Moon and its sister companies came to be . . . The conditions that we were trying to address when we started Purple Moon no longer exist" (Donovan 2010, 273). What constituted the hegemony of play in the 1990s is different from what constitutes it now. While it may resist change, it is not impervious to it.

That Her Interactive's Nancy Drew games still sell millions of copies to all kinds of players gives us a chance to think about not only the challenges of coming up against the hegemony of play, but also the opportunities. In 2001, Her Interactive started tagging its games as "For adventurous sleuths" and finally "For mystery fans," rather than "For adventurous girls." Its initial reliance on an all-girls Teen Advisory Panel helped the company establish the alternative characters, narratives, and gameplay that continue to be key elements of its success. Because of, and not despite, its early focus on games for girls, Her Interactive managed to expand the boundaries of what counts as a successful game, and who count as players.

Actively diversifying creative teams can shape the success of the game and the broader gaming world. The girls' games movement demonstrated what gaming can gain by working around the structures of the industry. Revisiting corporate and independent strategies can broaden practices like open beta-testing and crowdfunding beyond free labor or financing and into more participatory pathways between cultures of production and consumption. The cultural and industrial conditions in which the early Nancy Drew games operated are vivid reminders than we cannot draw an effective boundary between our digital and physical spaces—we have never been able to do so, nor should we. Moreover, "our continued insistence on shrugging off the problems of the Internet as 'not real'—as something we can just log out of—is increasingly misled," as it can preclude our capacity to identify and counteract regressive attitudes toward difference (Lees 2016). While the gaming industry today may still wrestle with the place and presence of women and other marginalized groups, Her Interactive's history reminds us that their ideas can push the industry—and its cultural contexts—in more inclusive directions.

## ACKNOWLEDGMENTS

The author is grateful for the generous support of The Strong Research Fellowship and for the expertise of the Strong National Museum of Play's staff.

## WORKS CITED

Braithwaite, A. 2016. "It's about Ethics in Games Journalism? Gamergaters and Geek Masculinity." *Social Media + Society* 2 (4): 1–10.

Brown, J. 1996. "Girl Gamers: Sugar, Spice, Everything Profitable?" *Wired*, November 19. www.wired.com/1996/11/girl-gamers-sugar-spice-everything-profitable.

Caraher, L. M 1998. "An Interview with Lee McEnany Caraher (Sega)." In *From Barbie to Mortal Kombat: Gender and Computer Games*, edited by J. Cassel and H. Jenkins, 192–213. Cambridge, MA: MIT Press.

Cassell, J., and Jenkins, H. 1998. "Chess for Girls? Feminism and Computer Games." In *From Barbie to Mortal Kombat: Gender and Computer Games*, edited by J. Cassel and H. Jenkins, 2–45. Cambridge, MA: MIT Press.

Consalvo, M. 2012. "Confronting Toxic Gamer Culture: A Challenge for Feminist Game Studies Scholars." *Ada: A Journal of Gender, New Media, and Technology* 1. http://adanewmedia.org/2012/11/issue1-consalvo.

Cook, J. 1999. "Game Maker Counting on Nancy Drew." *Eastside Journal* (Bellevue, WA), April 5.

Correspondence from Users. 2005. Her Interactive, Inc. Collection, Brian Sutton-Smith Library and Archives of Play at The Strong, Rochester, NY.

Cote, A. C. 2015. "Writing 'Gamers': The Gendered Construction of Gamer Identity in *Nintendo Power* (1994–1999)." *Games and Culture* 13 (5): 479–503.

Debrief for *Nancy Drew: Message in a Haunted Mansion*. Ca. 2000. Her Interactive, Inc. Collection, Brian Sutton-Smith Library and Archives of Play at The Strong, Rochester, NY.

Donovan, T. 2010. *Replay: The History of Video Games*. East Sussex: Yellow Ant.

Duncan, T. 1998. "An Interview with Theresa Duncan and Monica Gesue (Chop Suey)." In *From Barbie to Mortal Kombat: Gender and Computer Games*, edited by J. Cassel and H. Jenkins, 172–91. Cambridge, MA: MIT Press.

Focus Group Discussion Guides. 1997. Her Interactive, Inc. Collection, Brian Sutton-Smith Library and Archives of Play at The Strong, Rochester, NY.

Fron, J., Fullerton, T., Morie, J. F., and Pearce, C. 2007. "The Hegemony of Play." In *Situated Play: Proceedings of the 2007 DiGRA International Conference*, volume 4, edited by Akira Baba, 309–18. University of Tokyo, September 24–27.

Gamboa, G. 1997. "Girls Online: The Undiscovered Territory." *Akron Beacon Journal* (Akron, OH), June 16.

Game Evaluation Forms, *Nancy Drew: Secrets Can Kill*. 1998–1999. Her Interactive, Inc. Collection, Brian Sutton-Smith Library and Archives of Play at The Strong, Rochester, NY.

Gray, K. L. 2014. *Race, Gender, and Deviance in Xbox Live: Theoretical Perspectives from the Virtual Margins*. London: Routledge.

"Her Interactive CEO Interview (Nancy Drew Series)." 2011. *Examiner*, March 14. www.examiner.com/article/her-interactive-ceo-interview-nancy-drew-series.

"Her Interactive Releases 32nd Nancy Drew Mystery—Nancy Drew: Sea of Darkness." 2015. *HerInteractive.com*, May 19. www.herinteractive.com/about-us /news/her-interactive-releases-32nd-nancy-drew-mystery-nancy-drew-sea-of -darkness.

Her Interactive Sample Reel. 2000. VHS tape. Her Interactive, Inc. Collection, Brian Sutton-Smith Library and Archives of Play at The Strong, Rochester, NY

Her Interactive Selected Press Coverage and Customer Feedback. 2008. Her Interactive, Inc. Collection, Brian Sutton-Smith Library and Archives of Play at The Strong, Rochester, NY.

Huntemann, N. B. 2013. "Women in Video Games: The Case of Hardware Production and Promotion." In *Gaming Globally: Production, Play, and Place*, edited by N. B. Huntemann and B. Aslinger, 41–57. New York: Palgrave Macmillan.

Jenkins, H. 1998. "'Complete Freedom of Movement': Video Games as Gendered Play Spaces." In *From Barbie to Mortal Kombat: Gender and Computer Games*, edited by J. Cassel and H. Jenkins, 262–97. Cambridge, MA: MIT Press.

Kirkpatrick, G. 2016. "How Gaming Became Sexist: A Study of UK Gaming Magazines 1981–1995." *Media, Culture, and Society* 39 (4): 453–68

Kline, S., Dyer-Witheford, N., and de Peuter, G. 2003. *Digital Play: The Interaction of Technology, Culture, and Marketing*. Montreal: McGill-Queens University Press.

Laurel, B. 1998. "An Interview with Brenda Laurel (Purple Moon)." In *From Barbie to Mortal Kombat: Gender and Computer Games*, edited by J. Cassel and H. Jenkins, 118–35. Cambridge, MA: MIT Press.

Lees, M. 2016. "What Gamergate Should Have Taught Us about the 'Alt-right.'" *Guardian*, December 1. www.theguardian.com/technology/2016/dec/01/gamer gate-alt-right-hate-trump.

Leonard, D. J. 2006. "Not a Hater, Just Keepin' It Real: The Importance of Race- and Gender-Based Game Studies." *Games and Culture* 1 (1): 83–88.

Nagle, A. 2017. *Kill All Normies: Online Culture Wars from 4chan and Tumblr to Trump and the Alt-right*. Winchester, UK: Zero Books.

*Nancy Drew: Secrets Can Kill* Reviewer's Guide. 1998. Her Interactive, Inc. Collection, Brian Sutton-Smith Library and Archives of Play at The Strong, Rochester, NY.

*Nancy Drew: Stay Tuned for Danger* Game Production Binder. 1999. Her Interactive, Inc. Collection, Brian Sutton-Smith Library and Archives of Play at The Strong, Rochester, NY.

Nash, I. 2006. *American Sweethearts: Teenage Girls in Twentieth-Century Popular Culture*. Bloomington: Indiana University Press.

Newson, G. 1997. "Solving the Girl Mystery." *New Media*, September 1.

Oshiro, S. 1997. "Computer World Has Started Catering to Girls' Special Interests." *Honolulu Advertiser* (Honolulu, HI), October 20.

Pearce, C. 1998. "Beyond Shoot Your Friends: A Call to Arms in the Battle against Violence." In *Digital Illusion: Entertaining the Future with High Technology*, edited by C. Dodsworth Jr., 209–28. New York: ACM Press.

Salter, A., and Blodgett, B. 2012. "Hypermasculinity and Dickwolves: The Contentious Role of Women in the New Gaming Public." *Journal of Broadcasting and Electronic Media* 56 (3): 401–16.

Shaw, A. 2013. "On Not Becoming Gamers: Moving beyond the Constructed Audience." *Ada: A Journal of Gender, New Media, and Technology* 2. http://adanewmedia .org/2013/06/issue2-shaw.

Taylor, T. L. 2006. *Play between Worlds: Exploring Online Game Culture*. Cambridge, MA: MIT Press.

Teen Advisory Panel Enrollment, Completed Questionnaires. 1998–1999. Her Interactive, Inc. Collection, Brian Sutton-Smith Library and Archives of Play at The Strong, Rochester, NY.

Walkerdine, V. 2006. "Playing the Game: Young Girls Performing Femininity in Video Game Play." *Feminist Media Studies* 6 (4): 519–37.

Zacharias, L. 1976. "Nancy Drew, Ballbuster." *Journal of Popular Culture* 9 (4): 1027–38.

# CHAPTER 8

# THE HORRORS OF TRANSCENDENT KNOWLEDGE

*A Feminist-Epistemological Approach to Video Games*

STEPHANIE C. JENNINGS

Early in my playthrough of *Bloodborne*, I knock outside the building at an alleyway's dead-end. A voice emerges from behind the locked doors. The woman inside turns me away.

"And besides," she tells me, "this is no place for ladies." I hear her low chuckle through the boarded window.

It takes me a moment to grasp what she meant. She is a prostitute, I realize. Her home is actually a brothel.

She has urged me to go on my way. On this moonlit night of rampant bloodletting—the night of a hunt—the denizens of Yharnam in their shuttered homes are wary of a foreign-born hunter like myself. I can't really blame them for not trusting me.

I do as I'm asked, and step away, back into the dank alley. It is a well-populated strip, but each of its inhabitants turns me away. Walking down it, I find my non-diegetic-self wondering if the prostitute's dialogue only occurs for women characters like mine, since it wouldn't make much sense to ward off a man by telling him that a brothel is no place for ladies.

But what really sticks with me is a different thought. Did she only mean that the brothel was no place for ladies? Or was there a second meaning beneath her words, beneath the chuckle that seemed to suggest that we were sharing a joke that only we women could understand? I wonder if she actually meant the entire world around us. This blood-slick night whose only rule is kill-or-be-killed: this is what is no place for ladies. I wonder if she was being ironic. Ironic because maybe according to the laws of men this is no place for ladies, but perhaps we ladies understand that this world is, in fact, ours for the taking. I am, after all, a brutal, unfaltering hunter in this crumbling society of hysterical men. The night is mine, ours.

I have my business to attend to. And as I do, I am left with the feeling that Arianna, woman of the night, has sent me on my way to carve out a space in a world that has told us we don't belong.

At the end of the alley, I run into a mob of feral men that have begun the transformation into beasts. I kill them.

THE ABOVE GAMEPLAY narrative originates from *Bloodborne* (2015), the fourth installment in the *Souls* series by game studio From Software and director Hidetaka Miyazaki. It enters a legacy of notoriously violent and difficult-to-play video games. The *Souls* series has enjoyed international success, having sold millions of copies and received widespread critical acclaim. However, the games have also faced criticism for the inaccessibility of their extreme—and inflexible—difficulty. Each game in the franchise chronicles the rotting of powerful, opulent civilizations. Players adopt the roles of lone, wandering, customizable protagonists who have been tasked with ending cycles of societal chaos and decay. They navigate hostile environments, facing and defeating creatures that tower over the seemingly insignificant player-characters—but these monsters always represent a promise to players: an assurance that they can be subdued, defeated, triumphed-over. They can be killed, as long as players have the skills to kill them.

As such, *Bloodborne* could easily be critiqued as a system that promises its players opportunities for conquest, and that therefore invites and engenders masculine sensibilities of power. It could easily be condemned as yet another AAA title that enables and glorifies violent power fantasies for men. But playing through *Bloodborne*, I wondered if its ferocious difficulty and its guarantees of conquest could be an expression of femininity—or other performance or understanding of gender—rather than one exclusively of masculinity. Couldn't I be experiencing a power fantasy of my own by playing *Bloodborne*? Couldn't there be a feminist epistemology of those designs, of that world, of that play space?

## RETHINKING TRADITIONAL WAYS OF KNOWING AND BEING

Epistemology, the philosophy of knowledge, has had a troubled history in Western culture. In seeking to understand how human beings produce knowledge, it has solidified strict notions of what kinds of knowledge are legitimate and what kinds are illegitimate. Along its way, traditional epistemology has reinforced an oppressive gender binary by dividing legitimate knowledge and illegitimate knowledge along gendered lines. As Mary Flanagan (2002) summarizes, "In Western tradition, knowledge has been characterized with reason, identified as masculine and separated from the corporeal body. This paradigm has excluded women, who have commonly been identified with the body and thus lie outside the scope of knowledge" (425). Against these longstanding assumptions that have dominated Western thought, Donna Haraway (1988) sought to reclaim embodied knowledge as both legitimate and feminist. To do so, she posited a theory of situated knowledge. Situated knowledge could account for knowledge production in ways that traditional, patriarchal epistemology had overlooked and excluded: by rooting knowledge in the standpoints of partial, situated experience. Rather than operating under the false pretenses of some unachievable transcendent truth, situated knowledge could recognize that knowledge arises from bodily experience and in standpoints produced by class, race, gender, and sexuality in a highly stratified society. In this way, knowledge production could recognize its own historical, cultural contingency while also formulating a different sort of objectivity, a different sort of truth. As Haraway explained, "Feminist objectivity is about limited location and situated knowledge, not about transcendence and splitting of subject and object. It allows us to become answerable for what we learn how to see" (582–83).

Both Haraway and Sandra Harding (1991) pointed out that traditional epistemology—in particular, the knowledge production within the realm of the sciences—had not been so aware of or answerable for what it had learned how to see. Harding critiqued the biases lodged in masculine notions of objective knowledge. The prevailing epistemological models had their foundations in men's needs, interests, experiences, and world-views. Contrary to traditional epistemology's claims to disembodied, rational, transcendent objectivity, knowledge production had always already been partial, distorted, bodily, and subjective—but in a way that reproduced men's notions of the truth while silencing the viewpoints of women and oppressed groups. With situated knowledge at its core, feminist epistemology would expose androcentric epistemology's denial of its own skewed perception of truth. Moreover, as Harding declared, in order to remove men's partial knowledge as the center of epistemology, "it is also necessary to decenter the preoccupations of white, economically advantaged, heterosexual, and Western feminists in the thinking and politics of feminists with these characteristics. No longer should their needs, interests, desires, and visions be permitted to set the standard for feminist visions of the human or to enjoy so much attention in feminist writings" (13). In this way, situated knowledge would not just serve a privileged segment of women's perspectives. Instead, it could further enrich the breadth and depth of human knowledge by elevating the experiences, understandings, and subjectivities of countless marginalized groups and identities. As a result of this approach, knowledge would be recognized as increasingly heterogeneous and diverse.

But that does not mean that such knowledge would then somehow be invalid because it cannot accomplish a transmission of objective truth. Rather, it means that we need to modify our expectations for objectivity. According to Haraway, we must come to recognize and embrace that the partiality of our knowledge constructs a new understanding of objectivity that ensures that we are responsible for our own lenses, biases, cultural perceptions, experiences, frameworks, and approaches. On that note, Harding introduced the concept of *strong objectivity* to advance the understanding that "in a society structured by gender hierarchy, 'starting thought from women's lives' increases the objectivity of the results of research by bringing scientific observation and the perception of the need for explanation to bear on assumptions and practices that appear natural or unremarkable from the perspective of the lives of men in the dominant groups" (150). Strong objectivity would emerge out of the many diverse perspectives and heterogeneous approaches of situated knowledge, shedding new light on truth and reality.

## FEMINIST EPISTEMOLOGY IN GAMING CONTEXTS

Feminist epistemology is one possible way of orienting methods of games criticism toward justice: it excavates the counter-hegemonic voices that are so often buried beneath the detritus of dominant industry discourses. Narrow market assumptions have over-determined the directions of games research, to the point that "the vast majority of player-centered research, whether cognitive, behavioral, psychological, or sociological, whether quantitative or qualitative, concerns male players; this fact is seldom, if ever, articulated" (Fron, et al. 2007, 2). Game studies—and games criticism more generally—require methodological approaches the primary concern of which is elucidating the experiences of non-white, non-male players. As David Leonard (2006) writes, "An important step that game studies must undertake is toward intersectional analysis" (85).

There are, however, significant bodies of game studies scholarship, especially within feminist game studies, that have devoted themselves to the analysis and critique of video game representations and structures. These have frequently treated play as the activation of designer-embedded ideologies that the game's rules afford. Noting this trend, Adrienne Shaw (2014) insists, "We cannot look at representation by looking just at game texts, because the intertwined aspects of representation and play necessarily involved audiences' use of texts" (37). There have been periodic invocations to remedy this oversight—for instance, by calling on game scholars to refocus on the potentialities of play. In one such instance, Miguel Sicart (2011) emphasizes:

> Play is not only a performance. Play does not only include the logics of the game—it also includes the values of the player. Her politics. Her body. Her social being. Play is a part of her

expression, guided through rules, but still free, productive, creative (para. 79).

Yet very few contributions to game studies literature seem to take such claims into account. The ways that players make meaning—the ways that they incorporate their subjectivities and their values into their play, the ways that they generate knowledge while playing, and the styles of play that they adopt—are under-theorized and persistently overlooked areas in studies of video games. Exacerbating this issue is the very fact that little has been done to actively develop a methodological system for the qualitative, critical analysis of video games as texts (Consalvo and Dutton 2006).

My previous work has sought to address this dearth, providing an analytical approach "in which the subjectivity of the critic is accepted as central, unavoidable, and necessary" (Jennings 2015, 2). In it, I emphasize the notion that players are parts of the video game text—which would then mean that a critic's subjectivity is part of the game text that they read, examine, and analyze. The present chapter foregrounds feminist epistemology as an added component of this approach; it therefore further facilitates critical analyses of the *situated play* of video games. By regarding play as an appropriative activity that is situated in subjectivity, identity, and experience, this method expands opportunities for intersectional analysis, illuminates diversities of play styles, and avoids the reinforcement of an essentialist gender binary.

My playthrough of *Bloodborne* demonstrates possible uses of this framework. Here, I conduct a critical analysis of my own situated play. Important to note, then, is that I am a white, middle-class woman—for it is this subject position that informs the meanings that I have generated through my embodied actions as my *Bloodborne* character. Consequently, this chapter's focus is on the ways that women may create meaning through their own playful experiences of feminine performance, and on the ways that games may be productive of feminist ways of knowing. However, my intersectional standpoint and my view of feminism are necessarily limited. On one hand, I represent a marginalized position in that I am a woman in a patriarchal culture. But on the other, I also occupy a hegemonic position in that I am white, middle-class, and cisgender. Thus, although my examination of *Bloodborne* reveals possible pleasures of playing a violent and difficult video game as a woman, its conclusions are necessarily problematic.

And, indeed, *Bloodborne's* morbidity is among its aspects that I find most satisfying. Later in my playthrough,

> I pause to admire my avatar's lithe, bloodied body. I swing the camera around to see her in full: the stained armor, crimson-splashed cheeks and nose and hair, the rifle held casually in her left hand and cane in her right. She seems to smirk, which I enjoy. I'm good at this game. And I perceive the amount of blood that coats my in-game body as proof of this. I admit that I like this feature of the game: the more beasts I kill, the bloodier I become. It is concrete evidence that I am a practiced hunter, a conqueror, a killer.
>
> I have made her look as close to myself as I could: slender frame, high cheekbones, glasses. I'm proud of this projection of myself. I like watching the way she moves. The intuitively precise, expert way she wields her weapons; her swift strides, impeccable dodges; the swish of her cape. I like that she is small and wiry, fighting against creatures far bigger than she and seeming unfazed by it all. In fact, we—I—have just come out of a string of tough battles against some especially hor-rifying creatures. It wasn't easy, of course. But here we are, swelling with victory and shimmering with fresh blood, shredded bodies mark-ing our path.
>
> Violence isn't supposed to be feminine, though. It isn't supposed to be a feminine expression, a feminine solution to a problem, a femi-nine experience or way of knowing. Yet, for me, there is an undeni-able allure to playing a game as a powerful, untouchable, indomitable woman who is able to express herself in ways that I do not, would not, cannot outside of the game.

Specifically mentioning her experience of *Bloodborne*, Aevee Bee (2015) interpreted violence as a metaphor for interpersonal conflict. "So often," she said, "games' expressive qualities are limited to the violent motion of virtual bodies, yet they can be extremely articulate within that vocabu-lary." To her, violence in video games could be a bodily language of power, a mastery over form and technique and struggle that games allow players to speak and to perfect. She concluded, "It's not that I want to *really* hurt anyone. I just want to speak with the language of that power." Violence, then, can be recast as a language—a language not often afforded to women, a power that they are often not permitted to speak.

At the Canadian Game Studies Association conference, I saw Jon Saklofske (2015) give a presentation on the idea of feminist war games. The presentation contended with a number of difficult-to-approach questions, such as whether the violent environments of war video games could incorporate feminist values. Could there be feminist war games at all? As Saklofske asserted, "Not only *can* there be feminist war games, but such experiences *need* to be made available to players to provoke perceptual flexibility." Adding to the discussion in the Twitter backchannel, Nicholas Hanford (2015) also asked what a feminist power fantasy would be. My experience of violence in *Bloodborne* is, I believe, one example of how to understand the possibilities of feminist power fantasies and feminist knowledge-making in video games.

I do not think I would feel quite this way were I not able to play as a woman. My choice of woman avatar is key to how *Bloodborne* produces feminist knowledge for me, unlocking a uniquely feminine—that is, my own performance of femininity—way of experiencing violence and power through my situated acts of play. Mary Flanagan's (2002) take on feminist epistemology in video games is rooted in this connection between player and avatar; thus, her analysis is centrally focused on an embodied form of knowledge-making. "Through relationships to 'avatars,'" she argued, "we have a new kind of interaction with knowing" (427). At the end of her essay, Flanagan stresses the crucial importance of these subject positions for a feminist epistemology of play: "For users, especially female users, the shattering or opening up of the position of receiver—of the subject position—offers a situation in which alternative ways of seeing, hearing, listening, and understanding can develop through awareness and redesign" (450).

As both Kennedy (2002) and Flanagan (2002) have argued, feminist ways of knowing in a video game are not just about that game's representation of women. Representation is only one element in a complex web of features and experiences that make up video games—so better representation of women alone is not sufficient for incorporating feminist values into video games. We cannot overlook the significance of play: of different play-styles, of the variability of experience, of players' subjective outlooks that lead them to diverse ways of knowing. Moreover, feminism itself is not some rigid yes-or-no checklist of goals or a single, static system of beliefs—it is also shifting, intersectional, and varied. Adding subjective methods and concepts of feminist epistemology to our analytical toolkits for games criticism can aid us not only in understanding diversities of play and experience, but also diversities of feminisms.

With regard to the relationship between player and avatar, "the type of knowledge established through these virtual characters becomes a way of 'knowing' through performance" (Flanagan 2002, 439). Without my woman avatar and my relationship to her, without my performative acts as my avatar, I would not come to know *Bloodborne* as both a feminist and feminine experience in the way that I do. Through violence, we—my avatar and I—establish a language of power in the world around us. Though we may be small, our abilities—my quick fingers on the controller and the adept swing of her cane—hold the promise of a vocabulary that I cannot express as myself alone. We can conquer any colossus that stands before us. We can be untouchable. We can be powerful.

## THE HORRORS OF TRANSCENDENT KNOWLEDGE

Eventually, Arianna takes me up on my offer for help. I have returned to her boarded window; this time, she wants my protection. Day has not come. Night has remained night, lasting well longer than it should. The city is collapsing as inhumanity crawls into every human mind. Yharnam's homes are no longer safe, and Arianna and others need shelter. I tell them of the Cathedral Ward, whose thick clouds of incense stave off the roaming beasts. There, they should be safe—at least, for a while. At this point in the game, I've come to understand that salvaging the city is hopeless.

Later in the game, I return to the cathedral to visit the refugees with their fraying nerves. I find Arianna doubled-over, moaning in pain. She no longer speaks to me, so great is her agony.

Later still, I find that her usual spot is vacant. But I discover her in the tomb beneath the cathedral. She is sobbing, but otherwise almost lifeless. Next to her, scrabbling along the tomb's watery floor, is a grotesque creature, a Celestial Larva. Arianna has given birth to the offspring of the alien gods that occupy Yharnam. I kill it and take an item from its body: One Third Umbilical Cord. Doing so also kills Arianna. (The truth is: I have read online beforehand that I must gather these cords if I want the game's "true ending." My murders of Arianna and her child are not arbitrary but planned in advance).

On a menu screen, the umbilical cord's description tells me that the alien gods cannot reproduce on their own and must seek a surrogate for the birth of the next Great One. They impregnated Arianna without her knowledge—but her child is a warped human-alien hybrid, a failed attempt that will not ascend to godhood. Especially now that I have killed it.

Arianna is not the only woman in the game that endures forced impregnation. The same happens to Iosefka, a cruel scientist who seeks a cure for the malady that is turning humans into beasts; and to Queen Yharnam, the ruler of an ancient civilization for whom the city was named. The horrors of *Bloodborne*, I have come to understand, are the horrors of being a woman with a body capable of bearing children in a Western, patriarchal society. *Bloodborne* recognizes these fears, makes them real, gives them legitimacy. And in so doing, it points a damning finger at androcentric epistemology.

Although *Bloodborne* is a game developed by a Japanese studio, it enters a long, strong legacy of Western mythology: women being forcibly, and sometimes unknowingly, impregnated by gods to bear their divine children. The trope was prevalent throughout Greek mythology, often with Zeus taking the form of an animal to rape women, who would then give birth to his demi-god progeny. And, lest we forget, this very trope is one of the pillars of Western civilization: The god of Christianity impregnated the virgin Mary so that she would give birth to his son-as-himself, Jesus. But the horrors into which *Bloodborne* taps are not bizarre, unreal dreads of being impregnated with god-children. They are the terrors of rape, of pregnancies against our will and against our knowledge, of being forced to carry a child to term that we do not want and did not will into existence. They are the real and ever-present fears of women's bodies—and their very selfhood—being reduced to sexual objects and child-bearing vessels. Of patriarchal notions that define womanhood as the capability and willingness to procreate—that then exclude many people who identify as women. Of the perpetual surveillance, monitoring, and policing of women's bodies. Of the absolute deprivation of women's bodily autonomy.

The myths of god-induced-pregnancy point to the patriarchal assumptions that have constructed these fears. Anne Balsamo (1996) pointed to three key features of cultural thinking on reproduction in her analysis of the surveillance of pregnancies: 1) "A pregnant woman is divested of ownership of her body, as if to reassert in some primitive way her functional service to the species," 2) "The entity growing in her, off of her, through her . . . has some sort of ascendant right . . . that the maternal body is beholden to," and 3) "The state of being pregnant is so 'wondrous' . . . that she would endure any discomfort, humiliation, or hardship to experience this 'blessed event'" (80). Each of these points is mirrored in ancient Western god-child myths, as well as in the narrative of *Bloodborne*. In *Bloodborne*, the impregnated women have no ownership over their bodies, as they are not told or aware that they are pregnant. Their functional service to the species is to become the surrogate that will produce a human-alien Great One and thus allow the species to ascend to godhood. The entity growing off her is assumed to have an ascendant right to her body, as it is the child of a god. And bearing the god-child would be regarded as an ineffable triumph of humanity—a pregnancy so wondrous and blessed that it produces an actual apotheosis.

The horrors of *Bloodborne* are also the horrors of H. P. Lovecraft, an idea that cannot be overlooked or forgotten. Alluded to in the short story "The Call of Cthulhu" (1999), the Cthulhu mythos consists of a pantheon of Great Old Ones, ancient alien deities that once ruled Earth but that now lie dormant. These gods will eventually re-emerge, sending humanity into chaos. Knowledge of these gods is too much for the human mind; to try to understand them would be to shatter one's own consciousness. Lovecraftian horror is thus the horror of the unknowable, the dread that there are forces in the universe beyond human comprehension. The first paragraph of "The Call of Cthulhu" articulates this theme:

The most merciful thing in the world, I think, is the inability of the human mind to correlate all its contents. We live on a placid island of ignorance in the midst of black seas of infinity, and it was not meant that we should voyage far. The sciences, each straining in its own direction, have hitherto harmed us little; but some day the piecing together of dissociated knowledge will open up such terrifying vistas of reality, and of our frightful position therein, that we shall either go mad from the revelation or flee from the deadly light into the peace and safety of a new dark age (139).

Lovecraftian horror preys upon the will to transcendent knowledge, pointing out as it does that our knowledge is fragmented and partial. If these fragments were to be pieced together, humanity would discover its own frailty and insignificance in the cosmic framework and be driven mad with this awareness and knowledge. But perhaps this "madness" is only a threat for those humans arrogant enough to believe that their existence and knowledge is paramount, those who could not bear to have their power and superiority dethroned.

To me, *Bloodborne* is therefore about the encounter of Western, androcentric epistemology with the unknowable. It is about how, when faced with the terrors of what its knowledge does not encompass, Western patriarchy will strive to map its own oppressive worldviews onto what lies beyond its own explanation. In the game's narrative, the male-dominated institutions of Yharnam are responsible for the city's downfall. The College of Byrgenwerth—run by a group of men—was the first to discover evidence of the Great Ones' existence. Eventually, the Healing Church grew up around this discovery. It was formulated on the practice of blood ministration, whereby Yharnamites attempted to infuse their own blood with the blood of the alien beings to increase their lifespan, rid themselves of disease, and find a way to make themselves closer to the gods. The Healing Church came to be both religious pillar and governing body, creating a sort of theocracy that worshiped the alien entities. An offshoot of Byrgenwerth and the Healing Church, the School of Mensis, dedicated itself to discovering a way to produce a surrogate for the Great Ones' child.

The men of these knowledge-producing institutions pursued the Eldritch Truth, seeking a way to line their minds with eyes that would allow them to know in ways that the Great Ones could know.

They undertook these endeavors with the goal of elevating the species; but they did so at the cost of women. While the men sought the gods' knowledge, Yharnam's women were merely the vessels that would give birth to a human-god. They were impregnated without their consent, often without their knowledge. Yet these births always resulted in failures: stillbirths or the mutated Celestial Larvae. Hence, in many ways, the men's efforts to grasp the Eldritch Truth act as stand-ins for traditional epistemology's pursuit of objective, transcendent knowledge. Both of these aims have resulted in—and been built upon—the exclusion and exploitation of women. But in *Bloodborne*, the ruthless quest for Eldritch Truth—for transcendent knowledge—results in societal destruction and the transformation of humans into beasts. With most of *Bloodborne's* human-to-beast enemies apparently masculine-presenting—including the founders of Byrgenwerth and the School of Mensis—and most of the few remaining still-human characters feminine-presenting, the game creates an inversion of the classic trope of female hysteria. A cruel, incessant theme throughout Western epistemology and culture, the notion of hysterical women has explained away women's violence, characterized the chemicals and biology of their bodies as out-of-control, reduced them to irrational perversities unable to attain the detached logic of men.

*Bloodborne*, however, turns the knowledge-hungry men into wild, inhuman creatures that have lost all capacity for their treasured rational thought. While women had been victimized in Yharnam, the bedlam of its eternal moonlit night provides women a new opportunity: to demolish the oppressive patriarchal system. This is not only visible in my player-character herself, but also characters such as Eileen the Crow, Hunter of Hunters, who sets about killing hunters (almost exclusively men) who have begun the descent into beasthood. Here, my violent actions as a woman take on particularly potent meanings. The power fantasy in which I am engaged is not simply one of killing for fun. Rather, it is the power fantasy of being able to tear down an oppressive system that has objectified, excluded, and victimized me.

*Bloodborne's* narrative details and mechanics are too convoluted, intricate, and scattered for any one person to uncover on their own. If you want to understand *Bloodborne*, then you must take to its community. A comprehensive view of the game cannot be accomplished in a single playthrough by a solitary player. It takes the collaboration of many players and their countless, varied, subjective playthroughs to collect and archive the knowledge necessary to even begin to understand the game. Online communities weave together the partial knowledge of many players to start crafting the tapestry that will help to explain the game's vast and contorted expanse. The piecing together of fragmented knowledge is the only way to start grasping *Bloodborne*. The collecting of fragmented, partial knowledge is not only a narrative theme but is central to the game's mechanics. As players explore Yharnam, they gradually gain a quantified characteristic called Insight. Players can obtain Insight in a number of ways, including by discovering new areas, by defeating bosses, by helping other players, and by using items called Madman's Knowledge.

The connection between Insight and aiding other players suggests another aspect of the game's affection for partial knowledge, pointing again to the significance of the threaded-together fragments of individual, subjective experience and communal ways of knowing. The narrative hints that the player's world is only one of many intersecting parallel universes, an aspect emphasized by the players' ability to leave notes with bits of cryptic information for others to find and use. Players may summon other player-hunters into their game when they need help, though at the cost of Insight. Being summoned into another player's game to aid them, on the other hand, results in an increase in Insight.

As players gain more Insight over the course of the game, previously concealed details become apparent. With a high level of Insight, players are eventually able to hear the crying of a baby throughout their journey. Insight also allows players to ultimately witness the silent, lurking presence of giant aliens known as Amygdalas. The Amygdalas are clearly designed after Lovecraft's description of Cthulhu, and it is no doubt significant that they have been named after a part of the human brain. But Insight also has its drawbacks—the more of it the player has, the more susceptible the player is to being inflicted with a status effect called Frenzy, a clear insinuation of the loss of the player-character's humanity.

It is a nod, again, to Lovecraftian horror, to the cosmic dread of discovering the insignificance, limitations, and fragility of one's own mind.

Perhaps the umbilical cords are another mechanical instantiation of fragmented knowledge, I think. Humanity has failed to produce its own ascendance into godhood. The umbilical cords represent these failed attempts and the ways these attempts have exploited women. They are the fragmented experiences of the women that were forced to bear the Great Ones's warped, abominable offspring. Using them at the end of the game summons the Moon Presence and a battle against it.

After I kill the Moon Presence, the Doll—a constant companion throughout the game—lifts a wet, gleaming, sluglike creature from the ground. The slug is the player-character, my avatar, now in alien form. In this moment, have I ascended to godhood? Have I become the surrogate for the next Great One? Was my avatar an alien all along? Or is this some mockery of that godhood, a reminder of the pathetic attempts of human beings to transcend the boundaries of their own capacities to know? I want to think that I have become a goddess, that I have brought down the patriarchal constructs that have sought to bind me and define my womanhood for me.

But I am reminded that I have achieved this—whatever this is— through the brutalized experiences of other women. I have ascended at their expense. In fact, it is I that have killed them for my own gain. Were these murders acts of compassion and liberation? Was I ending their suffering, releasing them from the infliction of their alien infants, of their victimization by Yharnam's heinous epistemological conquest? Was I bringing together their partial knowledge into a new form of transcendent awareness, respecting their unwilling contributions to this catastrophe by bringing about a new form of human knowledge that none of us could have achieved alone?

I doubt this. Instead, I understand that I too have trampled on the experiences, lives, and bodily autonomy of others to produce my own tragic, pitiful godhood. I have assembled what was not mine to own or to know. As the Doll chuckles at my writhing body, and tells me "Oh, good hunter," the way one would speak to an errant child, I realize that this is the knowledge I have been left to discover.

## CONCLUSION

While a video game's structures of rules and regimes of representation may appear masculine, exclusionary, and hegemonic, the meanings of those forms are not static. They do not float in transcendent isolation. They come into being as texts only with the presence of the player, only through the act of play. When I played *Bloodborne*, I filled its playful space with meanings that the game's rules and representations did not suggest on their own. I brought my situated position and a mode of play that my subjectivity influenced; I then negotiated the game's rules through my play. As my situated knowledge collided with *Bloodborne's* systems and designs, I came to feminist ways of knowing through my feminine, performative play within the game's structured constraints and representations.

Incorporating feminist epistemology into interpretations of video games opens possibilities for new understandings of players and play, new ways of reading game texts. Moreover, such approaches encourage players to give voice to their own experiences, to speak the ways that they have come to know through their own engagements with video games. Embracing fragmented knowledge as a component in methods of criticism can, thus, lead to an opportunity for justice in studies of video games: a strong objectivity of player experience. As we develop new vocabularies to characterize and examine our styles of play and our modes of intersectional, subjective involvement, we arrive at radical reformulations of what video games and playing them might mean.

## WORKS CITED

Balsamo, A. 1996. *Technologies of the Gendered Body: Reading Cyborg Women*. Durham, NC: Duke University Press.

Bee, A. 2015. "I Love My Untouchable Virtual Body." *Offworld*. http://boingboing.net /2015/05/06/i-love-my-untouchable-virtual.html.

Consalvo, M., and Dutton, N. 2006. "Game Analysis: Developing and Methodological Toolkit for the Qualitative Study of Games." *Game Studies* 6 (1). http://game studies.org/0601/articles/consalvo_dutton.

Flanagan, M. 2002. "Hyperbodies, Hyperknowledge: Women in Games, Women in Cyberpunk, and Strategies of Resistance." In *Reload: Rethinking Women + Cyberculture*, edited by Mary Flanagan and Austin Booth, 425–54. Cambridge, MA: MIT Press.

From Software. 2015. *Bloodborne*. Playstation 4. Sony Computer Entertainment.

Fron, J., Fullerton, T., Morie, J. F., and Pearce, C. 2007. "The Hegemony of Play."
In *Situated Play: Proceedings of the 2007 DiGRA International Conference*, volume 4,
edited by Akira Baba, 309–18. University of Tokyo, September 24–27.

Hanford, N. [nicholashanford]. 2015. A question to add to the list of those that
have been thrown out here, what's a (feminist) power fantasy? @jsaklofske
#WarGames #CGSA2015 [Tweet]. https://twitter.com/nicholashanford/status
/606856538737770496.

Haraway, D. 1988. "Situated Knowledges: The Science Question in Feminism and the
Privilege of Partial Perspective." *Feminist Studies* 14 (3): 575–99.

Harding, S. 1991. *Whose Science? Whose Knowledge?: Thinking from Women's Lives*. Ithaca,
NY: Cornell University Press.

Jennings, S. C. 2015. "Passion as Method: Subjectivity in Video Games Criticism."
*Journal of Games Criticism* 2 (1). http://gamescriticism.org/articles/jennings-2-1.

Kennedy, H. 2002. "Lara Croft: Feminist Icon or Cyberbimbo?: On the Limits of
Textual Analysis." *Game Studies* 2 (2). www.gamestudies.org/0202/kennedy.

Leonard, D. J. 2006. "Not a Hater, Just Keepin' It Real: The Importance of Race-
and Gender-Based Game Studies." *Games and Culture* 1 (1): 83–88.

Lovecraft, H. P. 1999. "The Call of Cthulhu." In *The Call of Cthulhu and Other Weird
Stories*, edited by S. T. Joshi, 139–69. New York: Penguin.

Saklofske, J. 2015 "Are There (Can There Be/Should There Be) Feminist War Games?"
Presentation at the meeting of the Canadian Game Studies Association, Ottawa,
Ontario, Canada, June 2015.

Shaw, A. 2014. *Gaming at the Edge*. Minneapolis: University of Minnesota Press.

Sicart, M. 2013. "Against Procedurality." *Game Studies* 2 (3). http://gamestudies.org
/1103/articles/sicart_ap.

PART 4

# GAMING AGAINST
# THE GRAIN

CHAPTER 9

# PLAYING WITH PRIDE

*Claiming Space Through Community Building in World of Warcraft*

KAREN SKARDZIUS

O N JANUARY 5, 2014, a *World of Warcraft* (*WoW*) player going by the
character name Ooyl posted this comment in the *WoW* forums:

> I understand that in the real world, it's not picture perfect and I
> don't expect it to be that way in this game. I'm not here to lecture
> you or shove it down your throats but I'm here to tell you that
> there's injustice in this gaming community. In this community the
> lgbt [player] is sometimes looked down upon. In trade this morn-
> ing, random kids were comparing the gay community to beastality
> and that's not right. We are regular people who enjoy World of
> Warcraft just like the rest of you and our sexual preference does
> NOT affect how we play. Please treat us like humans. (Ooyl 2014)

This particular forum post elicited 501 responses from players within
eight hours, reaching Blizzard Entertainment's "post limit" for any given
thread. In resorting to the forums as a venue for expressing frustration at
the social conditions within the game, Ooyl is struggling to provide a
platform for a discourse that is not often heard and is regularly silenced
within *WoW* culture.

Importantly, Ooyl's request for a more just gaming community was made only a few months before the Gamergate campaign emerged as a rallying cry for anti-feminists who felt disenfranchised by the push for a more equitable gaming culture (Lees 2016). Those who supported Gamergate perceived the goal of equity as an attack on "true gamers" by those people they called "social justice warriors." Gamergate's main accomplishment was, and continues to be, the harassment of women and other minorities as an outlet for their frustrations. While in 2014 many dismissed Gamergate as just being "angry boys on the internet" who were only concerned with video games, we now see the same language, tactics, and values being espoused by those identifying with and sympathetic to the alt-right political movement. Game scholars have been arguing for years that video games play an important role in how we learn about and understand social, political, economic, and cultural organization (Leonard 2006). Perhaps now more than ever, it is imperative that we take seriously what goes on in and around video games, particularly through a lens of equity and justice.

Video game culture is commonly understood as white, masculine, and heteronormative, and the culture within and surrounding WoW is no exception. Alexis Pulos points out that although there is no purpose or requirement for it, a constructed sexual binary has been embedded in the design of the game and is reinforced through precise regulation (Pulos 2013). Further, several scholars have argued that heteronormativity is often harshly enforced by players and game policies/moderators, creating an atmosphere of oppression for those who do not conform (Sunden and Sveningsson 2012). Pejorative language regarding sexuality is commonplace in-game and in WoW-related player-created texts. Referring to her WoW guild's private chat channel, Bonnie Nardi writes, "It was as though the ether of the chat channel must be regularly refreshed with the recitation of sexualized, homophobic words" (Nardi 2010, 157). Many players seem to feel the need to prove their "straightness" by reciting their aversion, dismissal, or outright hatred of homosexuality to whoever is willing to listen. Kishonna Gray discusses this kind of behavior as well as racism and sexism in online games in terms of deviance and online disinhibition (Gray 2014). Online spaces, she argues, afford a level of anonymity that prompts people to act and speak in ways they would not if their identity was known to the people around them. Sometimes, the disinhibition is benign and can result in an individual showing uncommon kindness or generosity. Other times, the disinhibition is toxic and can result in angry, rude, or hateful outbursts. One such toxic outburst is what initially inspired this paper.

One night while I was playing *WoW* and casually chatting with guildmates, one guildmate announced that he was sick and tired of hearing about LGBTQ-friendly groups advertising recruitment in public chat channels on the Proudmoore server. He then complained that he did not understand why "they" could not leave "their" sex life out of the game. My curiosity piqued, I did a quick Internet search for Proudmoore and was surprised to find pages of results including forum posts, recruitment advertisements, fan-site interviews, and assorted other webpages proclaiming Proudmoore as the "unofficial LGBT-friendly server in *World of Warcraft*" (Archer 2014). *WoW* is a highly social game where a fun game experience typically depends on social participation in-group activities. Like in many other contexts outside of gaming, LGBTQ people who play *WoW* are often confronted with heteronormativity and homophobia that can result in marginalization and act as a barrier to full social participation. As a reaction to this exclusion, an alternative community within World of Warcraft has come into being. This alternative community can be interpreted as an act of resistance against a mainstream culture that has not only been insensitive to LGBTQ players' requests to be treated justly but has also been outright hostile and violent in their responses to these requests. Blizzard Entertainment has continually failed to offer all players adequate protections from harassment, hostility, and oppression, so some players have come together to create their own informal protections. Robin Kelley writes about the importance of imagination and the ability to imagine a new society, to imagine new ways of living and being in the world (Kelley 2002). Instead of accepting, or simply being angry about the conditions within which they were expected to play, these players dared to imagine a different way of engaging with *WoW* and its culture.

This chapter aims to understand how players endeavor to overcome oppression within *WoW*. First, drawing on Judith Butler's notion of precarity, I discuss how LGBTQ players have been positioned as precarious subjects in *WoW* culture. Second, I outline how players on the Proudmoore server work to mitigate this precarity through server-wide community-building events like the Proudmoore Pride Parade (Butler 2009). Finally, I discuss the importance of community, the relationship between equity and citizenship, and shared identities in establishing meaningful and inclusive social policies. I argue that players on the Proudmoore server have encouraged an equitable gaming environment and fostered a meaningful, inclusive community in *WoW* by providing players protections from bigotry and a space where marginalized players can become part of the center.

## PRECARITY AND PERFORMATIVITY

Judith Butler explains precarity as people and groups of people who "suffer from failing social and economic networks of support and become differentially exposed to injury, violence, and death" (Butler 2009). She adds that precarity "also characterizes that politically induced condition of maximized vulnerability and exposure for populations exposed to arbitrary state violence and to other forms of aggression that are not enacted by states and against which states do not offer adequate protection" (ibid). Importantly, Butler's notion of precarity is closely linked with her conception of performativity. Performativity, she says, is "repetition and ritual, which achieve its effects through its naturalization in the context of a body, understood, in part, as a culturally sustained temporal duration" (Butler 1990). Where performativity is an explanation of agency, precarity concerns the conditions over which individuals have no control. This notion of precarity and its link to performativity provide a useful framework for understanding how LGBTQ players are positioned in *WoW* culture, as well as how players on the Proudmoore server have taken on the responsibility of creating a fun, fair, and safe gaming environment for themselves.

## COMMUNITIES OF PLAY AND CITIZENSHIP

Online games such as *WoW* encourage us to question our assumptions about what communities are and how they operate. *WoW* players circulate within and between several communities at any given time and each of these communities is tied to certain aspects of identity. Players may identify with and feel they are a part of the broader gaming community, the *WoW* community, their server's community, a guild community, or a variety of other communities represented in-game (e.g., the LGBTQ community). The ways players interact and participate within these various communities greatly influences their understanding and experience of *WoW* culture and the meaning they derive from the game. Celia Pearce's communities of play framework is one that is particularly helpful for understanding community in the *WoW* context (Pearce 2009).

There are several defining aspects of a community of play that differentiate it from other conceptualizations of community. Pearce draws on Huizinga's description of play as a non-serious activity that is separate from ordinary life but absorbs the player intensely, and Tönnies's idea of community as a group of people who individually act out a collective will, to ground the term *community of play* (Pearce 2009). She rejects the negative connotations often associated with play as being wasteful or childish, instead arguing that play is highly social and productive both through the requirement of creative capacity and through the necessity of community building (ibid., 12). Borrowing from Csíkszentmihályi's concept of *flow* and DeKoven's concept of *CoLiberation*, Pearce discusses the concept of *intersubjective flow* as integral to a community of play. Csíkszentmihályi's *flow* is "the feeling of complete and energized focus in an activity, with a high level of enjoyment and fulfilment" (ibid., 130). *CoLiberation* deals with the balance between an individual and a community or isolation and conformity. Pearce's notion of *intersubjective flow* is when these feelings of flow occur between individuals rather than within an individual. Intersubjective flow, she says, "serves to accelerate a form of intimacy that is unique to play" (ibid., 133). The final aspect of a community of play is group cohesion, which is an integral part of a community of play and is substantiated through shared values. This notion of a community is particularly well-suited to an analysis of guild communities in conjunction with the concept of citizenship.

*Citizenship* has been used in a great many contexts with a variety of meanings and applications. The one commonality in most uses of the concept is that it refers to membership in a political community (Joppke 2010). In general, citizenship involves debates concerning status, rights, and identity: Who can hold citizenship? What rights are afforded to citizens? What does being a citizen of a particular community mean? How are citizens different from non-citizens? Historically, the purpose of citizenship has been to provide security and protection to those who hold it (ibid., 2). It also allows its members to operate within a defined space and to access resources that typically cannot be accessed by others. Marshall defines *social citizenship* as "basic human equality associated with the concept of full membership of a community" (Marshall 1992, 6). He further articulates that it "requires . . . a direct sense of community membership based on loyalty to a civilization which is a common possession" (ibid., 24). This version of citizenship is particularly helpful for understanding how guilds are uniquely positioned to shape their member's gaming experience.

METHODS

This project utilizes a Foucauldian interpretation of discourse analysis to do a case-based analysis of two guilds, The Stonewall Family (TSF) and The Spreading Taint (Taint), on the Proudmoore server to gain a better understanding of how players who do not conform to heteronormative ideology can (and do) resist and challenge it. For Foucault, discourse, power, and knowledge are inextricably linked (Foucault 1990, 100). In this sense, discourse consists of much more than simply language, texts, and images. Discourse involves the production of meaning and the creation of knowledge that produces the power and forms that people understand as truth. Discourse, he says, is "made up of a limited number of statements for which a group of conditions of existence can be defined . . . posing its own limits, its divisions, its transformations, the specific modes of its temporality" (Foucault 1972, 17). As such, discourse establishes meaning and its boundaries; it is the means by which knowledge is conveyed and objects, identities, and ideas are formed.

Foucault is careful to articulate that "we must conceive discourse as a series of discontinuous segments whose tactical function is neither uniform nor stable" (Foucault 1990, 100). He then instructs:

It is this distribution that we must reconstruct, with the things said and those concealed, the enunciations required and those forbidden, that it comprises; with the variants and different effects—according to who is speaking, his position of power, the institutional context in which he happens to be situated—that it implies; and with the shifts and reutilizations of identical formulas for contrary objectives that it also includes. (ibid., 100)

It is through discourse that we make meaning; it shapes how and what we know. There is no meaning outside of discourse and therefore no way of knowing beyond it. Foucault explains that discourse is made up of "practices that systematically form the objects of which they speak" (Foucault 1972, 49). This makes discourse analysis useful in understanding how dominant discourse, like heteronormativity, sustains its dominance and becomes naturalized as the norm. Similarly, discourse analysis can also provide insight into how resistance to dominant discourse operates.

## OOYL'S PLEA TO BE TREATED LIKE A HUMAN

Drawing on Butler's theory of precarity, Jenson and de Castell argue that women are positioned as precarious subjects in video game culture (Jenson and de Castell 2013, 72). Although Butler explains that precarious populations are "at heightened risk of disease, poverty, starvation, displacement and of exposure to violence without protection" (Butler 2009, 2), Jenson and De Castell are careful to point out that playing, creating or consuming video games obviously does not come with the risk of death due to starvation or poor living conditions that Butler speaks to in her work. They do however argue that there is a very real problem of women being targeted by violence and aggression within the video game industry and culture (Jenson and de Castell 2013, 73). The same can be argued in the case of LGBTQ players in *WoW* culture.

Revisiting Ooyl's post (quoted at the beginning of this chapter) and its accompanying responses sheds light on the precarity experienced by players who do not conform to heteronormative standards. Respondents generally did not regard Ooyl's concern as a problem that required attention or a solution outside of the individual experiencing the distress. Player responses to the post took three common forms: 1) that players witnessing vitriolic behavior or experiencing harassment should report it to Blizzard Entertainment and let the system take care of it; 2) that *WoW* is just a game and players should leave their (queer) sexuality out of it; and 3) the behavior is simple trolling and the target should "grow a thicker skin."

Many respondents suggested that Ooyl should simply report the inappropriate behavior to Blizzard Entertainment through the in-game reporting function. Keeping in mind that Blizzard Entertainment aims for a "fun, fair and safe game environment," they advise that "If you see another player violate these policies, please immediately report the incident to a Game Master for investigation" (Reporting Bad Behavior). Effectively, players are encouraging Ooyl to trust and rely on a system that has been perpetually failing to foster the gaming environment it claims to pursue. Although the players instigating this "bad behavior" (as Blizzard Entertainment calls it) may eventually be reprimanded, the current policies clearly do not foster the "fun, fair and safe game environment" they are supposed to for *everyone*. Many players have made forum posts calling for stronger enforcement of the current policies or some kind of change to better protect current players; however, they are almost always met with a response that the existing mechanism for dealing with "bad behavior" is sufficient. The existing reporting process is a reactive one, where players who witness another player breaching official game policy are burdened with the responsibility to submit a report to Blizzard Entertainment (ibid.). There is no further information provided about how the report is handled after submission other than to say that a Game Master will investigate.

Given that many players have the impression that the in-game reporting function does not make a difference in their play experience, it is unlikely that they will continually submit reports. It is also reasonable to assume that being required to submit frequent reports to Blizzard Entertainment in order to police other players would erode the supposedly "fun" experience the player is supposed to be having. By placing the burden on players targeted by bigotry to report the incidents, Blizzard Entertainment is reinforcing their precarious position within *WoW* culture. This precarity is seen particularly when victims of harassment and bigotry are blamed by other players for not using in-game reporting enough.

Another common form of advice given to Ooyl was that "No one gives two $#$@s leave it outside the game" (Moredrasia 2014). The suggestion is similar to the reasoning behind the repealed "don't ask, don't tell" US military policy: If players do not have to consider the idea that other players may identify as LGBT or Q, heterosexual players will not feel uncomfortable and therefore will not participate in hostile behavior towards them. Under the "don't ask, don't tell" policy, lesbian and gay people were only allowed to serve in the US military if they kept their sexual orientation hidden from others (Trivette 2010, 215). Part of the justification for the policy was grounded in the assumption that heterosexual personnel would be uncomfortable serving with openly homosexual personnel and this would disrupt social cohesion, putting the military's effectiveness at risk (ibid., 218). In *WoW*, this same assumption is exemplified by comments like, "If anything, the LGBT [community] shoves themselves down everyone's throats. I have nothing against gay people, but they want to be treated equally right? But they are always the first to reveal their sexual orientation" (Kwizzlix 2014). In a military context, personnel are expected to form strong friendships and social bonds with their comrades through sharing and a lack of personal privacy, creating a paradox for personnel who were required to maintain secrecy about their identity. The policy's purpose was to promote solidarity and social cohesion among military personnel, but instead it created tension and forced people to lie about their personal life and hide parts of themselves—in fact, weakening social connections (Trivette 2010, 219).

Similar to problems with the "don't ask, don't tell" policy, there are several ways suggestions that LGBTQ players should leave sexuality out of the game are problematic. First, *WoW* is a highly social game and general information about players' personal lives can be difficult to conceal. Players frequently spend time chatting about topics unrelated to the game as they complete in-game tasks and activities. When someone tells an LGBTQ player to leave sexuality out of the game, they are denying them the claim to the social existence in *WoW* that attracts so many players to the game in the first place. As the player Kanzeon explains, "Gay people aren't going to shove their lifestyle down your throat. . . . It might be a mere mention of a guy saying, 'Okay guys, boyfriend aggro, gotta go~' This instantly outs them as gay (assuming people know he is male), which can and does lead to problems in *WoW*. Why should a gay or transgender person have to hide?" (Kanzeon 2013). This sentiment about not wanting to hide one's identity was common in forum posts and interview comments made by players indicating that it is an important part of the *WoW* social experience. Second, the idea of leaving sexuality out of the game is firmly entrenched in a heteronormative perspective where heterosexuality is so common it is no longer perceived as sexuality. Heterosexuality is firmly embedded in *WoW*. For example, male quest-givers require players to rescue their missing wives, non-player characters flirt with each other during interactions, and players play out a quest line that culminates in a cutscene in which one of the most prominent non-player characters marries his female romantic interest Aggra. This is not to say that the game does not also include sexually driven content that is non-gender specific. Flirtatious character animations exist for players to interact with each other, and there is an annual in-game Valentine's Day celebration where players can participate in events, gain rewards, and earn achievements through participation with whoever the player chooses. The idea that any player, regardless of their sexual preferences, should (or even could) leave sexuality out of *WoW* is impractical to the point of absurdity. The idea that people who identify as LGBTQ should leave "their" sexuality out of the game reinforces their precarity by encouraging social distancing between themselves and other players, decreasing sociality, and increasing their vulnerability.

Another troubling common response was for respondents to equate Ooyl's experience with trolling or any other kind of griefing rather than acknowledging the homophobia Ooyl was describing. Bishop defines trolling as the "sending of provocative messages via a communications platform for the entertainment of oneself, others, or both" (Bishop 2013, 302). He points out that since the mid-1990s "trolling" has been used to describe intentionally transgressive humor, but that more recently it is becoming equated with more abusive behavior. A player going by the name Nixxia exemplifies this common player response by saying "[trolls] will say whatever it takes to upset someone. It may be !@#$%^_*!@ity today, women tomorrow, and everyone the day after with Hitler worship. That's what trolling is" (Nixxia 2014). In saying homophobic speech is simply a way for players to provoke a reaction, players whose responses are similar to Nixxia's are shifting the focus of the discussion from Ooyl's plea for a more equitable gaming space to the dominant discourse of normalized homophobia. Rather than placing importance on the discomfort, frustration, and/or misery for players targeted by homophobia, players like Nixxia are suppressing that discourse by bringing the "humor" back to the fore of the discussion.

Because Ooyl is speaking from a position at the fringe of established sexuality norms about other people holding a similarly precarious position, Ooyl's request that LGBTQ players should be treated more fairly is not taken seriously and is dismissed by many players. Given the overt hostility that many LGBTQ players face in *WoW*, some players actively seek out guilds that advertise themselves as "LGBTQ friendly" to find a place where they can play the game free from harassment. When players search for LGBTQ-friendly guilds through the *WoW* forums, they are more often than not met with suggestions to try out guilds on the Proudmoore server. One player, Nebliina, illustrated her experience as a self-identified lesbian playing *WoW*: "Much as I immediately loved this game, I was treated to the most obnoxious homophobia a virtual environment can provide. I hopped from realm to realm, simply cringing at what I was putting up with . . . in silence . . . to enjoy a game" (Nebliina 2014). Later in her post she echoed what many other players have written, saying, "Finally, I came to Proudmoore, which as many know does not support a homophobic culture. It might be the only realm that is proactively non-homophobic" (ibid.). As mentioned previously, Proudmoore is home to both TSF and Taint. These guilds each work toward creating a gaming space where LGBTQ players are protected from precarious conditions.

## PROUDMOORE PRIDE

Arguably one of the most boisterous and obvious ways these guilds work together to represent LGBTQ players, articulate queer discourses, and claim space within the game is through the organization and execution of the annual Proudmoore Pride Parade. The high level of publicity for the event attracts attention to Proudmoore as a server that promotes gaming equity and also to the presence of the LGBTQ community in *WoW* as a whole. As player Benjamin Hardin said in an interview, "I think it is important to remind other players that the person behind the avatar next to yours in–game might not want to hear you say how "gay" something that you dislike is" (Huge 2009). This is in keeping with Gabriela Richard's notion of increasing visibility and playing with resiliency for marginalized players (Richard 2014, 174). She explains that membership in a gender-supportive online gaming community can afford players the resilience needed to cope with those players that engage in harassment or create a toxic environment. The Proudmoore Pride Parade is an event designed specifically to accomplish these goals.

In past years, organizers have used the Proudmoore Pride Parade as a venue for circulating discourse that otherwise is not brought into the purview of most players. The 2013 Proudmoore Pride Parade was themed to reflect the pursuit of marriage equality (Paldadin 2013). Participants were encouraged to attend the parade with their avatars dressed in what would commonly be perceived of as wedding attire. The in-game parade disrupts normal gameplay for players who witness it, prompting the potential to generate a conversation or at least provoke thought about marriage equality. In a social space where many people believe discourse about sexuality has no place, the Proudmoore Pride Parade makes non-normative sexuality the focus, bringing marginalized players to the center, even if only for a short time.

The accepting and friendly reputation that Proudmoore enjoys is largely made possible through the efforts of several guilds on the server that work to publicly and actively promote an alternative social experience to that offered by Blizzard Entertainment. Much of this work is seen in the way(s) these guilds manage their communities. This distinction between the *WoW* experience and a *WoW* on Proudmoore experience points to the success of TSF and Taint in creating a fun, fair, and safe gaming environment for their members where Blizzard Entertainment has largely failed.

## COMMUNITY AND CITIZENSHIP
## IN *WORLD OF WARCRAFT*

Contrary to the stereotype of the lonely gamer playing video games alone in a dark room, players have often extoled the importance of community for their enjoyment of video games. In *WoW*, one of the most obvious forms of community can be found within guilds. In their early research about the social life of guilds in *WoW*, Williams et al. found that most players find merit in being part of a guild (Williams et al. 2006, 351–52). They explain that for some it is a way of maintaining relationships that already existed outside the game. For others, a guild is a tool for seeking and connecting with other people who share a common interest. Several years later, Jenny Sundén described her LGBT-inclusive guild as "a safe haven of sorts, a home away from home in *World of Warcraft*, a place with warm hearts and sharp tongues" (Sundén and Sveningsson 2012, 177). Although her guild is LGBT-inclusive, and she emphasized that it is a friendly place for women and trans people, she was careful to point out that even in such a safe space, players were consistently assumed to be male. To identify as female was to become a minority in the group. In her ethnography of an online LGBTQ gaming community, Adrienne Shaw cited several players who described the communal conditions of their play (Shaw 2012, 74–75). They talked about their desire to seek others who share similar interests (video games), the need to avoid the homophobia found in many online spaces, and a space where they did not need to censor their LGBTQ identities. This is in fact central to her argument that finding a space safe from gay-bashing is of more importance to most LGBTQ players than finding LGBTQ representation in the actual game texts. Notions of community as discussed in these studies are echoed in the ways TSF and Taint from Proudmoore discuss community.

TSF and Taint both serve as examples of communities of play in several ways. Both guilds are based around playing *WoW* in a social environment with particular collective goals, namely to provide an inclusive space for LGBTQ players without any of the common heteronormativity and harassment commonly found in *WoW*. These guilds deal with tension between individual and group identity by making *difference* the foundation of their group identity. Incorporating difference is important to these guilds not only in terms of sexuality but also in terms of playstyle. Guild recruitment advertisements for both Taint and TSF describe the guilds in a way that indicates that regardless of a player's playstyle, initiates and members will find others in the guild who enjoy the same activities. This is important for developing occurrences of intersubjective flow, which is the foundation of closeness within online gaming guilds. Intersubjective flow is achieved between players who share an identity based on shared values (i.e., guild identity) while doing enjoyable in-game activities together. While difference is a focus for both guilds, there is more involved in defining them as distinct communities. These guilds both refer to themselves as *families* in several areas of their websites, indicating the type of intimacy Pearce refers to in her discussion of communities of play (Pearce 2009, 133).

The shared values that gel these guilds together and work to maintain group cohesion are easily discernable from their respective guild charters. They each emphasize the privilege of being a member of their guild (and that it is a privilege that can be taken away), the necessity to advance inclusivity within *WoW* culture, and the requirement that players respect both each other as well as players outside the guild. Ironically, the very goal of creating an equitable and inclusive gaming environment for their members relies on the practice of excluding people from participation. Both guilds refer to membership in their guild as *citizenship*.

Referring to membership as *citizenship* in TSF and Taint is quite fitting for several reasons. Much like current-day nations that offer liberal citizenship, there is a bureaucratic process to obtaining citizen status within these guilds—to determine who merits admittance to the community. Before a player can become a member of either guild, they must first submit a formal application through the respective guild's website, which is then assessed by guild officers (The Stonewall Family 2015; Rough Trade Gaming Community 2015). Both applications require that applicants read and agree to adhere to the guild's charter and to explain why they wish to join an LGBTQ-friendly guild. Further, TSF has applicants type the following statement on their application: "I am 100% comfortable in a diverse social guild that includes gay, lesbian, str8, bisexual, transgendered & questioning members" (The Stonewall Family 2015). The applications also request information regarding the player's membership in past guild(s) and the reason(s) for leaving them.

The information gathered from these applications is very specific and allows guild leadership to make informed decisions about whether they believe the applicant shares the same values the community embraces and also whether they will adhere to the guild's charter. TSF also implements a fourteen- to twenty-one-day probationary period for new members, during which time initiates are restricted from access to the guild's resources and are expected to prove to current members that they are worthy of membership. Upon successful completion of the probationary period, initiates are promoted to the rank of "family member." This application process allows the guilds to be selective in who they admit into their community and sets clear expectations for their members' behavior. Most importantly, this process likely insulates members from other players who engage in homophobic practices. While this strategy of admittance may seem exclusionary on the surface, a closer look at the guild charters demonstrates the inclusive nature of these particular guilds as well as the protections they offer their members.

Interestingly, TSF has specific policies regarding dual-citizenship, leaving the guild, and rejoining the guild after having left. If a player wishes to have one character in TSF and another in a different guild, TSF considers this dual-citizenship. They have a very strict policy of not allowing their members to maintain dual citizenship with guilds that they are not on friendly terms with. In their own words, "If you are found to violate this policy, or we determine that you are recruiting our members for the guild you are dual-citizenship'd with—you will be shown the door quickly, plain and simple" (ibid.). These policies demonstrate the continuous process of maintaining and reproducing the communities of play. They also point to the fact that while the players do not come out explicitly and say it in their charter, or even elsewhere on their websites, loyalty is another value central to these communities of play. Collectively, the group expects its members to assume guild citizenship as part of their individual identity, which in turn works to sustain the guild's collective identity. When a citizen sheds their individual identity as a member, it is interpreted as a betrayal of the collective.

As communities of play with shared values, guilds are able to better control who gains access to their communities and regulate acceptable behavior. As such, guilds are better positioned to shape the gaming experience of players and provide a more equitable gaming environment if they so choose. In the case of TSF and Taint, the values that hold these particular communities of play together are part of the protections offered by citizenship in the community. Equity is fundamental to the maintenance and reproduction of these guilds.

## CONCLUSION

Broadly, the goal of this chapter was to gain some insight into how LGBTQ players have shaped their own cultural experience of *WoW*. The first goal was to demonstrate how LGBTQ players are positioned precariously within dominant *WoW* culture by examining Ooyl's forum post. This precarity is exemplified by the common responses players had to Ooyl's plea for equity. There were three dominant responses: affected players should 1) report to a system that does not work, 2) pretend sexuality does not exist in the game, or 3) simply deal with it. In short, Ooyl's concerns were effectively dismissed as unimportant or misread as something that is a problem with the "complaining' player, not the culture at large. In the following two sections, some strategies of resistance to the conditions that foster this precarity were examined. This was done through an analysis of how LGBTQ players have come together via events such as the Proudmoore Pride Parade, where queer sexualities are made highly visible and, as a result, the LGBTQ community on the server is made more resilient. Finally, the TSF and Taint guilds were analyzed more closely as communities of play who utilize citizenship as a tool for establishing and maintaining equity within their communities. Through these strategies, Proudmoore players have: 1) successfully created their own system for dealing with bigotry and harassment for when that of Blizzard Entertainment fails, 2) made queer sexualities visible and reinforced the idea that they are important, and 3) provided players with alternative spaces and tools to be resilient when they cannot control the behavior of others.

Given the overt hostility LGBTQ players commonly encounter in the *WoW* community, perhaps it should be unsurprising that an alternative community like the one on Proudmoore coalesced. It would also be interesting to seek out other alternative communities, particularly outside of the massively multiplayer online (MMO) game genre, to see how their experiences and practices compare to those of the Proudmoore guilds. Projects like these would be a step toward answering Jenson and De Castell's call for scholars to move beyond "being content to amass descriptions of how dreadful things are and finding or devising explanations of existing states of affairs" (Jenson and de Castell 2013, 80) and would focus more concertedly on how to achieve an equitable and inclusive video game culture for all.

WORKS CITED

Archer, J. 2014. "Proudmoore: The Gay WoW Server." *gaygamer*, May 1, 2014. http:// gaygamer.net/2014/05/proudmoore-the-gay-wow-server.

Bishop, J. 2013. "The Art of Trolling Law Enforcement: A Review and Model for Implementing 'Flame Trolling' Legislation Enacted in Great Britain (1981–2012)." *International Review of Law, Computers, and Technology* 27 (3): 301–18.

Butler, J. 2009. "Performativity, Precarity and Sexual Politics." *AIBR: Revista de antropologia iberoamericana* 4 (3): 1–3.

Foucault, M. 1972. *The Archaeology of Knowledge*. London: Routledge.

Foucault, M. 1990. *The History of Sexuality: An Introduction*. New York: Random House.

Gray, K. L. 2014. *Race, Gender, and Deviance in Xbox Live: Theoretical Perspectives from the Virtual Margins*. London: Routledge.

Hugh, R. 2009. "Pixelated Pride." *Advocate*, June 10. www.advocate.com/news/2009 /06/10/pixelated-pride.

Jenson, J., and De Castell, S. 2013. "Tipping Points. Marginality, Misogyny and Videogames." *Journal of Curriculum Theorizing* 29 (2): 72–85.

Joppke, C. 2010. *Citizenship and Immigration*. Malden, MA: Polity Press.

Kanzeon. 2013. "Females on WOW." *General Discussion*, March 24, 2013. http://us .battle.net/wow/en/forum/topic/8414572226?page=16#305.

Kwizzlix. 2014. "The LGBT Community." *General Discussion*, January 5. http://us .battle.net/wow/en/forum/topic/11159496053?page=3.

Lees, M. 2016. "What Gamergate Should Have Taught Us about the 'Alt-right.'" *Guardian*, December 1.

Leonard, D. J. 2006. "Not a Hater, Just Keepin' It Real: The Importance of Race- and Gender-Based Game Studies." *Games and Culture* 1 (1): 83–88.

Marshall, T. H. 1992. *Citizenship and Social Class*. Concord, MA: Pluto Press.

Moredrasia. 2014. "The LGBT Community." *General Discussion* January 5. http://us .battle.net/wow/en/forum/topic/11159496053?page=3.

Nardi, B. 2010 *My Life as a Night Elf Priest*. Ann Arbor: University of Michigan Press.

Nebliina. 2014. "Blizzard Donates $10K to GaymerX Convention. . . ." *Gaming, Hardware, and Entertainment*, August 26. http://us.battle.net/wow/en/forum/topic /14059365855?page=10.

Nixxia. 2014. "The LGBT Community." *General Discussion*, January 1. http://us.battle .net/wow/en/forum/topic/11159496053?page=2.

Ooyl. 2014. "The LGBT Community." *General Discussion*, msg.1, last modified January 5, 2014. http://us.battle.net/wow/en/forum/topic/11159496053#1.

Paldadin. 2013. "Proudmoore Pride 2013—Official Info." *Proudmoore*, last modified May 13, 2013. http://us.battle.net/wow/en/forum/topic/8796350895.

Pearce, C. 2009. *Communities of Play: Emergent Cultures in Multiplayer Games and Virtual Worlds*. Cambridge, MA: MIT Press.

Pulos, A. 2013. "Confronting Heteronormativity in Online Games: A Critical Discourse Analysis of LGBTQ Sexuality in World of Warcraft." *Games and Culture* 8 (2): 77–97.

"Reporting Bad Behavior and Bad Names." 2015. *Battle.net*, last modified December 17, 2015. https://us.battle.net/support/en/article/reporting-bad-behavior-and-bad-names.

Richard, G. 2014. "Supporting Visibility and Resilience in Play: Gender-Supportive Online Gaming Communities as a Model of Identity and Confidence Building in Play and Learning." In *Identity and Leadership in Virtual Communities*, edited by Dona J. Hickey and Joe Essid, 170–86. Hershey, PA: IGI Publishing.

Rough Trade Gaming Community. 2015. "RTGC Application." Accessed December 15. http://rtgc.enjin.com/application.

Shaw, A. 2012. "Talking to Gaymers: Questioning Identity, Community and Media Representation." *Westminster Paper in Communication and Culture* 9 (1): 67–89.

The Stonewall Family. 2015. "Membership Process and Guidelines." www.thestonewallfamily.com/membership.

Sundén, J., and Sveningsson, M. 2012. *Gender and Sexuality in Online Game Cultures*. New York: Routledge.

Trivette, S. A. 2010. "Secret Handshakes and Decoder Rings: The Queer Space of Don't Ask/Don't Tell." *Sexuality Research and Social Policy* 7 (3): 214–28.

Williams, D., Ducheneaut, N., Xiong, L., Zhang, Y., Yee, N., and Nickell, E. 2006. "From Tree House to Barracks: The Social Life of Guilds in World of Warcraft." *Games and Culture* 1 (4): 338–61.

CHAPTER 10

# CURATE YOUR CULTURE

*A Call for Social Justice-Oriented Game Development
and Community Management*

AMANDA C. COTE

A S 2014'S GAMERGATE movement linked racism, sexism, and discrimination to video game culture, journalist Leigh Alexander cautioned game developers, "When you decline to create or to curate a culture in your spaces, you're responsible for what spawns in the vacuum" (2014). Overall, developers and creators have largely declined to curate their spaces or have done so in ways that are ineffective. As a result, game culture has become toxic in many ways. From texts that underrepresent or stereotype women and people of color to online spaces where racism, sexism, and homophobia are the norm, numerous aspects of gaming reify straight, white, cisgender young men as "gamers" and exclude everyone else.

These problems are particularly prevalent in online spaces. Players of all types face interpersonal trash-talk while gaming, but it often becomes more virulent when the targeted player does not possess the characteristics of a traditional "gamer" (Cote 2015; Gray 2014; Nakamura 2009, 2012; Salter and Blodgett 2012). Female players often find that male players condescend to them, assume they are terrible at games, or sexually harass them. Players of color face similar problems. As Nakamura (2009, 2012) and

Gray (2014) recount, minority players frequently find their own team-mates turning on them, killing them in game, and lambasting them with racial slurs.

Even more significantly, this negativity is dismissed as a standard part of game culture: When players fight back against discriminatory language, others accuse them of overreacting and taking trash-talk too seriously. This falsely limits the impact of trash-talking to the game itself, assuming targeted players will be able to dismiss threats, insults, or other slurs as soon as the game session ends. It also normalizes aggression and dis-crimination within this sphere, allowing gaming to function as a bastion for unequal power structures. In other words, "games and game culture not only reflect entrenched inequality and lived white/male privilege, but serve as an important instrument in the reproduction of hegemony" (Gray 2014, xiv).

I would argue that these discriminatory patterns culminated in 2014, with Gamergate, which ostensibly focused on improving ethics in gam-ing journalism, yet resulted in the harassment of female gamers, devel-opers, cultural critics, and their allies. However, culmination implies an end or a peak. In reality, the problems first witnessed in game spaces have not peaked or gone away; rather, games' discriminatory practices have spread to broader sociopolitical spheres through the rise of white supremacist politics and the alt-right. In fact, the alt-right platform shares many explicit links with Gamergate, from "a range of pernicious rhetorical devices and defenses to distance themselves from threats to women and minorities" (Lees 2016) to the significant role played in each by Breitbart News executive Steve Bannon (Gross 2017). As Leonard (2006) argues, games—and I would include game culture—are "cultural products saturated with racialized, gendered, sexualized, and national meaning" (83).

Thus, the question of how to curate a culture in gaming is one with larger implications, as doing so becomes a microcosmic attempt at curat-ing American culture more broadly. It has become almost essential for activists and developers who desire greater equity in game communities to push for social-justice oriented game development and community management strategies in which all players have an equal ability to exist free of harassment and discrimination. As matters stand, many players have developed nuanced coping strategies for avoiding or managing harassment. However, the majority of these are individual, based on personal efforts such as avoiding online games, not playing games with strangers, or hiding one's identity from others in game spaces (Nakamura 2012; Cote 2015).

While these are effective on a private level, many of them further problems by masking minority gamers' presence, contributing to perceptions of games as masculinized and traditional "gamers" as dominant. As Gray (2014) points out, "Gamers can stay away from players they choose to avoid. However, this creates a problem in addressing meaningful solutions to verbal abuse within this space" (xxi). Individual coping methods do little to undermine the hegemony of trash-talk. Relying on players to combat their own harassment also puts the onus of solving toxicity on its victims, forcing those who are already marginalized to try to make improvements. This is unlikely to be effective, as "groups unequal in power are correspondingly unequal in their access to the resources necessary to implement their perspectives outside their particular group" (Hill Collins 1990, 83–84).

Enlisting the help of game creators and leveraging their power over game culture could take the burden of undermining games' toxicity off those who are already marginalized. It is true that many game developers are part of the same poisonous culture that plays out in their communities, and some, particularly those who promote stereotypical representations through their games, may even thrive on the discrimination that gaming culture has normalized. In these circumstances, one could argue, as Audre Lorde did, that "the master's tools will never dismantle the master's house," and that turning to developers for assistance is a wasted effort.

At the same time, the rise of social, mobile, and casual games over the last decade indicated to many developers that their audiences do and should span beyond traditional "gamers," and that it is in their own interest to diversify. As Jesper Juul (2010) argues in his book, *A Casual Revolution*, "The rise of casual games has industry-wide implications and changes the conditions for game developers, pushing developers to make games for a broader audience" (7). The success of casual games, Juul argues, demonstrates that diverse individuals and audiences buy games, which should fundamentally alter the structure of the game industry and its products.

Activists therefore have an opportunity to take advantage of this moment, to push for greater social justice in gaming when developers are likely to recognize its benefits. The question, of course, is what recommendations to developers should be. How can game creators and community managers create more equitable gaming spaces? To answer this question, this chapter briefly assesses how gaming has become exclusionary, what is lost due to its discriminatory trends, and how individuals currently cope. Subsequently, it critically analyzes past community management attempts. Through this, the argument is made that successful interventions toward social justice require attention to where players already are and how they want to manage their own communities, a step that many game companies previously ignored. With this attention, however, real improvements to game culture are possible. Finally, because long-term change can be a slow process, the chapter draws on interviews with female gamers to suggest short-term strategies developers could use to protect players in the meantime.

## EXISTING STRATEGIES AND BACKGROUND

Throughout its history, gaming has been masculinized by a variety of forces, such as its birth in the military-industrial complex, the strong overlap of sports and pool hall culture with early video game arcades, and the deliberate marketing of games to a young, male audience (Dyer-Witheford and de Peuter 2009; Graner Ray 2004; Kiesler, Sproull, and Eccles 1985; Kocurek 2015; Newman 2017; Shaw 2014). These factors have led to a hegemony of play (Fron et al. 2007) that prioritizes the needs of young, straight, white, cisgendered men, or stereotypical "gamers," over the needs of other players. Although young men are not the only people who game and could even be considered a minority audience, the industry has long marked them as the most important. Gamers often reflect this ingrained privilege in their attitudes about games and their behavior toward other players.

Gaming culture is rife with instances of harassment, particularly directed at white women and players of color. These run the gamut from the private persecution individuals face when gaming online to intense public incidents. For example, cultural critic Anita Sarkeesian and game developer Zoe Quinn faced death threats and the online publication of their personal information for the respective crimes of proposing a video series critiquing female representations in games and developing a nontraditional game about depression. Individual players face gendered or racial slurs, in-game attacks from their own teammates, and more (Cote 2017; Gray 2014; Nakamura 2012; Salter and Blodgett 2012). Multiple female gamers interviewed for this chapter detailed how male gamers often made sexual advances toward them, asking for pictures, descriptions of their breasts, and details on their current underwear choices. Although each had developed strategies for evading these requests, the frequency with which sexual advances occurred was exhausting and off-putting. Such behaviors risk driving players out of gaming spaces, which would come with significant losses both individually and generally.

First, games provide more than simple entertainment. For many players, they strengthen relationships with friends and family members (Williams et al. 2006). For others, they connect players to friends they would not have met otherwise, allowing them to develop bonds that span the country or even the globe. As one interviewee stated, "It's kind of like going to a club meeting or something; you have a common interest and you go and meet people. And you meet people from all over the world: different countries, different states. And a lot of them are unique people who I don't feel you'd meet otherwise" (Katie Tyler). Another added, "[Gaming] also is, I think, a great way for people who have a social issue where maybe they're agoraphobic or maybe they just don't like meeting people, who can go online on a game and have friends that you actually go and visit eventually" (Alissa). In other words, games provide essential social opportunities, both for players with existing offline networks and those who struggle to develop in-person connections.

Additionally, gaming's often-fantastic nature allows players to take on or try out new identities without the costs of doing so in real life. As Bessière et al. (2007) point out in a discussion of massively multiplayer online role-playing games (MMORPGs, or MMOs), "MMORPGs are a mode by which the player, through a constructed character, can enact aspects of his or her ideal self—the physical or psychological self the player wishes to be" (531). As a result, they argue, players can reduce the discrepancy between their actual self (where they feel they are) and their ideal self (where they want to be), increasing their self-esteem and self-confidence.

Thus, individuals can suffer a real loss of opportunity when gaming culture excludes them through discriminatory trash-talk and content. Not only do excluded players struggle to connect more strongly to others, but they can also want for the strengthened psychological state players can achieve while gaming. As marginalized players often overlap with society's most marginalized groups, a lack of access to empowering psychological mechanisms is doubly fraught.

Furthermore, gaming's current culture affects society more broadly by allowing racism, sexism, and other forms of discrimination to perpetuate. As female gamers I interviewed pointed out, game culture normalizes behaviors that gamers do not see as acceptable in real life. Describing the sustained harassment her guild inflicted on her, Helix said, "The worst was when I won a roll on an item and the guild leader threatened to tear my breasts into bloody shreds. I met him a year later in person. He was pretty fucking embarrassed and apologized profusely—clearly this wasn't some-thing he thought was OK when he met me in real life, but it was something he thought was OK in a video game." Other incidents she recounted were similarly repulsive, but her guild did not penalize anyone for their behavior toward her. Thus, gaming reinscribed misogynistic violence as a regular, everyday behavior—even when players ostensibly knew better.

Considering other areas where misogyny has been studied more deeply, "research in the workplace has found that a misogynistic atmo-sphere has negative consequences for both men's and women's well-being. Additionally, those that perceive greater hostility toward women are more likely to leave their jobs" (Fox and Tang 2014, 318). These effects occur for those who do not experience direct harassment themselves, as well as for those who do. Thus, negativity in gaming spaces can lose developers cus-tomers, affect individual player's mental health and well-being, and sup-port destructive social norms more broadly. As such, problematic behavior patterns must be addressed.

Due to the discrimination they face, targeted players have developed nuanced strategies to manage online harassment. In a previous piece, I discovered five main strategies female gamers use to evade or respond to harassment (Cote 2015): they avoid online gaming entirely, play only with friends, hide their gender, use their skill and experience as a psychological shield, or fight fire with fire, killing or harassing negative players in retaliation. Female players are often skilled at managing their gameplay environment to try to ensure the most positive experience possible.

However, each strategy has potentially serious downsides. For instance, while women can hide their identity to avoid targeted harassment, this helps maintain gaming as a masculine space and perpetuates the exclusion of non-male individuals. Other strategies, such as facing trash-talk with aggressive come-backs, can result in further harassment and maintain aggressive, violent language as the cultural norm. These results reflect other studies of gamers of color, such as when Gray (2014) found that female Black and Latina players also struggled to manage their interactions with others. Interviewees recognized these weaknesses, referring to their strategies as "Band-Aids" rather than long-term solutions (Cote 2015).

Furthermore, my past work found that female players never mentioned turning to a game manager for help and rarely used built-in options like blocking mechanisms. They felt many of these solutions were too easy to circumvent or interfered with their ability to play the game well by hiding legitimate feedback from other players. Gray (2014) also found that marginalized players were frustrated by developers' poor responses to their harassment, arguing that game companies ignored their reports about toxic players or even punished them for complaining.

Existing coping mechanisms can protect the individual being harassed but do little to change the overall culture of gaming, where harassment, sexism, racism, and homophobia are currently normalized. Furthermore, gamers who commit acts of discrimination rarely face repercussions for those actions, and developers fail to prioritize marginalized gamers' concerns. This indicates a need for new approaches, as gamers currently feel alone in their efforts to protect themselves and to strive for greater inclusivity in gaming.

RESEARCH DESIGN

To show what new, successful approaches might look like, I began by researching game companies' past community management attempts to understand why marginalized gamers rarely found them useful. Through a broad overview of game magazines, developer websites and forums, and general gaming forums, I found that developers tended to take one of two strategies in managing game harassment: either removing player anonymity or instituting a reputation system to penalize toxic players. However, I also found that these strategies varied in their success. To indicate why this was the case, I conducted a deeper critical analysis of three representative strategies from Blizzard Entertainment, Xbox Live, and Riot Games, drawing on past research, players' feedback to the companies, and interviews with female gamers. I then sought to develop further suggestions for community management from the same interview data.

Overall, I used thirty-seven in-depth, semi-structured interviews with self-identified female gamers conducted for a larger humanistic study regarding games and gender. Interviewees were recruited primarily through online video game forums with some added via snowball sampling. The recruitment post for the study was deliberately broad, with no qualifications given as to what constituted a "gamer," to encourage the greatest possible diversity among participants.

Interviewees ranged in age from nineteen to forty-five but averaged just over twenty-five. Most were from the United States, but three were based in Canada, two in the United Kingdom, and one in Bahrain. Early interview guides did not ask about race, and as a result four women did not identify their ethnic background. Of the remaining thirty-three, twenty-five define themselves as non-Hispanic Caucasians, two as Arab, two as Mexican, and four as Korean, Chinese, or Asian American. Participants were primarily college educated, with many either holding or pursuing advanced degrees.

Because of this, interviews provide strong insight into the experiences of female gamers but cannot be generalized to marginalized players more broadly, given the participants' high levels of education, young overall age, and predominantly white racial backgrounds. Future projects that build on this work may need to use off-line venues or more specific online spheres to recruit participants of different backgrounds. However, this focus on gender provides a starting point into managing game harassment, because sexism is a major component of online toxicity.

## REMOVING ANONYMITY: BLIZZARD'S REAL ID

In studying contributors to online harassment, researchers have demonstrated that anonymity, especially in a competitive environment, can lead to high levels of negativity (Chisholm 2006; Fox and Tang 2014; Gray, 2014). The logic, of course, is that an anonymous individual avoids the negative consequences of violating social norms, making them more likely to do so through aggressive or insulting language and behavior. Because of this, some game developers have attempted to control the behavior of their online community through decreased anonymity.

Perhaps the most infamous of these attempts occurred in 2010 when Blizzard Entertainment, the company behind the MMO *World of Warcraft*, announced their intention to connect players' real names to their posts on official Blizzard discussion forums. This system, Real ID, was introduced in June 2010 as an option to give players a permanent identity across Blizzard's different online games and allow them to communicate with others more easily. By sharing email addresses, players could become "Real ID Friends" and then connect if they were on different servers or even in different games. It also helped them track friends' various characters or groups for cooperative events (Blizzard Entertainment 2015).

In July 2010, however, Blizzard intended to require Real ID for online forum posts, with the stated goal of decreasing "trolling," or posts that are meant to invoke a negative emotional reaction in others (Remo 2010). This decision led to a massive backlash. Specifically, players engaged in in-depth protests on the very forums Blizzard was trying to regulate. Not only did they see Real ID as an autocratic infringement on their rights as players, but they also demonstrated that anonymity served many purposes other than allowing trolls to troll.

Players showed that anonymity was one of the factors that helped them feel safe when engaging with strangers online. Posters' comments revealed "a general concern that players will not post freely anymore and therefore not contribute to upholding the WoW community by fear of identity theft, of being too exposed, and of possible account hackers" (Albrechtslund 2011). Players saw the removal of anonymity as a threat to their security, rather than as the intended shield against harassment or trolling. They advanced this argument particularly heavily with regards to non-"gamers." Gamers expected that having their real identities exposed would deeply threaten players who were female, ethnic minorities, transgender, homosexual, and/or disabled (Albrechtslund 2011, Roinioti 2011). Given how frequently female players report hiding their gender online (Cote 2015), it is not surprising that many players heavily protested the removal of their control over their online identity. Rather than just a tool for trolling, anonymity was a shield for targeted groups, and they deeply desired the ability to manage when, how, and to whom they revealed their offline identities.

In addition to concerns about safety, players objected to Real ID because they did not necessarily want their gaming identity linked to their offline identity in a searchable way. Gamers recognized that many negative stereotypes surround games, especially MMORPGs like *World of Warcraft*. Because of this, they wanted to maintain separation between work or social lives and gaming lives. In a study of players' relationships with mass-media representations of gamers such as those in *The Big Bang Theory* or *South Park*, Bergstrom et al. (2016) "found multiple instances where players expressed concerns about the potential negative consequences of having their legal name tied to their World of Warcraft character" (11). Because media sources frequently represented gamers as asocial, nerdy, or inept, players desired the ability to distance themselves from those stereotypes through identity control.

Finally, players objected to the mandatory Real ID system because character names are a key part of play for them. Players invest both time and energy in crafting identities for their characters and matching these to the context of their games. As a result, Hagstrom (2008), MacCallum-Stewart and Parsler (2008), and Crenshaw and Nardi (2014) all found that players were strongly attached to their character names. Players often had naming patterns that connected their characters across games, as when one interviewee told Hagstrom (2008) that his character names always began with his initials (271). Other players carefully constructed names that fit into game lore, using different linguistic styles for human characters than for orc or alien characters, to match the different languages these species spoke in-game. Players' connections to the resulting names and identities were strong enough that many lasted even after the player moved games or deleted an old character; friends would still refer to that individual by their original in-game name. Forcing players to abandon the names and identities they had carefully crafted was not a popular policy.

Overall, the reaction against Real ID shows that, although it appears logical due to the role of anonymity in harassment, simply removing the ability to be anonymous is not an acceptable approach to community management. Not only did players react negatively to Blizzard's announcement because it would decrease their immersion and their divide between gaming and other aspects of life, but they also displayed deep concerns about safety. Forum posts discussed marginalized groups in particular, arguing that the change set up these individuals for increased, rather than decreased, harassment. This is reflective of interview data, which shows women at least rely heavily on the ability to control when or if they reveal their gender.

It is, of course, true that allowing players who do not fit stereotypical "gamer" identities to hide decreases public awareness of their presence; however, removing their ability to control their online identity and forcing them to manage the potential harassment that would follow is also not a real improvement. Therefore, companies need to look elsewhere for legitimate community management strategies and need to draw on the actual desires of players to develop useful approaches.

## REPUTATION SYSTEMS

Another frequent approach to in-game community management relies on the level of investment players put into their characters or accounts, as well as the moderate degree of difficulty inherent in changing one's pseudonym online. Through semi-permanent accounts, it is possible to track player behavior and develop a reputation for that individual. Reputation systems within games provide information on how an individual has behaved in the past and should affect who chooses to play with that person. However, reputation systems can be either good or bad, as demonstrated through the comparison of two previous iterations.

Evidence from Xbox Live's early reputation system, instituted shortly after the introduction of the Xbox 360, shows that just having a reputation system in place is not sufficient to prevent harassment. The system relied on a five-star player rating. Players began at three stars and were expected to move down if they were reported for bad behavior and up if they were consistently good teammates or opponents. This did not always occur. For instance, video game writer Alexander Hinkley created two profiles and played each for thirty-five games. On one account, he was a good team-mate, while on the other he "hoarded power weapons, drove erratically in vehicles, and teabagged opponents after killing them" (Hinkley 2010). Following this trial period, he found that his "bad" profile ranking had risen, even though 90% of the people he played with indicated that they wanted to avoid him. His "good" profile remained unchanged. This reveals a fundamental problem with the algorithms that managed the reputation system, in that they did not respond to feedback along logical patterns. Furthermore, Hinkley found that Xbox Live frequently matched him with players he had requested to avoid. Overall, "the Xbox 360's matchmaking service tries to match you with people of a similar reputation, but if it can't find any, it will still pair you up with the miscreants" (Orland 2013).

Because reputation did not accurately reflect a person's behavior or change their patterns of play, it did little to curb negativity. There were also few mechanisms in place to prevent players who were engaging in harassing behavior from flooding their victim's accounts with false reports, damaging the reputation of an innocent player and creating a cycle of aggression and violence. Marginalized players were also frequently punished more heavily than traditional "gamers" when they responded to harassment aggressively (Gray 2014, 61). Simply instituting a reputation system is not enough to affect harassment patterns, and it can even pre-vent players who are discriminated against from defending themselves.

However, evidence from another reputation system, employed by Riot Games to oversee the MMO *League of Legends* (*LoL*) community, shows that a properly managed approach can make a difference. *LoL* possesses a noto-riously toxic community. However, Riot has taken extensive measures to address this problem. Specifically, the company has focused on protecting players from existing negativity, reforming or removing toxic players, and creating a culture focused on sportsmanship and positivity (Lin 2013). To protect players, Riot's Social System design team first made cross-team chat opt-in rather than opt-out. This meant that people had to turn on the ability to see anything their opponents said, preventing them from accidental exposure to trash-talk. The design team also created a Tribunal system to evaluate player behavior. Players could report others' positive or negative behavior; the Tribunal then brought the most negative cases to the attention of the community, which could vote on whether that behavior was acceptable in *LoL* or not. Behaviors flagged as unacceptable saw consequences such as a warning email, while cases that the community pardoned saw no punishment (Lin 2013).

Although such a strategy could backfire if unwelcoming players consistently mark discriminatory behavior as "acceptable," this has not happened in *LoL*. "According to Riot, the judgements of the players coincided with developer judgements on bad behavior eighty percent of the time, suggesting ethical isomorphism between the well-intentioned designers and the average player" (Cross 2014, 15).[1] Additionally, punishment through the Tribunal has led to clear, measurable improvements. When the system restricted chat abilities for *LoL* players who were being reported, Riot found that "bad language, as a whole, dropped 7 percent and that positive messaging actually went up" (Campbell 2014). Players who improve regain their full chat abilities, while those who do not face increasingly severe punishment, even if they are popular or professional players. For instance, Riot banned two professional players for six months in 2014 when they continued to abuse opponents even after their accounts were restricted (Farokhmanesh 2014). This high-profile case clearly indicates that all players are to be treated the same way.

As a result, the *LoL* community has measurably improved. According to Social System designer Jeffrey Lin, in the first three years of the Tribunal system, "incidences of homophobia, sexism, and racism in League of Legends [fell] to a combined 2 percent of all games. Verbal abuse [dropped] by more than 40 percent, and 91.6 percent of negative players change their act and never commit another offense after just one reported penalty" (Lin 2015).[2] The Tribunal system shows that how a company responds to the reports they receive dictates the level of success they can expect. By encouraging players to report problems, applying punishments evenly across all groups of players, and having clear guidelines for unacceptable behavior, Riot made player reports and reputations effective. Because of this, the company has seen considerable change in their online culture.

Riot's success, in comparison to the failure of the Xbox Live system, shows that social justice-oriented game spaces can occur when community management attempts are well-planned and encourage players to participate.

## FURTHER SUGGESTIONS FROM INTERVIEW DATA

The difference between successful interventions and failed interventions shows that an understanding of gamers and game norms, such as deep emotional connections to in-game identity, are necessary for effective community management. It also shows that more positive game environments are possible, as a well-designed system can create overall cultural change. However, cultural shifts take time. More immediate protective solutions could help ease the transition by increasing players' ability to avoid harassment. In their interviews, players expressed many preferences that developers can draw on to design more inclusive systems.

Female gamers often described playing with friends as a safe way to approach multiplayer. Known players were less likely to engage in discrimination, and they could also serve as a psychological shield against harassment from strangers, reminding the targeted player to ignore what was said. Because of this, interviewees appreciated both short-term grouping mechanisms and long-term guilds or clans that allow players to choose who to work with. For instance, interviewees enjoyed the ability to sign up for a *League of Legends* match as a team, ensuring that they were with at least a few friends. Similarly, Gray (2014) found that women playing Xbox Live games often grouped up to turn the tables on their harassers (67). In a group, they were better able to "grief," or intentionally harass other players as a way of exerting their presence and power (Gray 2014, 38).

Guild or clan structures also allowed players to group with friends and provided information on where they could find safe spaces. Guilds that do not allow female members, for instance, are very upfront about that information, while groups that do not tolerate insults or profanity also make that clear. Williams, et al. (2006), found, "Most players were keenly aware of the types of guilds and had ready, common labels for them (which we have used here, not created). For example, one player stated, 'We're a raid-oriented family friendly guild.'" (345–46). Players could thus find groups that matched their socialization priorities and play style. Grouping mechanisms are already features of many multiplayer games and networked systems, so developers have a foundation for adding these capabilities in the future.

Other favored coping strategies reveal the need for more creative design solutions. For instance, many interviewees used their skill or experience with games as a barrier against harassment; when they were harassed, they could laugh it off as jealousy from an opponent who was not as good a player. However, using skill as a means of protection is difficult, requiring players to commit large amounts of time and effort to continual improvement. Many players would quit a favorite game the moment they did not have time to excel at it, feeling like they had lost their safe space. This is a particularly significant issue for women, who face the pressure of the "second shift," or the continued double burden of frequently managing both work and a household (Hochschild and Machung 1989; Schulte 2014). The requirements of the second shift can deeply interfere with their ability to relax and find time for entertainment, including games.

To help players maintain a high level of skill and experience, game developers could provide badges or account histories so that a player can display their past achievements even if offline pressures such as school or work decrease the time they have for gaming. New leveling systems could be another useful change. Once a player reaches the top levels of many types of games such as MMOs, the time commitment required to maintain those levels is enormous, which places a lot of pressure on the player. A game in which players can continue to explore and progress without being bored or needing to play constantly would be ideal. *Guild Wars 2* allows for this using a dynamic level adjustment mechanic, which temporarily weakens a player whose level exceeds their current in-game zone. Therefore, players can return to old quests without finding them too simple, allowing them to continue to progress, to develop further skills, and to defend their position in the game.

Developers could also help players manage their online identities effectively. Currently, players use linguistic markers, both verbal and typed, to distinguish who is a stereotypical "gamer" and who is not; they then use these to direct their harassment more specifically toward outsiders. The ability to avoid giving these cues in the first place could protect marginalized gamers. "As many women and people of color explain, [voice] creates the most havoc in their virtual lives—racial and gendered hatred based on how people sound" (Gray 2014, 45). Although players can camouflage their gender or race by avoiding microphones, there are times when doing so interferes with multiplayer gaming, particularly in fast-paced games. Therefore, when starting at the basic design level, developers may want to include some way to communicate quickly without using voice. One option could be including pre-programmed phrases linked to a short keystroke rather than requiring players to type sentences. Such an offering would also help players avoid racial profiling via written communication, as players with poor spelling or grammar are often targets of harassment (Nakamura, 2009).

These suggestions provide short-term mechanisms for protection in the existing game environment but are unlikely to change gaming culture toward greater inclusivity and acceptance of diverse players. As such, they should be only one tool employed in addressing online harassment. However, their grounding in players' lived experiences demonstrates how understanding audience behavior can help developers create strategies and tools players will actually use.

CONCLUSIONS

In gaming culture, minoritized and marginalized players face high levels of negativity, including sexism, racism, and homophobia. On top of this, games primarily leave players to develop their own coping mechanisms, relying on individual strategies such as avoidance or direct confrontation of harassers. These provide personal protection but do little to undermine the normalization of discrimination and a hegemonic structure that ostracizes many players. At the same time, growing attention to these problems—and the fact that casual, social, and mobile games have made developers recognize that broad audiences play games—provide an opportunity through which activists, players, and even interested game designers can push for greater change. Leveraging a desire for higher sales figures and bigger audiences, it may be possible to encourage developers to improve their game communities and increase the consequences players face if they choose to harass others. The question is: What does social justice-oriented game design look like, and how should developers institute it?

Based on the analysis above, real change requires a combination of approaches. From a short-term perspective, the strategies that gamers currently employ can continue to help them manage harassment, and developers can create new tools for immediate intervention. However, to foster long-term cultural change and undermine gaming's exclusivity, developers need to push further. First, they need to prioritize "minority" players as much as "majority" players, providing them with the power and tools needed to manage their environment and supporting them when others harass them. Second, companies need to apply consistent consequences when players harass others, indicating that this behavior is unacceptable. Finally, they should avoid removing marginalized players' current means of self-protection, allowing them to play safely while cultural change occurs. Well-thought out measures such as Riot Games' Tribunal have the potential to curb toxic behavior, encourage players to reform, and undermine the cycle of aggression and violence that undergirds existing online game spaces. Through long-term community management solutions, social justice-minded activists and developers can intercede in gaming's toxic hegemony and change its priorities.

Individual players will then be able to enjoy games without discrimination, and curating gaming spaces could also work to improve overall cultural trends. Although games are not the sole purveyors of sexism, racism, and homophobia in modern society, they are a widespread and popular entertainment medium. As such, their current status as a bastion of discrimination allows these attitudes to spread more widely, and there is increasing evidence that the systems of discrimination developed in gaming spaces have affected broader sociopolitical arenas. Thus, promoting social justice-oriented game development, where all players have an equal opportunity to be treated well, should be a priority, as it is a small but significant step toward greater social justice overall.

NOTES

1    Demographic statistics regarding Tribunal participation could not be found. However, Riot player statistics shows that over 90 percent of *LoL* players are male and most are young (Lyons 2012). This reflects the overall demographics

of the game industry and could partially explain the high level of agreement between players and developers. Future studies should explore this connection further.

2    This is not to argue that *LoL* has solved all its problems. Negativity does still occur and although the FAQ about the Tribunal attempts to lay out guidelines for punishable/pardonable offenses, it is likely that reports address only obvious, egregious incidents of harassment, rather than subtler exclusionary tactics and microaggressions. However, the Tribunal System still provides some evidence of consistent positive improvement that impacts the broader community, rather than just individual experiences. As such, it is a useful foundation from which to work.

## WORKS CITED

Albrechtslund, A. M. 2011. "Online Identity Crisis: Real ID on the World of Warcraft Forums." *First Monday* 16 (7). http://journals.uic.edu/ojs/index.php/fm/article/view /3624/3006.

Alexander, L. 2014. "'Gamers' Don't Have to Be Your Audience. 'Gamers' Are Over." *Gamasutra: The Art and Business of Making Games,* August 28. www.gamasutra.com /view/news/224400/Gamers_dont_have_to_be_your_audience_Gamers_are_over .php.

Bergstrom, K., Fisher, S., and Jenson, J. 2016. "Disavowing 'That Guy' Identity Construction and Massively Multiplayer Online Game Players." *Convergence* 22 (3): 233–49.

Bessière, K., Seay, A. F., and Kiesler, S. 2007. "The Ideal Elf: Identity Exploration in World of Warcraft." *Cyberpsychology and Behavior* 10 (4): 530–35.

Blizzard Entertainment. 2015. "Battle.net Social Community." http://us.battle.net/en /realid.

Campbell, C. 2014. "How Riot Games Encourages Sportsmanship in League of Legends." *Polygon,* March 20. www.polygon.com/2014/3/20/5529784/how-riot-games -encourages-sportsmanship-in-league-of-legends.

Chisholm, J. F. 2006. "Cyberspace Violence against Girls and Adolescent Females." *Annals of the New York Academy of Sciences* 1087 (1): 74–89.

Cote, A. C. 2017. "'I Can Defend Myself': Women's Strategies for Coping with Harassment While Gaming Online." *Games and Culture* 12 (2): 136–55.

Crenshaw, N., and Nardi, B. 2014. "What's in a Name? Naming Practices in Online Video Games." *Proceedings from CHI Play 2014,* pp. 67–76. Toronto, ON, October 19–22.

Cross, K. A. 2014. "Ethics for Cyborgs: On Real Harassment in an 'Unreal' Place." *Loading . . . The Journal of the Canadian Game Studies Association* 8 (13): 4–21.

Dyer-Witheford, N., and de Peuter, G. 2009. *Games of Empire: Global Capitalism and Video Games.* Minneapolis: University of Minnesota Press.

Farokhmanesh, M. 2014. "Riot Continues to Crack Down on 'Toxic' League of Legends Pro Players." *Polygon*, June 2. www.polygon.com/2014/6/2/5772642/riot-league-of-legends-ban-pro-players.

Fox, J., and Tang, W. Y. 2014. "Sexism in Online Video Games: The Role of Conformity to Masculine Norms and Social Dominance Orientation." *Computers in Human Behavior* 33: 314–20.

Fron, J., Fullerton, T., Morie, J. F., and Pearce, C. 2007. "The Hegemony of Play." In *Situated Play: Proceedings of the 2007 DiGRA International Conference*, volume 4, edited by Akira Baba, 309–18. University of Tokyo, September 24–27.

Graner Ray, S. 2004. *Gender Inclusive Game Design: Expanding the Market*. Hingham, MA: Charles River Media.

Gray, K. L. 2014. *Race, Gender, and Deviance in Xbox Live: Theoretical Perspectives from the Virtual Margins*. London: Routledge.

Gross, T. 2017. "Inside the 'Shakespearean Irony' of Trump and Bannon's Relationship." *NPR*, July 18, 2017. www.npr.org/2017/07/18/537885042/inside-the-shakespearean-irony-of-trump-and-bannons-relationship.

Hagström, C. 2008. "Playing with Names: Gaming and Naming in World of Warcraft." In *Digital Culture, Play, and Identity: A World of Warcraft Reader*, edited by Hilde Corneliussen and Jill Walker Rettberg. 265–86. Cambridge, MA: MIT Press.

Hill Collins, P. 1990. *Black Feminist Thought: Knowledge, Consciousness, and the Politics of Empowerment*. New York: Routledge.

Hinkley, A. 2010. "Xbox LIVE Reputation Does Not Work." *Examiner.com*, September 20. www.examiner.com/article/xbox-live-reputation-does-not-work.

Hochschild, A.R., and Machung, A. 1989. *The Second Shift*. New York: Penguin Books.

Juul, J. 2010. *The Casual Revolution: Reinventing Video Games and Their Players*. Cambridge, MA: MIT Press.

Kiesler, S., Sproull, L., and Eccles, J. S. 1985. "Pool Halls, Chips, and War Games: Women in the Culture of Computing." *Psychology of Women Quarterly* 9 (4): 451–62.

Kocurek, C. 2015. *Coin-Operated Americans: Rebooting Boyhood at the Video Game Arcade*. Minneapolis: University of Minnesota Press.

Lees, M. 2016. "What Gamergate Should Have Taught Us about the 'Alt-right.'" *Guardian*, December 1.

Leonard, D. J. 2006. "Not a Hater, Just Keepin' It Real: The Importance of Race- and Gender-Based Game Studies." *Games and Culture* 1 (1): 83–88.

Lin, J. 2013 "The Science behind Shaping Player Behavior in Online Games." Presented at the annual *Game Developers Conference*, March 26, San Francisco. http://gdcvault.com/play/1017940/The-Science-Behind-Shaping-Player.

Lin, J. 2015. "Doing Something about the 'Impossible Problem' of Abuse in Online Games." *Re/code*, July 7. http://recode.net/2015/07/07/doing-something-about-the-impossible-problem-of-abuse-in-online-games.

Lyons, S. A. 2012. "League of Legends Has 32 Million Monthly Active Players." *Destructoid*, October 12. www.destructoid.com/league-of-legends-has-32-million-monthly-active-players-236618.phtml.

MacCallum-Stewart, E., and Parsler, J. 2008. "Role-Play vs. Gameplay: The Difficulties of Playing a Role in World of Warcraft." In *Digital Culture, Play, and Identity: A World of Warcraft Reader*, edited by Hilde Corneliussen and Jill Walker Rettberg. 225–46. Cambridge, MA: MIT Press.

Nakamura, L. 2009. "Don't Hate the Player, Hate the Game: The Racialization of Labor in World of Warcraft." *Critical Studies in Media Communication* 26 (2): 128–44.

Nakamura, L. 2012. "'It's a Nigger in Here! Kill the Nigger!': User-Generated Media Campaigns against Racism, Sexism, and Homophobia in Digital Games." In *The International Encyclopedia of Media Studies*, Vol. 5. Hoboken, NJ: Blackwell Publishing.

Newman, M. 2017. *Atari Age: The Emergence of Video Games in America*. Cambridge, MA: MIT Press.

Orland, K. 2013. "Microsoft Gives a Damn 'bout Your Bad Reputation on Xbox One." *Ars Technica*, July 31. http://arstechnica.com/gaming/2013/07/microsoft-gives-a-damn-bout-your-bad-reputation-on-xbox-one.

Remo, C. 2010. "Battle.net 'Real ID' System to Require Full Names on Forums." *Gamasutra*, July 6. www.gamasutra.com/view/news/29297/Battlenet_Real_ID_System_To_Require_Full_Names_On_Forums.php.

Roinioti, E. 2011. "Blizzard Will Soon Display Your Real Name: Identity and Governance in WoW." *Proceedings of the Philosophy of Computer Games Conference 2011*.

Salter, A., and Blodgett, B. 2012. "Hypermasculinity and Dickwolves: The Contentious Role of Women in the New Gaming Public." *Journal of Broadcasting and Electronic Media*, 56 (2): 401–16.

Schulte, B. 2014. "'The Second Shift' at 25: Q&A with Arlie Hochschild." *Washington Post*, August 6.

Shaw, A. 2014. *Gaming at the Edge: Sexuality and Gender at the Margins of Gamer Culture*. Minneapolis: University of Minnesota Press.

CHAPTER 11

# THE LEGENDS OF ZELDA

*Fan Challenges to Dominant Video Game Narratives*

KATHRYN HEMMANN

*THE LEGEND OF ZELDA* is one of the bestselling franchises in video game history, with more than 82 million games sold worldwide (List of Best Selling Video Game Franchises). The series includes nineteen main titles and roughly a dozen spin-off games. Many of these games re-enact versions of the same story, which recounts the exploits of the heroic Link, who saves the princess Zelda from the clutches of the evil Ganon. Due to the unchallenged repetition of this plot, the Zelda series serves as an archetypal example of what influential game critic Anita Sarkeesian has called "damseling," a term she uses to refer to the common trope of the disempowerment of female characters as a motivation for the male player-protagonist. What do female-gendered players make of this story? Is it necessary to take these narrative elements at face value, or are other interpretations possible? How might the games look from Zelda's perspective?

The games in the *Legend of Zelda* franchise have consistently enjoyed an enthusiastic critical reception, and over time the series has developed a large and constantly expanding fanbase. Fans from around the world have been inspired by the *Zelda* series, creating their own parodies, commentaries, and transformative works based on the worlds and characters

213

appearing in the games. This chapter investigates *Zelda*-related fan work from North America, Australia, and Japan, focusing on how fannish creators deconstruct the damseling narrative of the games and recombine its elements in ways that reflect larger conversations surrounding gender, culture, and media. I argue that the activities of these fans reflect a tendency in many international fan cultures to view media properties not as passively consumable content but rather as templates from which more personalized and individually meaningful stories may be created. I will begin by introducing the *Zelda* series and explaining its importance before justifying critical interest in video games in relation to contemporary political trends and social activism. I will then examine a sample of fanworks and conclude with a broader discussion of transnational fan cultures and the potential of fannish voices to shape and transform mainstream media.

## THE LEGEND OF ZELDA AS A BOSS
## KEY TO A CULTURAL CONFLICT

*The Legend of Zelda* series began in 1985, two years after Nintendo released its first home video game console, which it called the Famicom, a portmanteau of "Family Computer" (*Famirī Konpyūta*). In the United States, this console later became known as the NES, or Nintendo Entertainment System. Shigeru Miyamoto, the creator of Nintendo's iconic Mario character, the senior executive director of Nintendo Corporation at the time of this writing, and the general producer of the *Zelda* series, was working on a new *Super Mario Bros.* game, but a disc system periphery for the Famicom was slated to be released soon. Miyamoto was thus asked to help develop a new title that would take advantage of the technology, which allowed the player to "save" a game so that she could return to a previous moment in her playthrough, thus preserving her progress even after the machine had been turned off (Thorpe 2013, 2). The game that ultimately came out in 1986 was the original *The Legend of Zelda* (*Zeruda no densetsu*), which Miyamoto directed along with Takashi Tezuka, who wrote the game's script and scenarios.

A sequel, titled *The Adventure of Link* (*Rinku no bōken*), was released the following year; and, in 1991, the third title in the series, *The Legend of Zelda:*

*A Link to the Past* (*Zeruda no densetsu: Kamigami no Toraifōsu*), went on to become one of the most commercially successful and critically acclaimed games in the series (*The Legend of Zelda: A Link to the Past*). As a testament to the continuing cultural relevance of *the game*, a YouTube "let's play" web series hosted by Arin "Egoraptor" Hanson and Daniel "Danny Sexbang" Avidan called *The Game Grumps* posted a thirty-seven-episode playthrough of *A Link to the Past* in the summer of 2015, and each video received more than two hundred thousand views within the first twenty-four hours of its release (Hanson and Avidan 2015). In 1993, *The Legend of Zelda: Link's Awakening* (*Zeruda no densetsu: Yume o miru shima*) was released for the Game Boy, significantly boosting the handheld console's sales and helping to ensure its longevity on the market (Rumphol-Janc 2014).

Despite the broad appeal and international success of these four games, the major turning point for the *Zelda* franchise came in 1998, when *The Legend of Zelda: Ocarina of Time* (*Zeruda no densetsu: Toki no okarina*) was released for the N64, a home console whose upgraded 64-bit processor facilitated 3D graphics. Although Miyamoto produced *Ocarina of Time*, the game was directed by Eiji Aonuma, who had overseen a 1996 Super Famicom game called *Marvelous: Another Treasure Island* (*Māverasu: Mō hitotsu no Takarajima*) that was strongly influenced by the *Zelda* series. Aonuma has continued to be involved with every main *Zelda* title, in part because *Ocarina of Time* immediately attained an appropriately legendary status. Not only did it break records for video game preorders and first-week sales in Japan, the United States, and Europe, but it also received perfect scores from game critics in publications such as *Electronic Gaming Monthly*, *Famitsū*, and *Edge*, as well as gaming websites such as *GameSpot* and *IGN* (*The Legend of Zelda* 2017).

As the *Zelda* series has continued to move from strength to strength across subsequent Nintendo consoles, each individual game has garnered respect and acclaim from critics and gamers alike, and the franchise boasts widespread brand-name recognition. Nevertheless, it is still worth investigating the question of why these games matter as narrative texts, especially when the attention of the gaming press has been primarily focused on their gameplay.

To begin with, the gaming industry as a whole earns a significant amount of money and only continues to make more as the market expands.

At the end of 2013, the information technology research and advisory company Gartner valued the worldwide video game industry at US$93 billion, with a projected increase of at least US$10 billion for every subsequent year based on past performance (van der Meulen and Rivera 2013). In other words, more people have been buying more games, and more types of games, with each passing month. To give a comparison, according to the professional services network PricewaterhouseCoopers, the worldwide cinema industry generated revenue of US$88.3 billion in 2013 (Global Entertainment and Media Outlook). Therefore, even if we consider nothing more than the revenue they pull in from eager consumers, video games are just as much of a cultural force as movies.

As with any such cultural juggernaut, video games are orbited by countless discourses and debates on the purpose, future, and validity of the medium. Many of the more troubling of these discussions within the context of the English-language gaming community have in recent years been amalgamated under the moniker "Gamergate," which has become shorthand for heated Internet flame wars over the role of gender in video games and gaming cultures. The Twitter hashtag #Gamergate originated on the online bulletin board 4chan, where anonymous users heaped abuse on female game developer Zoe Quinn, whom they pursued across the Internet on various social media platforms (Johnston 2014). This outpouring of vitriol was then directed at Anita Sarkeesian, the founder of the media criticism website Feminist Frequency. In May 2012, Sarkeesian had launched a Kickstarter campaign to crowdfund a video web series titled "Tropes vs. Women in Video Games." Sarkeesian was able to raise US$158,922 from 6,968 donors, but accompanying this positive interest and support were violent threats from people on the Internet who were angry that she dared to subject their favorite video games to critical thinking, which they saw as challenging their understanding and appreciation of texts that were meaningful to them as individuals and as a subculture of self-identified "serious gamers." This online behavior escalated, and in October of 2014 Sarkeesian was forced to cancel a talk at Utah State University after the school received an email from someone claiming that they would commit "the deadliest school shooting in American history" if she were allowed to present her lecture (Parker 2014). This series of events clearly demonstrates that people take the stories told by video games both very seriously and very personally. Simply put, games and their stories have enormous cultural currency.

Although many outside observers may have once dismissed online communities of angry men as nothing more than ephemeral subcultures, their activities have coincided with an aggressive and transnational vocalization of libertarian and neoliberal ideologies associated with white supremacy and militaristic nationalism. YouTuber and game reviewer Matt Lees, writing for *The Guardian* in the immediate wake of Donald Trump's presidential campaign, argued that "The similarities between Gamergate and the far-right online movement, the 'alt-right,' are huge, startling and in no way a coincidence" (Lees 2016). Gamergate served as a focal point and rallying cry for economically and socially precarious young men, who collectively helped to boost the public profiles of media figures that supported their harassment of young women such as Steve Bannon and Milo Yiannopoulos, both formerly associated with the far-right website Breitbart News.

In her 2017 monograph *Kill All Normies: Online Culture Wars from 4chan and Tumblr to Trump and the Alt-right*, academic political philosopher Angela Nagle points out that "what we call the alt-right today could never have had any connection to a new generation of young people if it only came in the form of lengthy treatises on obscure blogs" (Nagle 2017, 13). Nagle demonstrates that, regardless of the underlying political leanings of the people who participated in various hashtag-centric flame wars on Twitter, the appeal of an identification with conservative movements lay primarily with participation in online communities characterized by irreverent meme culture. In addition, sociologist Whitney Phillips has documented the connections between the mean-spirited nihilism of Internet humor within gaming subcultures and the aggressive sensationalism of conservative news media in her 2015 study *This Is Why We Can't Have Nice Things: Mapping the Relationship Between Online Trolling and Mainstream Culture*. As Phillips explains, "Not only do trolls scavenge, repurpose, and weaponize myriad aspects of mainstream culture (all the better to troll you with), mainstream culture normalizes and at times actively celebrates precisely those attitudes and behaviors that in trolling contexts are aberrant, antisocial, and cruel" (Phillips 2015, 49). In other words, there is a feedback loop between online subcultures and mainstream news media that has had the effect of radicalizing disruption politics. Disenfranchised young people on both sides of the political spectrum are increasingly turning to subcultures in order to find a guiding narrative, and so it is important to examine both the prevailing narratives of these subcultures and the ways in which they are challenged, subverted, and transformed.

## REWRITING THE "LEGEND" OF ZELDA

Like any other narrative medium, video games are subject to gendered biases and interpretations. As previously mentioned, *The Legend of Zelda* is one of the video game franchises that Anita Sarkeesian critiques in "Tropes vs. Women," as many of the games are classic examples of an easily identifiable trope that she refers to as *damseling* (Sarkeesian 2013). Damseling, in its purest form, is the process by which a female character is rendered inert and thereby positioned as an object that will motivate the male player-character to complete his quest. The point of the game is therefore to rescue the damsel in distress, who is subordinate to the hero and not able to rescue herself, generally because she is "stranded in a hostile area, trapped, desperately ill, or suffering any number of terrible fates where she needs help to survive" (TV Tropes Contributors 2017).

In the *Zelda* series, Princess Zelda is frequently such a damsel. Although there are many variations, the *Zelda* games all share a basic story and a common mythology. The setting of these games is the land of Hyrule, which was created by three goddesses. As these goddesses departed from the land, they left behind a representation of their demi-urgical power called the Triforce. The Triforce is a magical relic so power-ful that it can grant the wish of any person who touches it, and so it has been hidden and sealed away. If it is threatened, however, the Triforce can split itself into three parts—Courage, Wisdom, and Power—with each part transferring itself to a chosen bearer who best embodies its virtue. Link, the player-character and hero of the games, is the bearer of the Triforce of Courage. Zelda, the princess of Hyrule, is the bearer of the Triforce of Wisdom. The primary bearer of the Triforce of Power is a man named Ganondorf, who is described as a thief from the desert and can take the form of a monstrous boar called Ganon. Although Ganondorf is not in all the games, Zelda is in most of them, and she is variously kidnapped, imprisoned, placed into an enchanted sleep, crystalized, zombified, and turned into stone. The player's job, as Link, is to acquire a weapon powerful enough to kill Ganon and save Zelda, thus returning peace to Hyrule. This is the eponymous "Legend of Zelda."

Fans from all over the world have created fanfiction, art, comics, crafts, videos, and cosplay based on the *Zelda* games. The English-language *Zelda* fandom of the 1990s and early 2000s primarily concerned itself with sharing gameplay tips, swapping information about glitches, and debating the chronology of the games in largely male-gendered online spaces (Duncan and Gee 2008, 85–101). As Mizuko Ito has argued, however, "The role of Japanese gaming in bringing girls into electronic gaming should not be overlooked," with franchises such as *Pokémon* and *The Legend of Zelda* appealing equally to male and female players (Ito 2011, 97). Since the rise of more gender-inclusive online communities on fannish blogging platforms such as LiveJournal and Tumblr, female fans have reconfigured canonical narratives to represent their own interests and experiences. Writing about the precedents of these female-dominated communities in the cultures of fanfiction writers who gathered around the *Star Trek* films and television series of the 1980s, Camille Bacon-Smith posits that, "In fiction, the women of the fan community construct a safe discourse with which to explore the dangerous subject of their own lives" (Bacon-Smith 1992, 203). Since Bacon-Smith's pioneering study, a growing body of academic literature has examined the works and cultures of English-language fanfiction writers, but very little attention has been paid to the self-published fan comics that started to pop up during the 2010s at conventions focused on Japanese popular culture, including Japanese video games. The games and characters of *The Legend of Zelda* series have emerged as popular subjects of these fan comics and fan art. Although everyone loves Link, the hero of the story, many of these comics give agency and interiority to the female characters of the various games.

In Canadian artist Louisa Roy's fanzine series *Zelda: The Dark Mirror*, a minor female character from *Ocarina of Time* named Malon is instrumental in saving Hyrule. In the original game, the young farmhand serves no other purpose than to introduce Link to her father and then to provide him with a horse. In *The Dark Mirror*, which is set several years after the events in *Ocarina of Time*, Malon has grown into a warrior in her own right.

-23-

**11.1.** A graphic image from the second issue of the fanzine prominently showing Princess Zelda being scoffed at by the commanding officer. Courtesy of Louisa Roy

When Link and Zelda vanish from Hyrule, she spurs the kingdom's soldiers into action. In the second issue of the fanzine, Malon rides into a military camp on the border between Hyrule and the Gerudo Desert, where Ganondorf's stronghold is located. Malon delivers a letter from Princess Zelda to the commanding officer, who scoffs at her.

Because Malon helped Link in the past and is fully aware of how precarious Hyrule's peace is, she will not allow the older man to dismiss her and her mission. "You may not take this seriously, but I do!" she asserts, forcing him to acknowledge the severity of the situation (Roy 2008, 23). Other female characters from *Ocarina of Time* are equally important to the story, and Roy's comic explores how they aid each other in achieving small victories in their shared struggle against Ganondorf. *The Dark Mirror* is thus a story less focused on a single male hero saving the world than it is on the concerted efforts of multiple female characters, most of whom are only accorded a few lines in the original game. Although the player can only see the events in *Ocarina of Time* from Link's viewpoint, Roy's fan comic reminds the reader that Link was only able to succeed in his quest because of the help and support of the female characters.

Similarly, in Australian artist Queenie Chan's novel-length "prose manga" *The Edge and the Light*, Link is in grave danger, and it is Princess Zelda who must rescue him, along with the three oracles from the Game Boy Color Zelda titles *Oracle of Ages* and *Oracle of Seasons* (2001, *Zeruda no densetsu: Fushigi no kinomi ~ Daichi no shō* and *Jikū no shō*). In these two games, the young female oracles are kidnapped and must be rescued by Link, but in Chan's fan comic they take the initiative to team up with Princess Zelda in order to solve mysteries and fight evil. At the end of the story, Zelda is forced to make a difficult choice concerning the ultimate fate of Link, who is trapped within his role as a hero regardless of his personal desires. This twist emphasizes the difficulties faced by the Zelda characters in the original games, who must often manipulate events in order to propel Link forward on his quest. *The Edge and the Light* also exposes the frustration Zelda feels concerning her own role as one of the divinely chosen bearers of the Triforce. After she has made her decision at the conclusion of the story, Zelda laments, "As a goddess, Din can never understand the pain of mortals" (Chan 2013, 300). Although Zelda often functions as a mysterious plot device in the games, Chan's manga offers the reader a glimpse into her thoughts and feelings, demonstrating that, within the context of the games' narratives, she is just as active a character as Link. Like *The Dark Mirror*, *The Edge and the Light* thus foregrounds the female characters of the *Zelda* series, allowing them to shape and transform the story through their active decisions instead of their passive misfortune.

The *Zelda* series is just as popular with gamers in Japan as it is elsewhere, and in Japan there are entire fan conventions devoted to *Zelda*-themed self-published fan comics, or *dōjinshi*. Such fan comics form the core of an enormous collective fan culture in Japan, with larger *dōjinshi* events attracting hundreds of thousands of participants and attendees (Lam 2010). *Dōjinshi* tend to fall into two categories. The first is *dansei-muke*, or "directed toward men," which is characterized by its proclivity for graphic heterosexual pornography; and the second category is *josei-muke*, or "directed toward women," which includes a broad range of genres, such as comedy, drama, and romance. A significant number of *josei-muke dōjinshi* based on the *Zelda* games are four-panel (*yon-koma*) gag manga meant to poke gentle fun at the characters, while others focus on the implied romantic relationship between Link and Zelda. As in the genre of *shōjo* manga, which is generally targeted at teenage girls and serves as an inspiration for many *josei-muke dōjinshi* (Hemmann 2015), relationships unfold through the eyes of the female protagonist—in this case, Zelda.

In Sakura-kan's 2012 *dōjinshi Wake Up!*, which is based on the Wii game *The Legend of Zelda: Skyward Sword* (2011, *Zeruda no densetsu: Sukaiwōdo sōdo*), the reader is presented with several touching moments between Zelda and Link. When Ghirahim, the primary antagonist of the game, shows up to kidnap Zelda, she swiftly attacks him in order to punish him for interrupting her time with Link. This is an interesting reversal that exposes both how creepy the antagonist is for wanting to kidnap Zelda and how strong Zelda actually is in *Skyward Sword*, a game in which she undertakes many of Link's trials before he does. Although the artist plays the conflict between Zelda and Ghirahim for its humor, she seems to be suggesting that, in a world in which Zelda were not required to act as a motivational reward for the male player-character, she would have no trouble dispatching the game's villain herself.

Likewise, a one-page short manga included in Hiromi Shiroyui's 2004 *dōjinshi Kaze dorobō* (*The Thief of Wind*) offers a sardonic interpretation of a scene from *The Legend of Zelda: The Wind Waker* (2002, *Zeruda no densetsu: Kaze no takuto*) in which Link storms into the final dungeon to find Ganondorf hovering over Zelda, who is lying in an enchanted sleep. *The Wind Waker*'s incarnation of Zelda has spent her life as a headstrong and highly competent pirate nicknamed Tetra, so it is disconcerting that she would be so incapacitated within the game's narrative. *Kaze dorobō* offers a symbolic resistance to this strangeness by mocking it, showing the brash and outspoken Tetra arguing with Ganondorf and refusing to sleep on his bed. In the process, she repeatedly insults him by calling him an *ossan*, a derogatory term for a pathetic middle-aged man. When Ganondorf and

**11.2.** A graphic image from another Princess Zelda fanzine where the artist is showing the challenge and refusal of portraying Princess Zelda as a kidnapped princess and damsel in distress. Courtesy of Shiroyui Hiromi

Tetra see that Link has arrived, they grudgingly assume their positions as villain and kidnapped princess, as if they were only staging a show for the player's benefit.

By highlighting the illogical artificiality of Tetra's damseling in her role as Princess Zelda, the artist offers her readers a veiled critique of a game that refuses to acknowledge the full complexity of its characters and themes, which it subsumes under the highly gendered tropes of male aggressor and female victim.

## THE FEEDBACK LOOP BETWEEN FANNISH
## DISCOURSE AND MAINSTREAM MEDIA

As many media producers are fans themselves, what happens in fandom spaces is of obvious interest to entertainment industry professionals, and a surge in feminist consciousness is fully capable of influencing the development of media properties. One response to female-positive discussions of the *Zelda* series is the 2015 graphic novel *Second Quest*, which is titled after a feature in the original 1986 *The Legend of Zelda* that allowed the player to start a remixed and more challenging game after she had mastered the first. *Second Quest*, which was funded by a Kickstarter campaign and published by Fangamer, was written by game critic Tevis Thompson and drawn by David Hellman, a professional game illustrator and concept artist. *Second Quest* is narrated from the perspective of Azalea, its Zelda character, who is torn between her desire to be a useful member of her society and her strident rejection of the "hero and princess" narrative that this society has imposed on her (Hellman and Thompson 2015a, 73). As Azalea struggles to come to terms with her place in the world, she tosses a treasure chest full of the hero's tools off a cliff and into a void, signifying that she doesn't want to be a damsel or the sort of hero who runs through the world killing things for fun and profit (ibid.).

By throwing away the standard set of adventure game items that allow the player to interact with the world only by destroying it, Azalea is symbolically discarding the narrative of the male play-character's progression toward omnipotence at the expense of the non-player characters given the artificial designation of "enemies."

*Second Quest*'s website states that it was inspired by one of Hellman's paintings, which depicted a Hyrule that was open to the player, allowing her to create her own narratives as she freely explores the environment (Hellman and Thompson 2015b). In an interview with the feminist geek media website *The Mary Sue*, Thompson added that he was motivated to examine the fate of the "missing woman" prevalent in so many video games. He says, "It's not so much a question of whether a princess—or anyone—needs to be saved or protected. It's that no one ever asks the princess what she wants to begin with. It's really a question of agency and subjectivity" (Carmichael 2015). This conversation followed on the heels

**11.3.** A graphic image from an artist showing character Azalea tossing her hero's tools, signifying a refusal to be a damsel or hero who kills things for fun and profit. Courtesy of David Hellman and Tevis Thompson

of the Gamergate controversy, making it highly likely that Tevis was responding, in part, to the work of feminist critics such as Anita Sarkeesian. *Second Quest* is therefore an example of how feminist discourse both within and supported by fandom has shaped the viewpoints and ideas of creators who have pushed their own fannish interests into the realm of professional production.

As a medium, video games are well on their way to becoming the same sort of big-budget, focus-group-oriented affairs with which Hollywood has made us familiar; but, as is the case with both live-action cinema and animation, there are also many independent creators using open-source technology to perform their own artistic experiments, some of which later become commercial products.

A number of career and aspiring game designers communicate through online gatherings called "game jams," many of which are organized around a common theme. One of the most outspoken and prolific advocates of game jams, Anna Anthropy, has compiled a guide titled *Rise of the Videogame Zinesters* that encourages amateurs to make their own games. She writes, "Every game that you and I make right now—every five-minute story, every weird experiment, every dinky little game about the experience of putting down your dog—makes the boundaries of our art form (and it is ours) larger. Every new game is a voice in the darkness" (Anthropy 2012, 160). For example, games like Alice Maz's *Average Maria Individual* (2014), a contribution to the defiantly anti-gaming-industry-themed Ruin Jam, reinterprets Nintendo's *Super Mario Bros.* (1985) and has been praised by the gaming press as having "denie[d] the traditional male power fantasy that so transparently defines what is considered a 'pure gaming experience'" (Joho 2014).

Feminist critique through media development is far from uncommon in the international gaming community. Twenty enthusiastic contributions were made to the 2015 Female Link Jam, which was organized partially in response to Eiji Aonuma's comment that the protagonist of the game then in development for the Nintendo Switch console, *The Legend of Zelda: Breath of the Wild* (2017, *Zeruda no densetsu: Buresu obu za wairudo*), was definitely not female (Hilliard 2014). According to the game jam organizer, "Female Link is something fans have always had floating amongst their collective super-brain," and the development of a female character named Linkle for the 2014 spin-off *Hyrule Warriors* (*Zeruda musō*) game from Konami encouraged artists and game developers to imagine what a *Zelda* game would look like with a female protagonist (Female Link Jam 2015). Even though large game development studios such as those associated with Nintendo tend to be conservative in the way they handle their intellectual property, fans are more than capable of putting forth interesting and viable alternatives to dominant video game narratives that marginalize both fictional women and female-gendered gamers.

The fans who thrive in social mediascapes therefore have voices that are heard not just by their peers but also by the senior media producers and developers whose positions they may one day inherit. After all, it requires a high level of passion and dedication to attain the skills to express a reinterpretation of video game narratives through writing, art, and design. Fans read against the grain of games such as those in *The Legend of Zelda* series, emphasizing the agency and interiority of female characters while deconstructing and finding alternatives to stories that objectify women while confining men to a narrowly defined concept of masculinity. Despite their strong admiration for the original titles, the writers and artists creating fan comics and amateur games have demonstrated an understanding of these digital texts as open-access narrative platforms to be challenged, and these fans deconstruct and reconfigure dominant narratives to better reflect social and political concerns and their own personal identities.

WORKS CITED

Anthropy, A. 2012. *Rise of the Videogame Zinesters: How Freaks, Normals, Amateurs, Artists, Dreamers, Drop-Outs, Queers, Housewives, and People Like You are Taking Back an Art Form*. New York: Seven Stories Press.

Bacon-Smith, C. 1992. *Enterprising Women: Television Fandom and the Creation of Popular Myth*. Philadelphia: University of Pennsylvania Press.

Carmichael, S. 2015. "Review: Finding Zelda, Nintendo's 'Missing Woman,' in *Second Quest*." *The Mary Sue*. May 11. www.themarysue.com/second-quest-review.

Chan, Q. 2013. *The Legend of Zelda: The Edge and the Light*. www.queeniechan.com.

Duncan, S. C., and Gee, J. P. 2008. "The Hero of Timelines." In *The Legend of Zelda and Philosophy: I Link Therefore I Am*, edited by Luke Cuddy, 85–101. Chicago: Open Court.

"Female Link Jam." 2015. http://jams.gamejolt.io/femalelinkjam.

"Global Entertainment and Media Outlook: Filmed Entertainment." n.d. *pwc*. www.pwc.com/gx/en/industries/entertainment-media/outlook/segment-insights/filmed-entertainment.html.

Hanson, A., and Avidan, D. 2015. "Zelda A Link to the Past." YouTube video series posted by "GameGrumps." May 21 to June 27. www.youtube.com/watch?v=ymJoxJeVYJY&list=PLRQGRBgN_Enq1TqUAalUd87CLsE5PNWvH.

Hellman, D., and Thompson, T. 2015a. *Second Quest*. Tucson, AZ: Fangamer.

Hellman, D., and Thompson, T. 2015b. "About." *Second Quest*. www.secondquestcomic.com/about.

Hemmann, K., 2015. "Queering the Media Mix: The Female Gaze in Japanese Fan Comics." *Transformative Works and Cultures* 20. http://dx.doi.org/10.3983/twc.2015 .0628.

Hilliard, K. 2014. "Link Is Not a Woman in Zelda on Wii U." *Game Informer*. June 12. www.gameinformer.com/b/news/archive/2014/06/12/is-link-a-girl-in-zelda-on-wii-u.aspx.

Ito, M. 2008. "Gender Dynamics of the Japanese Media Mix." In *Beyond Barbie and Mortal Kombat: New Perspectives on Gender and Gaming*, edited by Yasmin B. Kafai et al., 97–110. Cambridge, MA: MIT Press.

Johnston, C. 2014. "Chat Logs Show How 4chan Users Created #GamerGate Controversy." *Ars Technica*. September 9. http://arstechnica.com/gaming/2014/09/new -chat-logs-show-how-4chan-users-pushed-gamergate-into-the-national-spotlight.

Joho, J. 2014. "*Average Maria Individual*, the Game 'Ruining' Your Favorite Classic on Purpose." *Kill Screen*. November 11. https://killscreen.com/articles/average-maria -individual-game-ruining-your-favorite-classic-purpose.

Lam, F. Y. 2010. "Comic Market: How the World's Biggest Amateur Comic Fair Shaped Japanese Dōjinshi Culture." *Mechademia* 5 (1): 232–48.

Lees, M. 2016. "What Gamergate Should Have Taught Us about the 'Alt-right.'" *Guardian*. December 1.

"*The Legend of Zelda: A Link to the Past*: Reception." 2017. *Wikipedia*, last modified September 29, 2017.

"*The Legend of Zelda: Ocarina of Time*: Reception and Legacy." 2017. *Wikipedia*, last modified October 9, 2017.

Nagle, A. 2017. *Kill All Normies: Online Culture Wars from 4chan and Tumblr to Trump and the Alt-right*. Alresford: Zero Books.

Parker, R. 2014. "Anita Sarkeesian Cancels Utah State Speech after Mass-Shooting Threat." *Los Angeles Times*. October 14.

Phillips, W. 2015. *This Is Why We Can't Have Nice Things: Mapping the Relationship between Online Trolling and Mainstream Culture*. Cambridge, MA: MIT Press.

Roy, L. 2008. *Zelda: The Dark Mirror II*.

Rumphol-Janc, N. 2014. "Zelda: Sales Numbers in Context." *Zelda Informer*. July 4. www.zeldainformer.com/articles/zelda-sales-numbers-in-context.

Sarkeesian, A. 2013. "Damsel in Distress (Part 1) Tropes vs Women." *Feminist Frequency*. March 7. http://feministfrequency.com/2013/03/07/damsel-in-distress -part-1.

Thorpe, P. 2013. *The Legend of Zelda: Hyrule Historia*. English edition. Translated by Michael Gombos et al. Milwaukie, OR: Dark Horse Books.

TV Tropes Contributors. 2017. "Damsel in Distress." *TV Tropes*. http://tvtropes.org /pmwiki/pmwiki.php/Main/DamselInDistress.

van der Meulen, R., and Rivera, J. 2013. "Gartner Says Worldwide Video Game Market to Total $93 Billion in 2013." *Gartner Newsroom*. October 29. www .gartner.com/newsroom/id/2614915.

# PART 5

# EMPATHETIC AND INCLUSIVE GAMING

# CHAPTER 12

# AVATARS

*Addressing Racism and Racialized Address*

ROBBIE FORDYCE, TIMOTHY NEALE,
AND THOMAS APPERLEY

I love this app. You feel *powerless and helpless.*

APPLE STORE REVIEW OF *EVERYDAY RACISM*

WRITING FOR *Kotaku* in 2012, John Scalzi produced the article "Straight White Male: The Lowest Difficulty Setting There Is." Irrespective of the goals of the article, the argument presented at the surface is that marginalized identities in some sense "play through real life" in a more difficult mode than straight white men and should be respected accordingly. Scalzi's argument, a version of which was already well-established within the field of Critical Whiteness Studies, proceeded to set off a conversation in games culture. One aspect of this was the common conflation of discussions of phenotypical difference with racism, while another was the framing of real experiences of racism—especially for people with darker skin tones—as having a rule-based nature. This moment was one of several key tributaries that fed into the swamp of 2014's vicious debates and attacks within the global game-playing community, when a fundamentally unjust, racist, and misogynist community was exposed within international games culture.

Scalzi's proposal for using a metaphor from video games to re-evaluate the experiences of marginalized and minorititzed communities in real life came full circle in 2017. *South Park: The Fractured but Whole* (Southpark Digital Studios/Ubisoft San Francisco) was released with, according to Metacritic (2017), generally favorable reviews from the digital game industry. The game, as with its television precursor, is known for being puerile, grotesque, and even cruel toward a wide range of people. The *South Park* franchise is also known for its social commentary, although this is often undermined or invalidated by the franchise's history of malice. Despite this, some reviews for the game contained substantial praise, noting that it had successfully combined the distinctive graphics and humor of the Comedy Central TV Show *South Park* with clear computer roleplaying game mechanics. The *South Park* game continued in the tradition of social commentary by including provocative game mechanics. In this, they apparently implemented the argument Scalzi had voiced: the skin color of the avatar and the difficulty of the game are proportional. The player is asked to choose a skin color for their avatar using a slider, which goes from white through shades of brown to black. The default setting is white, and as the slider is moved away from the white default toward a black avatar choice, the game's difficulty increases from "easy" to "very difficult."

Disappointingly, though, the game is still firmly within the bounds of white privilege because, as publisher Ubisoft put it, this feature is simply "a joke" (Weber 2017). As Winslow (2017) explains, the difficulty change is non-existent, and the gameplay itself is no different for any shade of skin tone for the avatar. The response to race, identity, and the structural complexities that underpin is simply a superficial aspect, with no greater interrogation or experiential shift. As David J. Leonard (2006) has previously pointed out, the inclusion of virtual Black bodies in video games "elicit[s] pleasure and play on white fantasies while simultaneously affirming white privilege through virtual play" (86). Reading the *South Park* game and Leonard's positions together, we can perhaps read the avatar choice as an ironic joke at the expense of the discriminated, "playing at" presenting an opportunity to use an in-game mechanic to interrogate the imbrication of privilege and race through an anti-racist pedagogy. As some described it, the engagement with anti-racist politics were merely "throw-away" (Clark 2017).

This chapter examines the imbrication of privilege that can potentially accompany using a virtual body in anti-racist pedagogy to educate white people about racism. The question that drives this approach is, "How does highlighting racialized experience through the lens of gameplay poten-tially entrench racist privileges?" We explore this issue by examining the mobile app game *Everyday Racism*, an activist anti-racist game developed to promote social justice. The chief concern we address in raising *Everyday Racism* as an example is to provoke thinking around anti-racist pedagogy in the context of video games: specifically, the problems that arise when white players "play race" (see also Fordyce, Neale, and Apperley 2016). This chapter addresses the issue of "playing race," both in the digital form as well as in offline spaces, and examines how the playing of race has become integral to the pedagogy of the anti-racist video game, *Everyday Racism*. In order to deal with these interrelated problems around race, racism, and games from the Australian context, the chapter begins by identifying how through playing race *Everyday Racism* addresses racist ideologies found across majority white settler colonial nations.

## SEEKING SOCIAL JUSTICE IN AUSTRALIAN GAMES

In the United States and elsewhere in the Anglosphere, including Austra-lia, there has been a new focus on issues of social justice and video games in the past decade: First, with a widespread recognition that specifically developed games could be used to communicate messages and inculcate habits, illustrated by the growth of serious games and games for health; and second, through a growing recognition of the concern that the main-stream commercial games industry has played a role in sustaining and perpetuating racist and sexist ideas and behaviors through industry prac-tices and through the games that are produced. Fron, et al. (2007), describe this latter issue as the hegemony of play, arguing that:

"Today's hegemonic game industry has infused both individuals' and societies' experience of games with values and norms that reinforce that industry's technological, commercial and cultural investments in a particular definition of games and play" (309).

In particular, Fron and her colleagues argue that these definitions are shaped by unexamined masculine and white privilege.

Since 2014, criticism of the games industry in the United States and elsewhere has been shaped by a Gamergate, a moment or movement that found "gamers" attempting to silence white women and women of color who had been speaking out against sexism, racism, and homophobia within the gaming industry, video games, and video game cultures.

The productivity and success of the game industry in expanding into new audiences and markets has not necessarily been followed by a changing understanding of the audience. Salter and Blodgett (2012) argue that women are only nominally included in the "new gaming public," which expects that they accept the hegemonic status quo. Nominal inclusion based on mute acceptance also characterizes the experience of African American gamers. Gray (2012), in her study of the experiences of women of color on Xbox Live (the online service associated with the Microsoft Xbox series of platforms), argues that they are subject to intersecting oppressions based on their failure to conform to the white masculine norm. Players were identified as women and of color through linguistic profiling over Xbox Live's voice channel and as a consequence were subject to racist, sexist, and homophobic harassment.

The significance of these practices of harassment and silencing are salient in the context of Trump-era politics. In the United States, elsewhere in the Anglosphere, and in the countries of the European Union, Gamergate illustrated the development of the kinds of rhetorical media techniques that were later deployed by the alt-right during the 2016 Trump election campaign. This connection is palpable and most convincingly illustrated by the role of Breitbart's Steve Bannon in both supporting and mainstreaming Gamergate in 2014, and then becoming the chief executive of Trump's election campaign in 2016 (Lees 2016). Other commentators have suggested that the alt-right used Gamergate as a way to recruit by radicalizing apolitical disenchantment (Sherr and Carson 2017).

In Australia, explicitly racist organizations—such as Reclaim Australia, The United Patriot Front, and the Great Aussie Patriot, among others— have also risen to renewed prominence in the past decade, at least in part buoyed by increased public discussion over migration and the nation's treatment of refugees. In one sense, such groups are continuous with Australia's long history of racism, in which indigenous nations and migrants of color have been subject to institutional and individual acts of violence ranging from state-sanctioned killing and arbitrary detention through to individual microaggressions; this legacy has not been surpassed (see Hage 2014). What is new about the present situation in Australia parallels the situation in the United States: the increased public presence of these groups, openly organizing over Twitter and Facebook, running web servers, and leading rallies and protests in the streets of cities. Online spaces have proved an effective venue for "overt" and "cloaked" publicity and recruitment (Daniels 2008, 129), providing a new medium to build support for old racial "technologies"; affording whites opportunities to dismantle protections for people of color, in this case under the (often passive) protection of those who administer such digital infrastructures.

These efforts have been paralleled with the attempts of anti-racist organizations in Australia—such as Warriors of Aboriginal Resistance and Blackfulla Revolution, among others—who remain frequently frustrated in their hopes to have racist conduct and content policed online. Australia also has a history of highlighting social justice issues through video games, or at least games that strive to discuss Australia's colonial legacy and foster inclusion. Well-known games such as *Escape from Woomera* (2004), a point-and-click adventure set inside an infamous detention center, and user-made mods of Australia for *Civilization V* are some examples.

*Escape from Woomera* is an artistic and activist project that has become something of a *cause célèbre* among scholars of serious games and game art (Apperley 2008, 225). The game was developed to highlight the dreadful conditions in the Woomera Immigration Reception and Processing Centre, located in South Australia. The role of the center was to hold "illegal" immigrants while their details and asylum applications were processed; it was operational from 1999 until its closure in 2004. *Escape from Woomera* was eventually released as an almost-finished downloadable online game in May 2004 after the closure of the center (although the Australian government continued the practice of detaining asylum seekers).

The Escape from Woomera Project Team received AUD$25,000 from the Australian Council of the Arts through the New Media Arts Board (Swalwell 2003). The government heavily criticized the funding decision, and the Federal Minister of Arts demanded an explanation. Michael Snelling, Chairman of the New Media Arts Board, attempted to diffuse the situation, claiming that the project was awarded funding based purely on its artistic merit (Nicholls 2003). When the Australian Council of the Arts dissolved the New Media Arts Board in 2004 in the wake of the furor, many believed that the funding of *Escape from Woomera* was the cause (Swalwell and Neil 2006).

More recently, the game *Everyday Racism* (*Everyday Racism*, 2014a, 2014b), developed by researchers across several universities, has sought to address racism both in terms of online/offline components of racist behavior and in terms of bridging between these two environments. *Everyday Racism* makes this attempt by directing racist actions and language in a didactic form toward the player. This occurs in the form of audio and video materials and short comics, and is mediated through the familiar interfaces of social media, email, and SMS messages. In this, the *Everyday Racism* game supports social justice by exploring what the experiences of discrimination are like for people of color, particularly as they are focused through mobile devices, in order to elicit anti-racist responses.


EVERYDAY RACISM

*Everyday Racism* begins with a free download, incidental setup procedures such as confirming that the player is aged over 18, and a survey to discover the age, gender, suburb, and ethnicity of the user. The player clicks I'm Ready and faces possibly the most important choice in the whole experience, a choice between one of four avatars: three racially coded individuals, and one "blank slate." The chosen avatar becomes the lens through which the player then experiences different forms of racist behavior. The three avatars represent significant minority groups that are subject to racism in the Australian context, and the app was built in consultation with these affected groups. They are:

- Aisha, a Muslim woman from Oman,
- Vihaan, a man from India, and
- Patrick, an Indigenous Australian man.

The specter of the central and privileged figure appears in the option to play as "yourself," a genderless silhouette that, in being unmarked, is the implicit white norm. This is reinforced by the "You" avatar's positioning as an onlooker. As You, the player watches the lonely Aisha from the window of a party to which she is not invited. If the player replays the game as Aisha, the character looking out the window is a young white bespectacled man with blond hair and a light beard. Otherwise, unlike the other avatars, the character of You is never visible and, in either case, never directly experiences racism in the course of the game. The unmarked You is always a bystander who is therefore immune to the direct pressures of institutional racism.

Outside the spectrum of ethnicity, the avatars are largely uniform. They are implicitly middle-class, aged in their mid- to late twenties, live city-based lifestyles, are interested in youth socialization, and appear to have no children, partners, or other dependents. *Everyday Racism* has eliminated almost every variable except ethnicity and gender. We can read from this an idea of a certain normative expectation about the players of smartphone games in terms of their age and their social desires. Once the avatar has been chosen, the player is then presented with a series of engagements that unfold in real time for players. Posing as phone alerts of new messages or notifications, the game interrupts the player's life to serve racialized content from the game for one week. The player experiences racial discrimination mediated through the phone as text messages, emails, radio conversations, and, at times, narrative videos and comics. The form that racism takes varies as events are sorted for each player. At times, the racism comes in the form of discriminatory epithets from passers-by, while, in others, the player watches retail assistants harass shoppers.

Within *Everyday Racism*, such events are used to interpellate the player into a response. The gameplay progresses in a similar manner to dating simulator games or the conversation mechanic employed by many RPGs and dating sims (e.g., the *Dragon Age* and *Mass Effect* series), where the player is called upon to select from a limited set of responses to the current situation. While normally these genres involve a substantial amount of narrative, *Everyday Racism* relies on short-form communication, and racism is communicated literally in almost every case. Characters are directly harassed or ignored on the basis of presumptions about their ethnicity, religion, or culture. This abuse may be shouted, written down, emailed, or tagged. In other cases, the abuse is more subtle, appearing in accusations of inappropriateness or lack of "cultural fit." In all cases, the player is served four of these events every day directly from their mobile device and is asked to respond. Almost all possible actions are communicative actions, cast into three different molds: a) take no action, b) seek remediation from an authority figure or social group, or c) directly intervene in the situation. The scenarios vary so widely it is worth giving several examples.

In one scenario universal to the racialized avatars, "You" receive an email from a prospective employer stating that "You" have not been employed because they "just don't feel that you would be a good *cultural fit* with the organization" (our emphasis). Reacting by filing a formal complaint (option b) leads to a pro forma email saying an investigation is pending, while replying with an email to the employer identifying their racism (option c) leads to their assurance that you have "misunderstood." In another scenario, you are not invited to socialize with workmates because they assume you do not drink alcohol, and direct action again leads to a denial of racist intent.

Alternately, as Patrick, you receive an email for a workplace function related to an annual celebration of Indigenous Australian culture that includes mocking suggestions to bring body paint and didgeridoos. Direct action again leads to denial and a suggestion the player is too "serious."

Against these, there are more dramatic audio-visual scenarios. In one segment, the player overhears racist radio broadcasts (a hazard endemic to Australian media, see Hanson-Easey et al. 2012), and is invited to complain to the broadcaster. In another, the player overhears a racist discussion by café staff before being asked, "How will you respond?" In this case, the supplied choices include either walking out, replying, "I just wanted to order a coffee," or asking, "Can I speak to the manager?" Choosing any option but that of direct action leads to the game asking, rhetorically: "Do you think acting like it doesn't matter will change anything?"

For players acting through the "You" avatar, the situations are more selective, yet the responses continue to fit the same pattern as before, even if the experiences are tangential and guilt is the predominant motivator for action. As Alana Lentin and Justine Humphry (2016) note, this form of gameplay is pedagogical and future-oriented, giving little capacity for immediate support during the moment that an event takes place. Do we sit silently while others are targeted? For the racialized avatars, the situation is less escapable.

## AVATARS OF COLOR

*Everyday Racism* is a game that seeks to achieve something different from many other games. It is much more experimental and "risky" than most other "serious" games. Its portrayal of race is radically different from most other interactive digital entertainment, yet significantly it still articulates some of the key issues around race that have been raised by game studies. Race has long been an object of research within games scholarship. Work by scholars such as Chan (2005), Jansz and Martis (2007), Galloway (2007), DeVane and Squire (2008), DiSalvo, Crowley, and Norwood (2008), Williams, Martins, Consalvo, and Ivory (2009), Shaw (2010), and Young (2015) has taken a variety of methodological approaches to understand different aspects of identity and video gaming through critical, quantitative, and qualitative lenses. The work by many of these scholars—particularly Williams et al. and Dietrich—has worked to measure the capacity of racial phenotypic representations to live up to the experiences of non-white video game players. In Williams et al. the approach contrasts the representational appearance of different racial categories within video games against the real population statistics provided by the United States Census (Williams et al. 2009). There are clear limits to such positivistic methods, not only because they conflate surveys with reality, putting aside other meaningful boundaries (locality, community, etc.), but also because representation only addresses those sorts of structural racism that are based around exclusion or colorblindness, not to mention the absence of a clear intersectionality in the approach.

Alternately, Dietrich (2013) investigates what range of nuance is allowed within racialized representations in video games by investigating character creation systems, finding that there is a greater degree of possible representation for people seeking white avatars than there are for any people of color. For example, when assessing for "African" hairstyle options, Dietrich finds that 30 percent had one or two hairstyles available, while half of the games surveyed allowed for no "African" hairstyle options whatsoever (2013, 93). In their ethnographic study of tween virtual world *Whyville*, Yasmin Kafai and Deborah Field (2013) similarly noted the dearth of avatar parts that represented Black bodies. One of Kafai and Fields' key case studies follows the experiences of an African American tween who struggled for weeks trying to trade, find, or buy African American body parts for her avatar before settling for using light brown "Latino" body parts in order to have matching body parts. Kafai and Fields estimated that 90 percent of the available avatar body parts in the game were a coded a white "peach" color, while the remaining 10 percent represented non-white identities. In this case, because of the social, multiple player context of *Whyville*, they point out that the inability to represent oneself in a way that is connected to other areas of an individuals' life (such as gender and ethnicity) have a profound impact on young people's socialization into digital publics.

Embedded notions of race and ethnicity aren't always such an obvious issue in video games. But the remediation and translation of the notion of race is relatively common and found in popular video games such as *Warcraft* (1994) and *StarCraft,* (1998) not to mention being a mainstay in pencil-and-paper tabletop role-playing games (cf. Higgin 2008; Kontour 2009). In a discussion of race in *StarCraft*, Galloway (2007, 94, 96) argues that "gamic" races are "altogether different from but in some senses determined by offline races" because they are represented by hardcoded, fixed statistics that do not vary with respect to gameplay, the consequence to this racial fixity being that "race is "unplayable" in any conventional sense for all the tangible details of gamic race (voice, visage, character animation, racial abilities, etc.) are quarantined in certain hard-coded machinic behaviors." As Young (2015) points out in the context of the games franchises based on Tolkien's work, the logics of race within many early fantasy video games come down to a binary black/white, good/evil distinction, but these divides become less clear due to a "neo-liberal colorblindness," furthering the idea that race is not something that can be played, as race is disassociated from any meaning other than the aesthetic (15). While Galloway is talking about a specific genre of game-play, namely real-time strategy games, the description applies in many other cases as well.

When the expression of race is taken away from a notion of essential character statistics and placed within a narrative, it is often used solely to justify moments of violence under the pretext of anti-racism. In other words, within the unfolding diegesis of the video game, racism is used to validate interventionist violence, for instance, in *Dragon Age: Inquisition* (2014), where players must engage in violence to protect elvish characters from racist abuse, a moment that is contextualized within a game for which the premise is the battle between two modernising colonialisms. Race can indeed be played, insofar as anti-racist violence is usually optional, but it tends to be in terms of acting violently in response to acts of racism. While this may well be a moment of cathartic relief for many players, this plays out differently in *Everyday Racism*. Because *Everyday Racism* seeks to faithfully represent everyday experiences staged with an anti-racist animus, physical violence is never given as a possible response to acts of racism. Instead, the role of narrative acts of racism in the game—the component that allows race to be played—is to provide space for education.

Whereas many games make avatars of color available to white people, *Everyday Racism* also makes the *experience of racism* available to white people. We will address this aspect through two important questions: First, can making experiences of racism available to white people function as a part of an anti-racist pedagogy? And second, should this even be attempted? This second point may seem obtuse, but the essence of this concern is that one tenet of white supremacist social structures is that there are no experiences that are denied to white people (Frankenberg 1993; Dyer 2013). The settler-colonialist history of countries such as Aus-tralia, Canada, and the United States have been founded on the expropria-tion of culture, land, religion, and identity from people of color (Veracini

2010). Today, as Moreton-Robinson suggests (2015), "white possession" of others continues through the presumed ability of whites to determine what is and is not racism, who is and is not indigenous, and what is and is not appropriate "reconciliation." The idea that not even experiences of racism can be denied to white people appears, on this account, innately suspicious. If the proposed benefit is that white people might gain a sympathetic understanding of the experiences of people of color—suggesting that the latter's own accounts are not already believed—the potential cost is that this will lead to the perpetuation of "whitesplaining," where white people become authorities on matters of racism.

For *Everyday Racism*, the answers to both questions are undoubtedly in the affirmative. Its designers are grounded in the fields of health and applied psychology, drawing on research that suggests that:

1. racism—typically understood as a moral or political wrong—has clear negative effects on mental and physical health (Paradies, 2006);
2. racist attitudes are sustained because they are not challenged; and,
3. confrontation can be an effective road to remediation.

Against the prevailing wisdom, scholars in the field of social psychology have argued that attempts to alter beliefs through collective guilt about past and present racism may be counterproductive (Halloran 2007), showing instead that "bystander" interventions to identifying racists acts when they occur frequently has productive effects for targets and bystanders, as well as being "politically significant" (264) in shifting "the burden of anti-racism away from targets" (Nelson, Dunn, et al. 2011, 264). The supposition here is that public condemnation can lead racist individuals to see they have overestimated community support, and, as such, a key aim of *Everyday Racism* would seem to be to encourage bystander behavior, though close attention to the underpinning assumptions suggests some limitations. In short, on behalf of what or whom does one intervene? One suggestion, following Nelson, et al. (2011), is to intervene on the basis of "superordinate group membership" (270), explicitly invoking "shared values, experiences, affiliations" (274). The suggestion is to recalibrate prejudice to the parameters of a more inclusive ideological formation, such as the nation or locality. This is a compelling strategy, though it is important to note nationhood and other "supervalent" norms that are highly contested grounds of social belonging, which in turn are capable of producing a substantial Othering effect.

Our interest is not in critically commenting on this specialized research but rather to highlight the politics of the avowed solution in the context of video games for social justice using moments of empathic imagination to stimulate social change. In short, making the experience of racism available to players implicitly not already submerged in the daily experiences of racism in the first place brings us to the key problem we identify in the experience of race within video games. There exists a strand of academic analysis that seeks to question what we might call the "adoption of race" within video games due to problematic similarities to the history of other practices of race-based mimicry that have existed across history (Leonard 2004, 2006; Shiu 2006). Drawing upon Adam Clayton Powell III's description of video games as "high-tech blackface," David J. Leonard (2004; 2006, 86) suggests that there may be a connection between the history of minstrelsy and the modern genre of basketball games: "Sports games reflect a history of minstrelsy," he notes, "providing its primarily white creators and players the opportunity to become black" (2004, 1). Specifically, such video games allow players to perform acts that would otherwise be wholly socially unacceptable. The argument presented is one that takes its case study from a game that, on top of utilizing "high-tech blackface" as a method of player/avatar interaction, is also filled with a very limited suite of racial tropes of Black people, particularly limited to "ghettoized" identities. Leonard's suggestion is that this leads to players being rendered as a sort of "virtual ghetto tourist" (2004, 4).

Leonard identifies the potential here for video games to simply reinforce racial stereotypes while allowing white players to play at being racialized. Adrienne Shaw (2014) draws on the work of both Leonard and Lisa Nakamura (2002) to identify the different forms that identity tourism can take. This includes forms that involve highly stereotyped performances of race and gender in order to gain acceptance in multiplayer games, or the more complicated relations between self and Other that are enabled in digital spaces, which are not mediated or shaped by multiplayer spaces (Shaw 2014, 139–40). We want to continue to develop this argument and look at how these issues play out within games where an anti-racist pedagogy is an important part of the game's operation. The core issue is the extent to which games enable a form of "blackface" and other types of appropriation of ethnicity in the cause of creating avatars. This is obviously a fraught question with tensions between, on one hand, the processes of inclusion, representation, and agency within video game spaces, but is tied off against the issues of fetishization, cultural and ethnic appropriation, and the long history of racist caricatures as exemplified by blackface.

## DOLEZAL-ING IT: THE AVAILABILITY OF RACE TO WHITE PEOPLE

The question as to what conditions create an appropriate ethical frame for white people to take on the identity of people of color in digital spaces gains a new light when put in the context of recent high-profile acts of public blackface. Two illustrative examples of this are Rachel Dolezal and Boglarka Balogh. Both are white women, Dolezal from the United States, Balogh from Hungary. Dolezal is infamous for attempting to "pass" as African American, while Balogh is known for a series of digitally-altered self-portraits in which she mimicked the outfits, makeup, and dress of people from different African nations. We focus upon these two examples because, unlike many other uses of blackface, the avowed purpose of their acts was not to mock people of color (which is not to suggest such intentions lessen the damage done by their actions).

Prior to being publicly outed by her white parents in June 2015, Dolezal was an instructor in Africana Studies at Eastern Washington University and president of the Spokane chapter of the National Association for the Advancement of Colored People (NAACP). Revealed as genealogically white, she met accusations of having fraudulently displaced others from engaging in self-determining politics by insisting on the validity of her experiences. This was achieved by, first, claiming to be the victim of nine acts of racism (Moyer 2015), and, second, claiming an affective Black identity; she maintains that "I was being me" in presenting as Black (McGreal 2015). Such reasoning has been criticized as highly offensive to people of color and devaluing others' experiences of overt and structural racism.

Balogh's appropriation, alternately, was more contained. In attempting to raise awareness of tribal women in Africa, she blended her own facial features into photos of different Mursi, Himba, Arbore, Turkana, and Karo women (Balogh 2015a). Balogh removed the photos following significant public criticism, claiming: "My intention was 100% pure."

Dolezal and Balogh's acts vary significantly in their scope: Dolezal worked for decades to accrete a cultural and phenotypical identity, misleading employers and others about her past, while Balogh made a series of images. When Dolezal was criticized, her initial reaction was to construct a fictitious family history in which her "real" father was Black, before then shifting the basis of her racial identity from genetics to one of affect and experience (Samuels 2015), whereas Balogh apologized immediately (Balogh 2015b).

Evidently, Balogh and Dolezal's acts diverge in terms of the damage done, but both illustrate the dynamics identified in the previous section. First, in both cases, the identities of people of color were assumed as *available* to white people, whether for momentary impersonation or, at a limit, long-term affective identification. Balogh's adoption of not just one but many racial identities demonstrates the flexibility with which white people take on other identities, often in the name of valuing or "respecting" them. This availability, second, underwrites the *fluidity* of relations of identification between white individuals and race, in that, in contrast to those who are racially interpellated, the basis of these relations is a matter of individual determination; the basis of racial identity can be less a matter of imposed categories than subjective selection. Thereby, third, those relations themselves are *disposable* or, alternately, inalienable. As Dolezal's example shows, the exposure of gross appropriation does not necessarily lead to repatriation or withdrawal.

We use these recent examples because they demonstrate the extension of the problems of avowedly "well-meaning" racial identification outside the space of video games. Within video games, players are routinely afforded the opportunity to identify with an avatar of color through which they experience the game world. Whereas games where non-white bodies are the only option have been subject to significant consumer criticism, any idea of limiting the availability of avatars of color has been received as censorship (see Fordyce, Neale, and Apperley, 2016, commentary on the game *Rust*). Avatars of color are treated as both disposable and inalienable or, in a phrase, they are objects of "white possession."

While these issues within video games may appear secondary in light of other forms of appropriation, our examples above gesture to the problems that arise when race is treated as something that can be adopted when wanted (even in the face of significant international criticism and repudiation) and discarded when no longer desirable. If *Everyday Racism* presents one possibility, where avatars of color enable socially progressive acts of empathy, the other is the socially regressive perpetuation of conditions in which whites feel they have a right to racialized bodies; in which race remains, for them, available, fluid, and disposable.

CONCLUSION

*Everyday Racism* effectively addresses the new contexts of racism in Australia. Built to simulate various forms of online and mobile interaction, the game effectively stages the experience of racism, particularly microaggressions. The app takes on a highly experimental approach to combatting racism that has been widely acknowledged to be effective. Among the various awards and accolades it has received are the United Nation's PEACEapp award (UNAOC 2014) and second place in the international Intercultural Innovation Awards (The Intercultural Innovation Award 2014). The game clearly provides opportunities for people to understand the social nature of racism as well as their own position *vis-à-vis* racist society (including, potentially, as perpetrators). The game's goal of motivating interventionist behavior is approached in a way that at least implicates individuals in moments of racism and forces a decision. We consider *Everyday Racism* to be an exemplar within anti-racist video games that connects players' game-based experiences to their experiences in the world.

But making racialized identities available to white people is politically and morally complex. The pedagogical benefits of a game like *Everyday Racism*, whose success may be exceptional rather than definitive, do not dissolve the innate problems of overcoming a form of white domination— racially discriminatory acts—by making the experience of racialization an object of white knowledge. This is a point that is underscored in the epigraph to this chapter, where the comment "You feel *powerless and help-less*" is open to interpretations of schadenfreude or disempowering pity as much as to empathy or processes of learning. The stories of Dolezal and Balogh are simply two in a long history of white people taking on the identities and/or appearance of people of color, much of it intended to mock, demean, own, or otherwise diminish the cultures and identities of people of color. The fact that there is a long history of treating the bodies of peoples of color as objects of white possession, whether through forms of entertainment for white people, means that the use of racialized bodies and experiences of racialization as a part of pedagogy has to be carefully managed. The potential for an app such as *Everyday Racism* to promote a true sense of justice is muted, relative to its remediation of respectable behavior over structural issues.

As is clear from the examples, we have discussed that making "non-white" bodies and identities available is a fraught process. But it appears that it can also serve a function as an explicitly counter-racist pedagogy, and furthermore, removing non-white identities within video games becomes exclusionary toward people of color. Clearly the capacity of "playing race" sits at a politically-charged intersection between education and mockery, representation and fetishization. So, to what extent can the practice of ally-construction and ally-empowerment be a reasonable goal for a video game? Anti-racist games may yet tell us.

## ACKNOWLEDGMENTS

A draft of this article was presented at the First International Joint Conference of the Digital Games Research Association and Foundation of Digital Games, Abertay University, Dundee, 1–5 August 2016. The authors would like to thank Emil Lundedal Hammar for insightful comments on an early draft.

This research was supported by the Australian Research Council Discovery Project Grant DP140101503 "Avatars and Identity" (2014–2016) led by Justin Clemens, Thomas Apperley, and John Frow.

## WORKS CITED

Apperley, T. 2008. "Videogames in Australia." In *The Videogame Explosion: A History from Pong to PlayStation and Beyond*, edited by M. J. P. Wolf, 223–28. Westport: Greenwood Press.

Balogh, B. 2015a. "I Morphed Myself into Tribal Women to Raise Awareness of Their Secluded Cultures." *Boredpanda*. December 26. www.boredpanda.com/i -morphed-myself-into-african-tribal-women-to-raise-awareness-of-these-secluded -culture.

Balogh, B. 2015b. "I Morphed Myself into Tribal Women to Raise Awareness of Their Secluded Cultures" *Boredpanda*. December 26. www.boredpanda.com/i -morphed-myself-into-african-tribal-women-to-raise-awareness-of-these-secluded -culture. NB: This reference refers to the updated post in which Balogh deleted her original photos.

Bioware. 2009. *Dragon Age: Origins* [Windows]. Electronic Arts.

Bioware. 2014. *Dragon Age: Inquisition* [Windows]. Electronic Arts.

Bioware. 2008. *Mass Effect* [Windows]. Electronic Arts.

Chan, D. 2005. "Playing with Race: The Ethics of Racialized Representations in E-Games." *International Review of Information Ethics* 4: 24–30.

Clark, J. 2017 "Southpark: The Fractured but Whole." October 18. www.slantmaga -zine.com/games/review/south-park-the-fractured-but-whole.

Daniels, J. 2008. "Race, Civil Rights, and Hate Speech in the Digital Era." In *Learning Race and Ethnicity: Youth and Digital Media*, edited by A. Everett, 129–54. Cam- bridge, MA: MIT Press.

DeVane, B., and Squire, K. D. 2008. "The Meaning of Race and Violence in Grand Theft Auto San Andreas." *Games and Culture* 3 (3–4): 264–85. DOI: 10.1177/1555412008317308.

Dietrich, D. 2013. "Avatars of Whiteness: Racial Expression in Video Game Charac- ters." *Sociological Inquiry* 83 (1): 82–105.

DiSalvo, B., Crowley, K., and Norwood, R. 2008. "Learning in Context: Digital Games and Young Black Men." *Games and Culture* 3 (2): 131–41. DOI: 10.1177/1555412008314130.

Dyer, R. 2013. *White: Essays on Race and Culture*. Hoboken: Taylor and Francis.

Escape from Woomera Project Team. 2004. *Escape from Woomera* [Windows]. Escape from Woomera Project Team.

Everyday Racism. 2014a. *Everyday Racism*. Apple. https://itunes.apple.com/au/app /everyday-racism/id726683275.

Everyday Racism. 2014b. *Everyday Racism*. Google Play. https://play.google.com/store /apps/details?id=com.atn.everydayracism.

Firaxis Games. 2010. *Civilization V.* [Windows]. 2K Games.

Fordyce, R., Neale, T., and Apperley, T. 2016. "Modelling Systemic Racism: Mobilising the Dynamics of Race and Games in *Everyday Racism*." Fibreculture 27. http://twentyseven.fibreculturejournal.org/2016/03/18/fcj-199-modelling -systemic-racism-mobilising-the-dynamics-of-race-and-games-in-everyday -racism.

Frankenberg, R. 1993. *White Women, Race Matters: The Social Construction of Whiteness*. Minneapolis: University of Minnesota Press.

Fron, J., Fullerton, T., Morie, J. F., and Pearce, C. 2007. "The Hegemony of Play."
In *Situated Play: Proceedings of the 2007 DiGRA International Conference*, volume 4,
edited by Akira Baba, 309–18. University of Tokyo, September 24–27.

Galloway, A. 2007. "*Starcraft*, or, Balance." *Grey Room* 28: 86–107.

Hage, G. 2014. "Continuity and Change in Australian Racism." *Journal of Intercultural
Studies* 35: 232–37.

Halloran, M. J. 2007. "Indigenous Reconciliation in Australia: Do Values, Identity and
Collective Guilt Matter?" *Journal of Community and Applied Social Psychology* 17: 1–18.

Hanson-Easey, S. A., and Augoustinos, M. 2012 "Narratives from the Neighbour-
hood: The Discursive Construction of Integration Problems in Talkback Radio,"
*Journal of Sociolinguistics* 16 (1): 28–55.

Higgin, T. 2008. "Blackless Fantasy: The Disappearance of Race in Massively Multiplayer Online Role-Playing Games." *Games and Culture* 4 (1): 3–26.

Intercultural Innovation Award. 2014. "Everyday Racism." https://interculturalin
novation.org/everyday-racism.

Jansz, J., and Martis R. G. 2007 "The Lara Phenomenon." *Sex Roles* 56: 141–48.

Kafai, Y. B., and Fields, D. A. 2013. *Connected Play: Tweens in a Virtual World*. Cambridge, MA: MIT Press.

Kontour, K. 2009. "Myths of Neo-conservatism and Privatization in World of Warcraft." *Refractory: A Journal of Entertainment Media* 16 (1). http://refractory.unimelb
.edu.au/2009/11/17/myths-of-neoconservatism-and-privatization-in-world-of-
-warcraft-%E2%80%93-kyle-kontour.

Lees, Matt. 2016. "What Gamergate Should Have Taught Us about the 'Alt-right.'"
*Guardian*. December 1.

Lentin, A., and Humphry J. 2016. "Antiracism Apps: Framing Understandings and
Approaches to Antiracism Education and Intervention." *Information, Communication, and Society* 20 (10): 1539–53.

Leonard, D. 2004. "High Tech Blackface: Race, Sports, Video Games and Becoming
the Other." *Intelligent Agent* 4 (2): 1–5. www.intelligentagent.com/archive/IA4
_4gamingleonard.pdf.

Leonard, D. 2006. "Not a Hater, Just Keepin' It Real: The Importance of Race- and
Gender- Based Game Studies." *Games and Culture* 1 (1): 83–88.

McGreal, C. 2015. "Rachel Dolezal: 'I Wasn't Identifying as Black to Upset People.
I Was Being Me.'" *Guardian*. December 14.

Metacritic. 2017. "Southpark: The Fractured but Whole." October 17. www.metacritic
.com/game/playstation-4/south-park-the-fractured-but-whole.

Moreton-Robinson, A. 2015. *The White Possessive: Property, Power, and Indigenous Sover-
eignty*. Minneapolis: University of Minnesota Press.

Moyer, J. 2015 "'Are You an African American?' Why an NAACP Official Isn't Saying."
*Washington Post*. June 12.

Nakamura, L. 2002. "After/Images of Identity: Gender, Technology, and Identity Politics." In *Reload: Rethinking Women and Cyberculture*, edited by Mary Flanagan and
Austin Booth, 321–31. Cambridge, MA: MIT Press.

Nelson, J. K., Dunn, K. M., and Paradies, Y. 2011. "Bystander Anti-racism: A Review of the Literature." *Analyses of Social Issues and Public Policy* 11: 263–84.

Nicholls, S. April 30, 2003. "Ruddock Fury over Woomera Computer Game." *The Age.* www.theage.com.au/articles/2003/04/29/1051381948773.html.

Paradies, Y. 2006. "A Systematic Review of Empirical Research on Self-Reported Racism and Health." *International Journal of Epidemiology* 35: 888–901.

Salter, A., and Blodgett, B. 2012. "Hypermasculinity and Dickwolves: The Contentious Role of Women in the New Gaming Public." *Journal of Broadcasting and Electronic Media* 56 (3): 401–16.

Samuels, A. 2015. "Rachel Dolezal's True Lies." *Vanity Fair.* July.

Scalzi, J. 2012. "Straight White Male: The Lowest Difficulty Setting There Is." *Kotaku.* May 17. www.kotaku.com.au/2012/05/straight-white-male-the-lowest-difficulty -setting-there-is.

Shaw, A. 2010. "What Is Video Game Culture? Cultural Studies and Game Studies." *Games and Culture* 5 (4): 403–24.

Shaw, A. 2014 *Gaming at the Edge.* University of Minnesota Press.

Sherr, I., and Carson, E. 2017. "GamerGate to Trump: How Video Game Culture Blew Everything Up." *Cnet.* November 28. www.cnet.com/au/news/gamer gate-donald-trump-american-nazis-how-video-game-culture-blew-every thing-up.

Shiu, A. S. 2006. "What Yellowface Hides: Video Games, Whiteness, and the American Racial Order." *Journal of Popular Culture* 39 (1): 109–25.

South Park. 1997–. *South Park.* South Park Digital Studios. Comedy Central.

South Park. 2014. *South Park: The Stick of Truth.* South Park Digital Studios/Obsidian.

South Park. 2017. *South Park: The Fractured but Whole.* South Park Digital Studios/ Ubisoft San Francisco.

Swalwell, M. 2003. "The Meme Game: Escape from Woomera." RealTime 55. www .realtimearts. net/rr55/swallwell.html.

Swalwell, M., and Neil, K. 2006. "'Unaustralia the Game' and the Possibility of Independent Satirical Videogames." Unpublished conference paper, presented at the Cultural Studies Association of Australasia, Canberra, December.

United Nations Alliance of Civilizations. 2014. "PEACEapp winners announced!" www.unaoc.org/peaceapp-blog/peaceapp-winners-announced.

Veracini, L. 2010. *Settler Colonialism: A Theoretical Overview.* Basingstoke, Hampshire: Palgrave Macmillan.

Weber, R. 2017. "*South Park: The Fractured but Whole*'s Race Choice Won't *Actually* Affect Difficulty, Says Ubisoft." *GamesRadar.* September 7. www.gamesradar .com/amp/south-park-the-fractured-but-wholes-race-choice-wont-actually-affect -difficulty-says-ubisoft.

Williams, D., Martins, N., Consalvo, M., and Ivory, J. D. 2009. "The Virtual Census: Representations of Gender, Race and Age in Video Games." *New Media and Society* 11 (5): 815–34.

Winslow, J. 2017. "The Darker the Skin, the Harder the Game: How South Park Pretended to Care about Race." *Polygon*. October 9. www.polygon.com/2017/10/9/16435592/south-park-race-difficulty.

Young, H. 2015. "Racial Logics, Franchising, and Video Game Genres: The Lord of the Rings." *Games and Culture*. Advance publication. DOI: 10.1177/1555412014568448.

# CHAPTER 13

# ACTIVISM IN VIDEO GAMES

*A New Voice for Social Change*

TAYLOR ANDERSON-BARKLEY AND KIRA FOGLESONG

V IDEO GAMES ARE a popular form of entertainment across a varying range of demographics. Women make up almost half of gamers (Grundberg 2014). The average gamer is thirty years old despite the general misperception that video games are a "children's medium" (Bogost 2007; Stokes, Seggerman, and Rejeski 2006). Huge AAA series like *Halo* and *Call of Duty* along with classic franchises such as *Super Mario* are recognizable names even among non-gamers. Because video games are such an immersive medium, they are widely used for distraction, amusement, and escapism, the inclination to flee one's reality typically through entertainment (Jansz and Martens 2005). However, in conjunction with providing players an outlet, video games have been able to push forward certain beliefs and ideologies about social and political issues. With organizations like Games for Change assisting video game designers in creating and distributing games for social change, activism in video games is steadily on the rise as a new genre of games that uses their themes, mechanics, and the medium's entertainment appeal to "campaign" for social change.

Video games offer a new platform for a new audience and, given how the millennial generation in particular yearns for the use of different and current media, it is easy to see why video game activism is increasing. Video games garner a lot of their popularity because of their interactive nature, setting them apart from other media like television, film, and literature, allowing designers to express ideas to this new audience in an immersive way. Additionally, video games have been shown to be powerful pedagogical tools. Yet the question remains whether this persuasion is limited when used for activism: Can video games promote awareness, encourage sympathy, and incite action? By traversing through the history of video game activism, observing previous studies on how video games persuade and help gamers learn, this chapter seeks to understand the potential and limits of this as an activist medium.

## THE MANY FORMS OF ACTIVISM

Activism is the act of using consistent and passionate campaigning to bring forth and incite social or political change. Thus, persuasion is key in shifting others' beliefs to viewpoints presented by an activist movement (Bogost 2007). However, activism must constantly be reimagined in an effort to appeal to the most possible people in the current culture. A few popular forms of activism today include commodity activism and online activism, which capitalize on the values placed upon consumerism and social media (Mukherjee and Banet-Weiser 2012). Commodity activism renders social change as a commodity through efforts to get consumers to support a cause by donating portions of proceeds that result from buying certain products. Activism becomes part of the role of consumer (Butler 2011). However, given that the only action on the consumer's part is the purchase of a product they may have already intended on buying, it begs the question of whether this should be considered "activism."

Online activism offers other ways for successful campaigning with the ability to reach many types of people all over the world, given that one-third of the world has access to the Internet (Butler 2011). "Clicktivism," a subset of online activism, involves the use of social media to promote change by organizing protests, boycotts, and petitions (Miloevi-orevi 2017). A recent and successful example was the Ice Bucket Challenge, where people made donations and shared videos on social media of buckets of ice being dumped on themselves in support of ending ALS, Amyotrophic

Lateral Sclerosis. This campaign funded enough research for scientists to make critical steps towards finding a cure (ALS).

However, some clicktivist movements are ineffective and criticized for disintegrating into "slacktivism," where one donates or takes actions online that ultimately contribute little or nothing to the cause (Jones 2013). An infamous example of clicktivism-turned-slacktivism was the movement around Kony 2012, a call-to-action video to stop Ugandan war criminal Joseph Kony (Evan 2012). While Kony 2012 gained a lot of initial support, receiving over 100 million views by the sixth day of its release (Jones 2013), it eventually tapered off after being accused of oversimplifying the issues in Uganda (Chalk 2012). It ultimately had little to no effect on the situation presented in the video.

Online activism is not perfect when it comes to inciting action, but the use of the Internet has had a profound impact on increasing social awareness. As the times continue to change and technology becomes easier for people to utilize, video games have been introduced into the world of activism as another way to reinvent these pursuits as a popular, persuasive, and effective medium.

## THE RISE OF "SERIOUS" GAMES

While *Pong* (1972) is often considered the first video game because of its commercial success, there were several non-commercial video game titles in existence before 1972. These games were meant for "serious" use, meaning they were not created for strictly entertainment purposes but for the sake of scientific research or professional training. For example, *The Oregon Trail*, a text-based game created by three teachers in 1971, sought to teach students about the period of American history of its namesake by casting the player as a pilgrim in 1848 who must traverse a trap-laden road in order to settle in Oregon. It was so popular among students that it continued to be developed and was even released commercially in 1985 (Djaouti et al. 2011).

Since stories provide a means to make sense of the world (Bogost 2008), game developers recognize the persuasive potential of video games to influence opinions and attitudes (ibid.). As such, both "serious" and games strictly for entertainment began to incorporate increasingly complex stories during the 1980s and 1990s (Djaouti et al. 2011). Video games began to incite social thought, and Chris Crawford's *Balance of the Planet* is a notable example of this trend. Released on Earth Day in 1990, the game simulated environmental issues and modeled their consequences based on players' solutions to the issues. Crawford wanted to illustrate how simple solutions to environmental issues often fail because the world is so complexly intertwined (Bogost 2006). *Balance of the Planet* was almost a failure commercially and critically until educators found it. While the average gamer "hated" the game (Crawford 2003) as it was short with little to do, educators loved it because it was "the most thorough and accurate simulation of environmental problems available" (Crawford 2003). Overall, *Balance of the Planet* was received more as an educational tool than a game.

## THE ORIGIN OF ACTIVIST GAMES

Video games communicate differently than other forms of media because they can simulate direct experience and thus have a new dimension for effectiveness as rhetorical tools (Bogost 2008). The level of agency offered to a player in the ability to move throughout a game of his or her own volition increases the level of immersion within the game as well as the chance to make his or her own conscious decisions and form opinions about issues outside of the game (Tanenbaum and Tanenbaum 2009). This unique and versatile medium sparked the creation of organizations like the Serious Games Initiative in 2002 in order to promote using games to foster social awareness and eventually social action, popularizing the term "serious games" (Djaouti et al. 2011). By 2010, the worldwide serious games market grew to $1.6 billion (ibid.). The Serious Games Initiative created a separate branch called Games for Change in 2004 expressly for developers to create games for activism. Since then, Games for Change has become the central hub for publishing games for social change. They work with nonprofits, educational institutions, and even government agencies to receive donations, advise projects, and host workshops for encouraging social game creation. Currently, there are 172 games published on Games for Change's website (About).

Along with Games for Change's efforts, one particular game propelled the current wave of activist games. In 2005, MTV partnered with the Reebok Human Rights Foundation and the International Crisis Group to host a contest for generating awareness around the genocide occurring in Darfur, Sudan. The winner, *Darfur is Dying*, a two-part game that shows the consequences of the player's decisions as a Darfurian refugee trying to survive situations based on the horrors going on in Sudan, was created by a team of graduate students from the University of Southern California led by Susana Ruiz. Even though the game was well-received and won MTV's challenge, it was accused of trivializing the issue by thinking a game could save the world (Muratet et al. 2009). Ruiz simply hoped to create an accessible game that brought awareness to audiences who wouldn't typically see a documentary or read a news article on the subject, but the game had little effect on the actual situation in Darfur (Jones 2009). With over a million downloads, *Darfur is Dying* did become a pioneer for using games as a successful rhetorical tool to reach out to a new demographic and untapped audience, but it also brought forth sentiments of those against the use of video games as a legitimate activist medium (ibid.).

## HOW GAMES TACKLE PERSUASION

Persuasion is the key reasoning behind using games for activism and is also its key attribute. Even though video games are another medium of expression similar to film, literature, and television, its immersive nature and use of persuasion creates a whole new meaning and format. Unlike these other media, video games have rule systems throughout their progression, and the players must successfully traverse through and understand these systems in a method known as procedurality (Bogost 2008). Combining this method with traditional rhetoric, it creates a new way to persuade through video games known as "procedural rhetoric," a term coined by Ian Bogost. Rather than using words or images, video games use the mechanics and rules to persuade its players as they navigate through the game (Lavender 2011), and players can unpack the arguments through play (Bogost 2008).

The most common use of persuasive games in education is for additional practice of material being covered that have repetitive processes to reinforce concepts in a player's mind (Squire 2003). Along with these "drill and practice" games, commercial games are sometimes used to teach, although they are not persuasive at heart. Teachers have used games like the *RollerCoaster Tycoon* and *Assassin's Creed* franchises for teaching subjects such as physics and history (Crecente 2015; Kirriemuir and McFarlane 2003). Learning through the use of games holds a greater appeal to students by motivating them and enhancing achievement and participation (Leonard 2008). Having a receptive audience primed by a medium to capture the audience's attention is a critical step for success in activism. And the success of persuasive games with students implies that an activist game may effectively reach this demographic.

Similarly, within the healthcare system, a majority of persuasive games still take on the role of educator. Persuasive games such as *Re-Mission* (2006), a game aimed toward child cancer patients who play as nanobots destroying cancer cells (Granic et al. 2014), have been used to increase modification of attitudes and psycho-education, for example. Research shows that these games are effective in improving compliance and behavior in patients as well as learning (Horne-Moyer et al. 2014). A multitude of games have been designed for other healthcare-related issues and produced similar effective results. As many of the games involved in healthcare have been researched and studied with the outcomes being positive, it is easy to see how persuasive games are beneficial to the healthcare system and, all in all, are appealing to many of the younger patients.

## HOW PERSUASIVE GAMES TRANSLATE TO ACTIVISM

Activist video games have the ability to convince players of their social or political importance because these games make arguments about how social and cultural systems operate by representing the systems in the game (Bogost 2008). There are different forms of activist games that have emerged since the Serious Games movement gained traction. *Darfur is Dying* is the most recognizable "original design" activist game. It is considered an "original design" game because it was created from scratch by game developers (Belman and Flanagan 2010). Another form is "engine appropriation" or "modding," where developers modify, or "mod," the code of an existing game software to fit their needs of activism. Elements typically changed include the level design, the gameplay, or even the rules (Jones 2009). For instance, *LayOff* (2009) is a mod of the classic game *Bejeweled* (2001), but instead of swapping gems, the player swaps workers as a corporate manager who sends sets of workers to the unemployment office. This is a cheaper, more accessible method of creating activist games as it requires few resources and already has the fanbase of the original game (ibid.). As shown, using either of these forms of activist games can convey the complex messages of a cause in a refreshing way, one of the challenges that face any activist movement.

## THE AUDIENCE, RECEPTION, AND OUTCOMES

Due to the limited reach and popularity of the activist genre, larger AAA game companies don't actively create activist games, as there is risk when deviating from their niche entertainment field. The majority of activist games, then, are created by indie developers who are either fully independent, supported by Games for Change, or commissioned by other organizations. They tend to specifically target youth and hope to partner with other social change organizations while doing so. The civic participation of youth has been in steady decline over the last few decades, and social organizations are believed to be a force that could foster this lacking civic action (Evans and Prilleltensky 2005). Also, not only are video games a popular and accessible medium amongst the technology-savvy younger generations, but youth are a major force in shaping the attitudes and behaviors of the current culture and receive a lot of attention as political constituencies in the future, two important factors for influencing social change (Stokes et al. 2006).

The reception of persuasive and activist games is varied upon release, and few case studies describe the effectiveness of their messages. When any form of media expresses a perspective that strays from dominant ideologies and narratives, backlash is likely. Activist video games are not immune from this reality. The social commentary of *Super Columbine Massacre RPG* (SCMRPG) (2006), where the player acts as the two shooters during the mass shooting at Columbine High School in 1999, prompted outrage because of the game's depictions of the tragic event. The game's creator, Danny Ledonne, wanted to push what a game could be and encourage the audience to self-introspect upon experiencing the events as the shooters, hoping to increase deeper understanding of the events that took place. Many people, including the families of the victims, thought the game trivialized the horror, disgraced the victims, and glorified the shooters. Oppositely, fans of the game praised *SCMRPG* for using a new medium to present the issue and attempting to legitimize video games as an expressive art form (Jones 2009).

Despite these negative reactions, there are a few games that have proven successful in increasing social awareness of certain topics, and their success might hint at the overall benefit and potential effectiveness of activist games. Even though few case studies exist regarding the effects of activist games specifically, there are plenty of case studies in the healthcare field regarding the impact of other types of serious games. These games were found to be successful and beneficial to patients with results indicating that the attitudes and behaviors of the subjects were influenced and changed after being exposed to the medium. Research showed that child cancer patients who played *Re-Mission* (2006) gained knowledge of their disease, paid attention to protocol, and had a greater self-efficacy (Granic, Lobel, and Engels 2014). Following the trend that games can actually influence behavior and attitudes, activist games can be projected to effectively incite social action.

Regarding intentionally activist games, a select few games do have statistics and case studies surrounding their reception and effectiveness. The first game of note was created solely for exploring whether a game could modify player attitudes towards a social issue. *Homeless: It's Not a Game* (2006) attempted to present the homelessness issue by casting the player as a homeless woman who must survive in a dangerous city. The study found that there were no significant changes in the overall knowledge or interest in combating homelessness, but there was an increase in sympathy for the homeless. Even though the empathy of the subjects was stagnant and players did not feel compelled to act on the issue of homelessness, once again games were shown to have persuasive effects. Perhaps even more importantly, though, there was a noticeable increase in the players' perceptions of recognizing video games as an effective means for raising awareness, which further reflects the potentiality of video games as means for social change (Lavender 2011).

Games for Change published two articles based on of the book *Half the Sky: Turning Oppression into Opportunity for Women Worldwide*, written by Nicholas Kristof and Sheryl WuDunn. The first game, *9 Minutes* (2012), addressed the issue of the high maternal and child mortality rate in India. The C-Change initiative created a mobile game for India about safe pregnancy and delivery, as it was believed that many of the deaths could have been avoided with increased knowledge and demand for appropriate services. A case study was conducted to measure the shifts in knowledge, attitudes, and behaviors toward promoting the best actions for a safe pregnancy and delivery by observing a group of over 900 pregnant women, women planning on becoming pregnant, and their husbands from Delhi, India. The results were exceptionally positive and the project's hypothesis that the mobile game would be effective was proven to be the case. Better yet, the game influenced the participants toward action, and many participants spread their knowledge to others including friends, family, and even their doctors. Shown by this case study, an activist game can succeed in provoking some form of action in individuals (Dasgupta et al. 2012).

The next game observed was a multi-million-dollar project funded by seven of the world's leading organizations for women and girl issues. *Half the Sky Movement: The Game* (2013) is an activist game designed to promote awareness for women and girls living under conditions of violence and inequality throughout the world. Unlike other activist games, players have the ability to make real-world change by activating events in-game as they play. For example, if players collect books for young girls in the game world, a real-life donation would be made to Room to Read. This is a similar concept to the passiveness of commodity activism but it is centered more around active play contribution over continued consumerism. The study of the initial launch of the game revealed that more than 20 countries were represented in the player demographics and nearly 2.8 million people viewed the game, while 1.1 million of those became players. The game had more than half a billion press impressions, and CNN's Piers Morgan even admitted, "The future of advocacy may well be gaming" (Games for Change, 2013). Beyond the immense scope of the project, the results were remarkable. In half a year, the game raised close to half a million dollars and nearly 250,000 books in total donations that went on to benefit girls living in the conditions represented in-game, as well as $160,000 for surgeries throughout the world. No other activist game has achieved this much positive press or positive real-world action to date (ibid.).

## ACTIVIST DESIGN PRINCIPLES

While the data compiled for the three aforementioned games may indicate a trend in how social activist games are generally received and where the genre is heading next in terms of outreach with its strategies and designs, these few case studies of specifically activist games cannot comprehensively speak for the genre as a whole. The impact of *Half the Sky Movement: The Game* was undoubtedly remarkable, but there may be some implications surrounding activism in video games if there has really only been this one major success. Persuasive games can elicit some type of change in its players, as shown repeatedly, but determining the overall success of an activist game is complicated. Many of the social and political issues discussed in activist games cannot change immediately, and some games that strive to be activist fail by merely promoting social awareness rather than inciting action. In that sense, these social awareness games are the slacktivists of the video game genre. Author Bryan Bergeron believes the best ways to assess the success and outcome of an activist game is to compare the goals set within the development stage to any behavioral changes within the players (Bogost 2007). Game designer Douglas Thomas believes in looking into the long-term impact of these games on players (Jones 2009). Because it has been shown that video games can cause shifts in behaviors, it is imperative that methods to assess video games like these be used to gather more research.

Since there is a lack of empirical data regarding the success of activist games in provoking players to act for a certain cause, it may be beneficial to look at several of the design features that many researchers believe will result in said outcome. Getting an audience to empathize with a cause is of utmost importance for spreading any activist pursuit, and authors Jonathan Belman and Mary Flanagan (2010) have proposed four design principles to accomplish this effect via games.

The first principle points out that only players who are empathetic at the start of a game are likely to be empathetic to the cause carried throughout the rest of the gameplay. The designer must encourage an empathetic viewpoint right at the beginning, so players are susceptible to being affected by the message. After invoking empathy, the next principle states that players need to be informed about how they can address the issue or else, with no solution to the problem at hand, their empathetic feelings will fade, and they will be less likely to be emotionally moved as they replay the game.

While short bursts of emotional empathy are the best design choices for games that only wish to invoke an emotional response, as states the third principle, the game design will need to consider the audience and focus on putting the player in the metaphorical "shoes" of the social or political cause if a significant change in behavior or action is desired. Lastly, pointing out the similarities between the player and the cause is another potentially effective way to incite empathy—but designers must be wary of provoking a defensive response from the player who may then reject the message of the game if too many similarities are brought forth. Using descriptions and pictures is a simple way to apply this principle effectively. For example, *LayOff* displays a short biography of the workers in a completed set so a player might relate and empathize with the workers they let go (Belman and Flanagan 2010). Other design goals include making the game immersive, so players do not become disinterested in the issues, as well as keeping the overall game mechanics simple for non-players to enjoy (Lavender 2011). On top of all of these, the most important design technique of an activist game is to make credible and objective representations (Swain 2007).

That being said, unfortunately, perhaps the greatest obstacle facing activist games is also one of the major obstacles facing the video game medium as a whole: accurate representation. Video games have been criticized for their portrayals of race, ethnicity, nationality, sexuality, and gender roles in their stories and characters. It may prove difficult to elicit empathy and action against stereotypes and injustice if the medium indeed perpetuates inequalities and violences in their own representations. This shortcoming, in part, reflects the lack of diversity within the gaming industry, as a majority of creators and designers are white and male, which can lead to the production of games that fit within this majority's perspective of society (Gray 2014) as well as games that are geared toward players that are also white and male. This can leave creators and designers feeling trapped as they seek creativity and innovation within a medium that tends towards a static "core market." For example, despite appeals from designers and females making up nearly half of all video game players, the persistent catering to (white heterosexual) male gamers not only contributes to the core market's unwillingness to change, but results in games that appear to ignore, or even misrepresent, a significant portion of their audience (Fron et al. 2007).

Because many stereotypes are still ever prevalent in video games, they tend to become normalized ideas to the players, which can unfortunately lead to the justification of oppressing minorities (Gray 2014). Studies have shown that video game use has increased problematic public attitudes toward minoritized and marginalized communities and even how these groups view themselves. For example, a study showed increased attitudes of hostility toward Black males often due to exaggerated violent displays in-game, potentially reducing the self-esteem and social expectations of these men (Topos Partnership 2011). The portrayal of women in video games has also produced similar negative results in that hypersexualized female characters tend to influence both male and female players to perceive women as objects with lesser cognitive abilities, which affects how men treat women and how women perceive themselves (Giulio n.d.).

Adding to the complexity of the issue, representations in video games can also be problematic outside of the portrayal of people. Looking at war games in particular, many players who will most likely never experience war obtain their knowledge of it through video games. However, most video games do not present an accurate portrayal of war. Many lack very present aspects of war today, such as Black soldiers and civilians who can end up caught in the crossfire, and war games created in the United States, for example, often portray the United States as being righteous or as the hero coming in to save the day. Because many view games based on reality, players are potentially unable to make informed opinions about certain subject matters related to such portrayals (Leonard 2004).

Now, outside of how games themselves influence beliefs, there is another stereotype that stigmatizes the video game medium itself. Because video games are typically seen as a "children's medium," it can be difficult for the public to recognize its uses outside of entertainment or for a broader audience, and, for lack of better words, take the medium "seriously." However, the general public is not the only entity who might view the legitimacy of video games in a low light and not fully understand the persuasive nature and power it has as a medium. Individual game designers may hold these views as well. When a game designer believes that their creation is only make-believe, they can be less likely to try to portray accurate and meaningful depictions of minority characters. It can seem to them that when set in a purely fantastical world, their depictions of characters and even those characters' surroundings hold no real impact, when in fact they do (Leonard 2006). This can lead to stereotypical portrayals that "make racism, sexism and poverty appear to be natural, normal and inevitable part of everyday life" (ibid.).

Although these examples posit the negative effects of video games and raise concerns for creators and users of the medium, this still shows the impact of video games and further proves their capabilities of expressing ideas and influencing a player's belief system, intentional or not. Thus, it is of utmost importance that the designers and the audience, who play a crucial role as well, negate these biases by creating games with authentic representations of people and social issues, by promoting video games as a form of legitimate speech, and by attracting or being a receptive audience who is willing to participate in the discussion despite the controversies currently surrounding the medium. By demanding games with accurate representations, players, as well as scholars and educators, can help the video game medium overcome one of its toughest obstacles. Then, as the medium has the ability to produce true activist games, overcoming these obstacles will allow for the production of more games that do not merely raise awareness but fully incite action and future change.

In the way of facing this already immense challenge, though, is another, perhaps even more challenging obstacle to overcome. Hindering the progress of the medium and the change within the industry include ideologies that are in opposition of diversifying video games. There are players who enjoy games exactly the way they are now. For example, the Gamergate campaign of 2014 led to the harassment of many females in the game industry, as supporters saw them as a threat to the industry and what they enjoyed about it. Instead of welcoming diversity, supporters of Gamergate sought to stop it before it progressed. Now post-2016, ideologies such as those of Gamergate, including sexism and racism, are becoming more prevalent in the United States, at least in the public eye. Thus, this obstacle in particular may prove to be more and more challenging to overcome, but a more representative video game industry depends on it (Lees 2016).

CONCLUSION

Change within the video game industry, especially in terms of diversity and accurate representation, should be welcomed, not feared. Not only can it help reduce the normalization of stereotypes, but it will also allow activist games to flourish within the medium and affect even more change throughout society. Activist movements in all forms have faced the issue of failing to incite action and thus fail to be truly activist. In online activism, this failure is slacktivism. In activist games, they devolve to social awareness games. Only by overcoming the barriers to inciting action can activist movements move into true activism. By observing the evolution of games and their abilities to persuade and provoke response, the significant role they can play on player's lives is seen. Despite the substantial effects that have been shown, video games have yet to be fully accepted as a meaningful cultural and social system, perhaps because of the state of social issues such as race, ethnicity, and gender representation in games currently. Video games are not afforded respect as a mature, expressive, or "serious" medium with a function in society and culture, either, because many still view video games merely as child's play or distractions for adults.

Although this is common with the introduction of new media, as similar occurrences happened with comics, television, and film (Bogost 2007), it is imperative for game designers, scholars, educators, players, and the public to see video games as influential, holding designers and other gatekeepers accountable for their representations. Collectively there must be a demand for activist games and efforts to provide opportunities for gamers and designers to take advantage of the potential of video games as instruments of change. In order for this to occur, more awareness needs to be brought to the shortcomings of the medium itself first. As the legitimacy of video games continues to be established, more widespread empirical data and research can be conducted related to the efficacy of specifically activist games, although strides have already been made in researching persuasive and other serious games. The only way the long-term efficacy of activist games can be discovered is through empirical research, and as the medium grows in popularity and continues to incorporate interactive entertainment with "serious" applications, activist games can carve out their much-deserved space within the world of critical analysis and research until they are seen as a legitimate medium of expression and a key player in affecting real change.

WORKS CITED

ALS Association. 2016. "Breaking Research News: Ice Bucket Donations Find New ALS Gene!" The ALS Association. www.alsa.org/fight-als/ice-bucket-challenge .html.

Annetta, L. A. 2008. "Video Games in Education: Why They Should Be Used and How They Are Being Used." Theory into Practice 47 (3): 229–39.

Bailyn, E. 2012. "The Difference between Slacktivism and Activism: How 'Kony 2012' is Narrowing the Gap." Huffington Post. May 19. www.huffingtonpost.com/evan -bailyn/kony-2012-activism_b_1361791.html.

"Balance of the Planet." n.d. The Games Machine. http://archive.org/stream/the-games -machine-32/TheGamesMachine32#page/n78/mode/1up.

Belman, J., and Flanagan, M. 2010. "Designing Games to Foster Empathy." International Journal of Cognitive Technology 15 (1): 11.

Bogost, I. 2006. "Playing Politics: Videogames for Politics, Activism, and Advocacy." First Monday. Last modified August 25, 2006. http://uncommonculture.org/ojs /index.php/fm/article/view/1617/1532#b3.

———. 2007. Persuasive Games: The Expressive Power of Videogames. Cambridge, MA: MIT Press, 2007.

———. 2008. "The Rhetoric of Video Games." In The Ecology of Games: Connecting Youth, Games, and Learning, edited by K. Salen, 117–40. Cambridge, MA: MIT Press.

"A Brief History of Storytelling in Video Games." 2012. Digital Raconteurs. Last modified February 29, 2012. https://digitalraconteurs.wordpress.com/2012/02/29 /a-brief-history-of-storytelling-in-video-games.

Butler, M. 2011. "Clicktivism, Slacktivism, or 'Real' Activism: Cultural Codes of American Activism in the Internet Era." Master's thesis, University of Colorado. http://individual.utoronto.ca/christine/sources/clicktivism.pdf.

Chalk, S. 2012. "Kony 2012: Success or Failure?" IBT. www.ibt.org.uk/documents /reports/Kony-full.pdf.

Clicktivist: Digital Campaigning, One Click at a Time. n.d. "What Is Clicktivism." www.clicktivist.org/what-is-clicktivism.

Crawford, C. 2003. *Chris Crawford on Game Design*. Boston: New Riders, 2003.

Crecente, B. 2015. "U.S. Department of Education: The Future of Education Includes Video Games in Classrooms." *Polygon*. April 13. www.polygon.com /2015/4/13/8401113/u-s-department-of-education-the-future-of-education -includes-video.

Dasgupta, P., Tureski, K., Lenzi, R., Bindu, K., and Nanda, G. 2012. *Half the Sky Movement Multimedia Communication Initiative: An Evaluation of the 9-Minutes Mobile Game and Video*. www.gamesforchange.org/g4cwp/wp-content/uploads/2013/03/Half-the-Sky-Mobile-Phone-Game-Evaluation.pdf.

Djaouti, D., Alvarez, J., Jessel, J. P., and Rampnoux, O. 2011. "Origins of Serious Games." In *Serious Games and Edutainment Applications*, edited by M. Ma, A. Oikonomou, and L. Jain, 25–43. London: Springer.

Eisen, A. 2015. "ASU Police Chief Deems 'Super Columbine Massacre RPG!' Creator a Public Safety Concern." *GamePolitics.com*. Last modified November 9, 2015. http://gamepolitics.com/2015/11/09/asu-police-chief-deems-super-columbine -massacre-rpg-creator-a-public-safety-concern/#more-20769.

Evans, S., and Prilleltensky, I. 2005. "Youth Civic Engagement." In *Handbook for Working with Children and Youth: Pathways to Resilience across Cultures and Contexts*, edited by Michael Ungar, 405. Thousand Oaks, CA: Sage.

Fron, J., Fullerton, T., Morie, J. F., and Pearce, C. 2007. "The Hegemony of Play." In *Situated Play: Proceedings of the 2007 DiGRA International Conference*, volume 4, edited by Akira Baba, 309–18. University of Tokyo, September 24–27.

Games for Change. n.d. "About." www.gamesforchange.org.

———. 2013. *Facebook Game Launch Report*. www.gamesforchange.org/g4cwp/wp -content/uploads/2011/06/HTS_ImpactReport_October_web.pdf.

Giulio, J. M. n.d. "Gender and Video Games: A Look at the Portrayals of Women and the Demographics of the Female Gamer." http://web02.gonzaga.edu/coml studentresources/Jordyn%20M.%20Giulio.pdf.

Granic, I., Lobel, A., and Engels, R. C. 2014. "The Benefits of Playing Video Games." *American Psychologist* 69 (1): 66.

Gray, K. L. 2014. *Race, Gender, and Deviance in Xbox Live: Theoretical Perspectives from the Virtual Margins*. London: Routledge.

Grundberg, S. 2014. "Women Now Make Up Almost Half of Gamers." *Wall Street Journal*. August 20.

Horne-Moyer, H. L., Moyer, B. H., Messer, D. C., and Messer, E. S. 2014. "The Use of Electronic Games in Therapy: A Review with Clinical Implications." *Current Psychiatry Reports* 16 (12): 520.

Jansz, J., and Martens, L. 2005. "Gaming at a LAN Event: The Social Context of Playing Video Games." *New Media and Society* 7 (3): 333–55.

Jones, C. 2013. "Activism or Slacktivism? The Role of Social Media in Effecting Social Change." http://citeseerx.ist.psu.edu/viewdoc/download?doi=10.1.1.467.6295& rep=rep1&type=pdf

Jones, R. 2009. "Saving Worlds with Videogame Activism." In *Handbook of Research on Effective Electronic Gaming in Education*, edited by Richard E. Ferdig, 970–88. Hershey, PA: IGI Global.

Kirriemuir, J. and McFarlane, A. 2003. "Use of Computer and Video Games in the Classroom." *Proceedings of the Level Up Digital Games Research Conference*, Universiteit Utrecht, Netherlands.

Lavender, T. J. 2011. "Video Games as Change Agents—The Case of Homeless: It's No Game." *McMaster Journal of Communication* 7 (1).

Lees, M. 2016. "What Gamergate Should Have Taught Us about the 'Alt-right.'" *Guardian*, December 1.

Leonard A. A. 2008. "Video Games in Education: Why They Should Be Used and How They Are Being Used." In "New Media and Education in the 21st Century," special issue, *Theory into Practice* 47 (3).

Leonard, D. J. 2004. "Unsettling the Military Entertainment Complex: Video Games and a Pedagogy of Peace." *Studies in Media and Information Literacy Education* 4 (4): 1–8.

———. 2006. "Not a Hater, Just Keepin' It Real: The Importance of Race- and Gender-Based Game Studies." *Games and Culture* 1 (1): 83–88.

Miloevi-orevi, J. S. 2017. "Civic Activism Online." *Computers in Human Behavior* 70 (C): 113–18.

Mukherjee, R., and Banet-Weiser, S. (eds.). 2012. *Commodity Activism: Cultural Resistance in Neoliberal Times*. New York: NYU Press.

Muratet, M., Torguet, P., Jessel, J. P., and Viallet, F. 2009. "Towards a Serious Game to Help Students Learn Computer Programming." *International Journal of Computer Games Technology* 3.

Persuasive Games. n.d. "About Us." www.persuasivegames.com/about.

Rose, F. 2011. "The Art of Immersion: Why Do We Tell Stories?" *Wired*. Last modified March 8, 2011. www.wired.com/2011/03/why-do-we-tell-stories.

Squire, K. D. 2003. "Video Games in Education." *International Journal of Intelligent Games and Simulation* 2 (1). www.scit.wlv.ac.uk/~cm1822/ijkurt.pdf.

Stokes, B., Seggerman, S., and Rejeski, D. 2006. "For a Better World: Digital Games and the Social Change Sector." In *Games for Change*, edited by Hsing Wei. www .gamesforchange.org/g4cwp/wp-content/uploads/2011/06/g4cwhitepaper.pdf.

Susi, T., Johannesson, M., and Backlund, P. 2007. "Serious Games—An Overview. Technical Report." HS-IKITR-07-001. School of Humanities and Informatics, University of Skövde, Sweden.

Swain, C. 2007. "Designing Games to Effect Social Change." In *Situated Play: Proceedings of the 2007 Digital Games Research Association*. www.lcc.gatech.edu/~cpearce3 /DiGRA07/Proceedings/107.pdf.

Tanenbaum, K., and Tanenbaum, J. 2009. "Commitment to Meaning: A Reframing of Agency in Games." In *Digital Arts and Culture Conference* (DAC 2009). Irvine, CA.

Topos Partnership. 2011. *Media Representations and Impact on the Lives of Black Men and Boys*. New York: The Opportunity Agenda.

CHAPTER 14

# DiscrimiNation

*A Persuasive Board Game to Challenge*
*Discriminatory Justifications and Prejudices*

MARESA BERTOLO, ILARIA MARIANI,
AND ELEONORA ALBERELLO CONTI

A s GAME DESIGN seeks answers to social problems, game designers must go beyond the simple goal of entertainment to become facilitators who raise awareness and activate reflection. They must design games to force players to respond to matters of concern, thereby affecting both attitudes and even behaviors once the game is long over. Intended to move the discussion to real context where the game can nurture progressive debates, *DiscrimiNation* is a persuasive boardgame on unjust or prejudicial treatments of some commonly known societal marginalized members and groups.

Conceived and designed by the authors of this chapter, *DiscrimiNation* has evolved through several playtests and iterative processes of design, underpinning on a data collection process that involved twenty-two persons in ten game sessions. It was born from a larger research project dealing with the topic of social change in general, and more specifically social inclusion and communitarian comprehension. In the Game Design group of Imagis Lab (Design Department, Politecnico di Milano), students and faculty members work together on the creation and analysis of games for social change (G4SC henceforth). Through games we explore challenging and complex social issues to lead players to interrogate bias, stereotype threat, and prejudices, aiming at raising their awareness on communitarian and/or individual matters of concern. As a result of this reasoning, we follow a "through design" approach, structured around iterative processes of research, design, prototyping, and evaluation of case studies (Laurel 2003; Cross 2006). Hence, to understand to what extent games can impact players and affect their attitudes, we conduct qualitative and quantitative enquiry.

Recognizing the significant role that games play in the contemporary cultural, social, political, and economic scenarios, we seek to utilize the popularity of gaming as a vehicle for social change. The current study highlights the potential of games to address substantive justice issues. Dealing with imagination and fictional world, plot, and narrative, we move across topics of key relevance such as violence and gender roles, race and racism (Leonard 2006). As powerful cultural products, games shape and contribute to structuring both individuals' and societies' perspective of the world (Fron et al. 2007). Because of their aim, the meanings they embed (Bogost 2007; Brathwaite and Sharp 2010) and the experience they engender (Sicart 2011), G4SCs exist as a powerful system that is able to represent, abstract, and reduce complex and articulated situations. The best possibilities of G4SC are those that enable players to have a first-hand experience of issues otherwise not easy to notice, analyse, or understand. Since we are particularly interested in the significant role G4SC can play in terms of suggesting critical reflection as part of an effort to improve societal sustainability and reciprocal understanding, we observe and craft these games as communication systems that often diverge from the hegonomic (game) culture (Fron et al. 2007).

ETHICS AND MECHANICS: EXPOSING SOCIAL
INJUSTICE AND INEQUITIES

Relying on a significant body of literature concerned with gaming stereotypes and the dehumanizing portrayals of communities of color within virtual landscapes (Leonard 2006; Burgess et al. 2011), we embed reasonings into a game intended to foster critical discourse. By integrating more complex dynamics and creating scenarios that force ethnical choices, we found the centering of discrimination within the game's mechanics and its embrace of stereotypes as a means of engaging the world around us allowed for critical conversations and introspection. In particular, rather than following the logics of "priggishness," we opted for a strongly and deliberately provocative approach.

Embracing a topic-oriented perspective, the field is fraught with games adopting a direct, explicit approach to connect players with serious social issues, often even presenting information in a didactic way. This approach, however, can turn problematic in that it can cause players to unconsciously create psychological barriers, preventing an optimal experience and meaning transfer. According to the research of Kaufman and Flanagan (2015), who stated that games such as *Cards Against Humanity* are actually able to reduce racist and sexist attitudes, such a direct approach lessens the communicative/persuasive impact of the game, as well as its ability to produce beneficial outcomes.

Building on this perspective, *DiscrimiNation* tries to covertly enact the transmission of knowledge/awareness by using a challenging and reverse approach. It encourages players to hinder other categories by discriminating them. Acknowledging the ongoing debate regarding (video) games, including the privileging of white cis-heterosexual and male experiences, as well as the dehumanization of minoritized communities (Fron et al. 2007), this game makes players adopt the perspectives of members of marginalized categories of which they have to strive to maintain the rights, no matter if someone else would lose something in the process. Further, they have to produce credible justifications to discriminate and build "persuasive" reasonings against the other groups. The players intent during gameplay is to divert the population's and governing body's hatred from themselves, addressing it to others, in a *best-defense-is-a-good-offense* strategy.

To question the social factors that encourage discrimination and lessen intergroup hostility and prejudice, the game embeds the discussion on rhetorical violence and prejudicial treatment of marginalized communities on both a procedural and semantic level. On this account it is crucial to investigate what Sicart (2011) argues about Bogost's *procedural rhetorics*, as the practice of using game processes persuasively, to convey ideas effectively, and affect/change players' opinions (Bogost 2007, 29). Sicart recognizes Bogost's contribution in pushing our understanding of games as persuasive systems forward, but he outlines the limits of procedural rhetorics when applied to the design and analysis of ethics and politics in games. Seeking a contribution that is more than a critique of the procedural, he expands on this framework. He suggests that the presence of the player and the play itself are fundamental elements of the political and ethical relevance of games (Sicart 2011). Building on Sicart, it should be clear that interpretation is nodal, and play experience analysis is a key aspect that must be addressed to comprehend how this provocative game and its meaning have been received.

Playing different roles from their usual ones, and aware of being in the safe area of the game, players can experience diversity. As the game goes on, they understand how certain categories are perceived in-game as well as personally, recognizing how easy it is to make unfair or prejudicial judgments. As described below, the design process puts bias and prejudices at the center of gameplay, challenging players to make non-ethical choices and questionable actions. As a result, the game exposes some traits of how discrimination works. It invites players to "walk in the shoes" of marginalized groups, paying particular attention to the larger picture, namely the way society—via media and strategies of communication—deals with minorities and "diversity."

JUSTIFYING BIAS: THE 3 NS OF JUSTIFICATION

As said, discrimination itself is *the* leading mechanic in *DiscrimiNation*, since there are three in-game statuses each player can cover: (1) *human*, (2) *sub-human*, and (3) *object*. These statuses are our translation of objectification, the first element in the so-called Cognitive Trio—objectification, deindividualisation, and dichotomisation. Joy framed the Trio in 2009 as a *normal* psychological mechanism on which human beings lean against to protect themselves from who or what is "different." However they can become defensive distortions when excessively applied, especially against human rights (Joy 2009, 117). According to Joy (2003; 2009), Normal, Natural, and Necessary (the 3 Ns) are the three key concepts that we tend to use to justify and legitimize our own violent, discriminatory ideologies. What we situate as normal, natural, and necessary is an interpretation

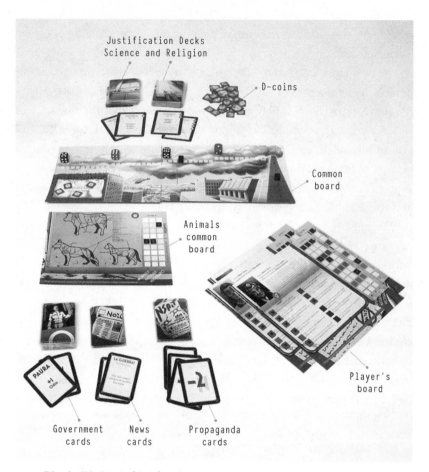

**14.1.** DiscrimiNation and its elements

reflecting dominant cultural values. Adopting a historical perspective, the 3 Ns of justification have been used to justify violent practices from slavery to male dominance, from racial segregation to heteronormativity. Not long ago, for example, it was considered "natural" to enslave Black people as their *very nature* deemed them inferior. It was also considered "necessary" to carry on the practice of slavery as the entire world economy would have collapsed without the labor provided by slaves. Finally, enslaving Blacks was considered "normal" because it was enabled by law and tradition: it was enforced and defended by authority. This kind of reasoning, according to Joy, can be extended and applied (even if to a different extent) to any

Character's description

3 Ns counter

Human rights

**14.2.** There are five player boards: four for each player/category and one for animals, a non-playing character. Each board contains 1) the description of the character and his/her social group to defend; 2) the 3 Ns counter, tracking the situation of the player's status; and 3) the human rights that can be lost during the game.

discriminatory ideology, to validate and justify questionable practices (ibid.). The more toward a social group the 3 Ns of justification are rooted, the easier it is to discriminate against that population.

In *DiscrimiNation*, the 3 Ns are the pivotal element around which revolves the entire game system. Their role and presence are clearly expressed on the players' boards (figs. 14.2 and 14.3).

Further, pivotal elements are immersion, projection (Gee 2003), and mimicry (Caillois 1958). Playing roles within the safe space of the game can influence our perception of a situation and create a fertile ground of debate: embracing diverse roles, we are enabled to explore other positions and grasp important perspectives.

In *DiscrimiNation*, each player represents a category among the African diaspora, Women, Atheists, and members from the Queer community, and is equipped with the correspondent board. The board describes the past and current situation of the group, and the "3 Ns counter" (containing three columns, one for each N) takes into account the progressive variation of the character's status during the game, and twelve rights that can

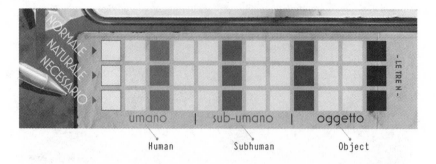

Human    Subhuman    Object

**14.3.** (*top*) Detail of the 3 Ns counter and the three statuses the player can reach losing her rights

**14.4.** (*bottom*) The board represents the capital city of Discrimi; the Scale of Hate tracks the level of the population's hate against the discriminated minorities (as a whole).

be lost or regained accordingly. To further clarify, what is made evident by the game mechanics and the board composition is that the more an "N" increases, the greater is the number of human rights the category loses. This demonstrates how discrimination against a category causes its objectivization (Joy 2009), namely its becoming considered as a subject subjugated to someone else's will.

The game creates a clear and inevitable correlation among the growth of players' N (the three discrete columns on the right of personal board; fig. 14.3), the resulting loss of human rights (central list in personal board; fig. 14.2), and the general increase of hatred among the population (stated in the common board). This last element corresponds to the so-called Scale of Hate (fig. 14.4), which is constantly updated to track the hatred of the population of Discrimi. As a matter of fact, this is a common

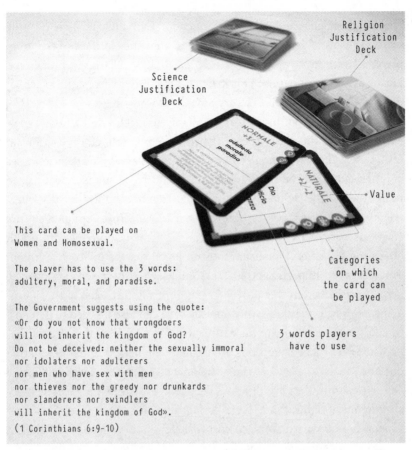

Religion
Justification
Deck

Science
Justification
Deck

Value

This card can be played on
Women and Homosexual.

The player has to use the 3 words:
adultery, moral, and paradise.

Categories
on which
the card can
be played

The Government suggests using the quote:
«Or do you not know that wrongdoers
will not inherit the kingdom of God?
Do not be deceived: neither the sexually immoral
nor idolaters nor adulterers
nor men who have sex with men
nor thieves nor the greedy nor drunkards
nor slanderers nor swindlers
will inherit the kingdom of God».
(1 Corinthians 6:9-10)

3 words players
have to use

**14.5.** There are two Justification Decks: Science and Religion. Players can use them to reinforce or weaken the 3 Ns of another player by giving a speech (with religious or scientific content, depending on the card drawn) using all three words noted on the card. Each card presents a numeric index that corresponds to the card effect on the Ns of the player to whom it is destined, and three simple words with remands to science or religion according to their deck of provenience.

value that positively or negatively responds to the players' actions. There is almost no need to say that players have to decide their own strategy, but in the meanwhile they can't avoid keeping a close eye on the Scale of Hate, trying to maintain the hate level quite low: if it reaches the maximum value, the game ends immediately and all players lose.

The game includes two elements of culture that are central to the justification systems, and of the 3 Ns in particular: science and religion

(Joy 2009). Science and Religion Justification Cards (fig. 14.5) are the only means in players' hands able to affect and alter the N values of the other players. However, to be effective, each player has to narrate a proper and persuasive descrimination. This mechanic is meant to depict the logic that prejudice generates action (Myers 2012).

In order to provide a satirical perspective on well-known stereotypes, each card asks the player to use the three words printed on its front to formulate a "logical" sentence that condemns, blames, and discriminates another category. The three words are meant to be stereotypically used to exaggerate the differences of marginalized and minorititzed groups, relying on concepts that have become normalized within dominant culture (Deskins 2013). This is the only way to interact with other players, and it arises the flawed and illogical motivations on the ground of discrimination, triggering important ethical reasonings. None of the groups involved are left unscathed in this provocative, politically incorrect, authoritative game. However, the three words on the card can also be used to defend a category and contribute to make the situation a little more bearable.

The win or lose conditions are clear: If the hatred of the population does not reach the end of the scale and at least one player still has a "human" status, the government is defeated, and the player with the highest amount of rights wins. However, it is also possible to chose for a total cooperation among players, to curb the population's hate and fight the oppressor together, as a united front. This is a non-explicit opportunity to ethically defeat the dictatorial government. Curiously, such a strategy that seems the most obvious choice has been undertaken only once across all playtests conducted.

RESEARCH DESIGN

Challenging the concept of diversity, *DiscrimiNation* is purposed to inquire as to the relationship between in-game actions and the player's real ethics, as well as between common bias and one's cultural roots. And in spite of moving toward the use of stereotypes for racist reinforcement (Deskins 2013), this game aims at deconstructing their basis, showing the presence of significant inconsistencies and misconceptions.

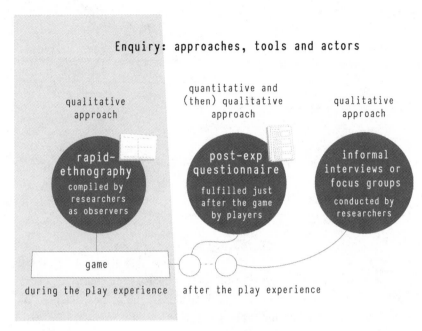

Enquiry: approaches, tools and actors

qualitative
approach

quantitative and
(then) qualitative
approach

qualitative
approach

rapid-
ethnography
compiled by
researchers
as observers

post-exp
questionnaire
fulfilled just
after the game
by players

informal
interviews or
focus groups
conducted by
researchers

game

during the play experience    after the play experience

**14.6.** Overview of the methods and tools employed and when they were used

As a consequence, we asked ourselves: Was it effective in pushing players to understand the psychological mechanisms (the 3 Ns) hidden behind the conscious or unconscious discrimination? Can such an understanding enable them to avoid their application in real life? And what did players feel during the game?

To understand the extent *DiscrimiNation* is effective and powerful in explaining and transfer its meanings, the play(er) experience has been tested and assessed utilizing both qualitative and quantitative approaches (Creswell 2007; Dourish 2006; Mariani, 2016). In particular, ten sessions were:

- observed conducting real-time rapid ethnographies (qualitative),
- immediately followed by questionnaires (quantitative + qualitative),
- and then further investigated through focus groups and semi-structured interviews (qualitative).

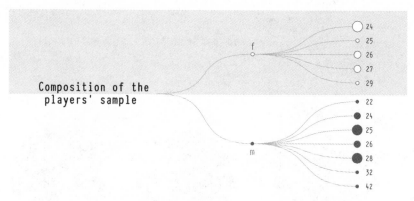

**14.7.** Composition of the sample of players we analyzed

To collect data, we structured a questionnaire that asks players to state their level of agreement (100) or disagreement (0) on a continuous scale (negative items have been inverted to uniform the values). Hence, the following data presents numbers around fifty as a statement of neutral position. Twenty-two players (fig. 14.7) attended the ten sessions conducted between September and December 2015. In the following, we present some moments of a singular, representative game session that is considered as inclusive of the data, in particular of the players' attitudes and practices.

## SOW THE WIND AND REAP THE WHIRLWIND: INQUIRING PLAYERS

Even before starting to play, we collected curious reactions. Upon explanation of the rules, players appeared shocked in discovering that the game mechanics consist of discriminating against other players. In particular, noticing that at the bottom of some *Justification Cards* there are *Government Tips* quoting statements of important scientists, philosophers, and scriptures that may be used to discriminate, players first showed incredulity, then aversion and dislike. These tips have often been described as being excessively "mean" and "unfair." One of the players even asserted: "I would never use these tips. I do absolutely not agree." However, when it was discovered that individual victory was connected to the decreasing of other players' rights, the interest in tips increased. Moreover, it became evident why players should fight. One player stated, "I finally understood why I should cane the others!" Then, explaining the process of objectivation, someone asked, "Well, but if I get to be an object, do *they* give me something for pity or mercy?", seeking for a sort of higher morality for the unluckiest players. This hope was quickly, absolutely cleared by the game system itself. No mercy, ever. The government is equally unscrupulous. Then the game starts.

From the opening rounds, the researchers observed a diffused sense of discomfort and uneasiness due to the dissimilarity between players' identities and the person the game requests them to be: persons who discriminate, perpetrators. Acknowledging that such a discrepancy can be hard to overcome, and that the motivational power of games is strong and empowering, we paid specific attention to the span of time players needed to mask the socially acceptable version of themselves (and related social desirability bias) and become the racist, stereotyped, shameless persecutor and hater. We observed a diffused, initial fear of saying something inappropriate and of actually hurting the feelings of other players.

Then, after about a turn, a shift occurred: Players embraced the peculiar values of Discrimi's fictional world, with evident benefits in terms of immersion. Out of the full number of players observed, a smaller number of individuals experienced an early, profound immersion that began early on. Perceivable examples we detected were: a player who started their first turn saying, "We, Atheists, want to buy science because it is never enough"; two players who started teasing each other, making full and despicable use of discriminatory stereotypes; Women-player pointing at Atheists-player using free bias such as "God will punish you," followed by the Atheists-player answering "Shut up, woman!" even if the Women-player was actually a male. Then Atheists-player said, "We chose to help animals and assail Women since Women are not useful," attesting once again how the player was fully immersed (and stayed immersed) in the role played. Even if the subject was far away from being misogynist and racist, he performed his part and attacked the group with the in-game necessary means.

Therefore, after the initial embarrassment resulting from the unusual requirement that players act prejudicial and evil, the original awkwardness and closure toward the topic were smoothed over, leaving space for brutal and sarcastic claims, charges, and blames. Their attitudes shifted, becoming, somehow, consciously and provocatively expressive of entire unfounded ideologies.

Moving the reasoning to the quantitative data gathered via a questionnaire, it was confirmed that the game's hypothesis is disruptively communicated. All players agreed in stating that playing was pleasant and fun (averages: 79.8 and 87.8)—an outstanding result considering that they spent their time insulting each other and coming to an understanding that bias and prejudice are deeply rooted in each of us, even if we are not aware. As shown in fig. 14.08, the data reinforce the presence of high levels of immersion in the fictional world of Discrimi, of a game narrative perceived as engaging, and of a coherent tone. In parallel, among the others, it is important to notice the high scores (fig. 14.8, right side) players gave to mechanics, triangularity (Schell 2008), and meaningful play (Salen and Zimmerman 2004). The game is considered balanced.

As shown in figure 14.8, it is not a coincidence that several players were neutral in defining the length of the game adequate. This is an interesting side effect we can associate with the large amount of time players spent throwing themselves into fights just to improve their situation or disguised as acts of spite. We also observed a constant need to explain one's actions to others, in an attempt to legitimize and often over-argue motives. As a matter of fact, a recurrent in-game dynamic consisted of players acting in selfish but unpredictable ways, building brutal justifications. We inquired into this feature through semi-structured interviews, finding out that players felt in tune with the mood of the fictional world, and accordingly they felt free to take some risks and explore the interplay with the others. Here, it highlights the concept of being aware that "this is a game," (Bateson 1956), of moving within a protected space where it is possible to explore new perspectives, even if it means exploring one's dark side (Sicart 2010; Antonacci 2011).

Players insulted one another, saying things they did not believe, because they felt motivated and justified by the game. But in every session, at a certain point of the gameplay, something occurred: a disclosure about the real meaning of what was going on. And each time the need to cooperate started to prevail, feeding a common discussion on hatred and pushing

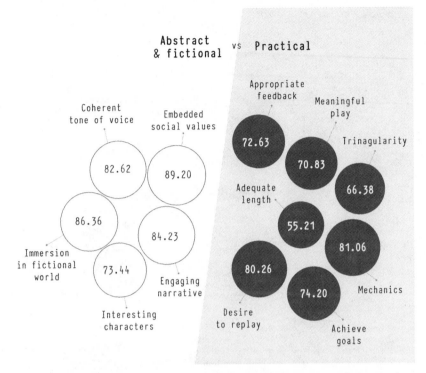

Abstract
& fictional   vs   Practical

Coherent
tone of voice        Embedded
                     social values

82.62            89.20

86.36
                 84.23

Immersion
in fictional    73.44
world                  Engaging
                       narrative

Interesting
characters

Appropriate
feedback          Meaningful
                  play

72.63                         Trinagularity

           70.83

Adequate                       66.38
length

           55.21
                          81.06

                 80.26

                      74.20    Mechanics

Desire
to replay         Achieve
                  goals

**14.8.** We asked our players to state their position according to some abstract and practical aspects of the game. The dimension of the spheres represents the average (expressed in their center) of how players situated themselves on the continuous line: under the threshold of 50 to state "I disagree with the given statement" or above it to assert "I agree."

the conversations about diversity and opportunities beyond the game, exposing and problematizing the ease of using rhetorics and historical references to feed injustice and oppression.

As shown in figure 14.9, all players agreed that the game challenged their moral sensibilities and ethical values, in that, while encouraging discrimination and hostility, it was also fun and gratifying.

Although just a few players were not able to deeply grasp the socio-cultural meaning beyond the 3 Ns, most of the players succeeded in comprehending their in-game and in-real-life function. What is more, once the real meaning embedded in the game and its mechanics were disclosed, it became a matter of collective discussion during the game session itself, attesting to how messages can stimulate reflection, opening up dialogue and

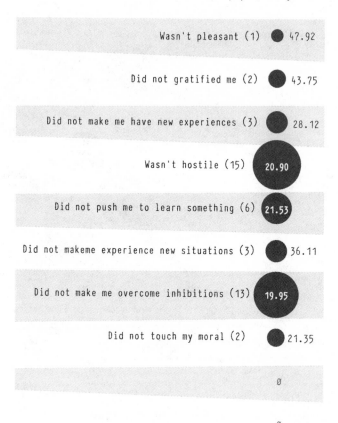

Info (n° players) Average

Wasn't pleasant (1) 47.92

Did not gratified me (2) 43.75

Did not make me have new experiences (3) 28.12

Wasn't hostile (15) 20.90

Did not push me to learn something (6) 21.53

Did not makeme experience new situations (3) 36.11

Did not make me overcome inhibitions (13) 19.95

Did not touch my moral (2) 21.35

0

0

**14.9.** The dimension of the spheres (also declared at the end of the sentences among brackets) represents the number of players who situated themselves below (left) or above (right) the threshold of 50. Inside the spheres there is the average in stating "I agree" or "I disagree." For example, two players stated the game did not impact their morals, and 21.35 is the average between 12.50 and 30.21.

critical debate. The 3 Ns used to start each of the justification sentences that were formulated by the players matter-of-factly correspond to the actual arguments employed to discriminate.

The game is an interactive representation, a simulation (Frasca 2001; 2003) able to reduce, abstract, emphasize, and problematize certain

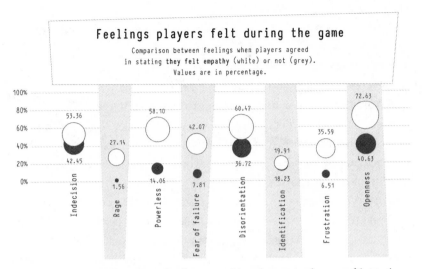

**Feelings players felt during the game**

Comparison between feelings when players agreed
in stating **they felt empathy** (white) or not (grey).
Values are in percentage.

**14.10.** The values differentiate the diverse positions between who agreed in stating "I felt empathy" (red) and who did not (blue).

situations or processes (Bogost 2007). Becoming a stage wherein players can experience other roles (Goffman 1974), this G4SC can influence through the logic and empathy it provokes (fig. 14.10): it has the power to shape and bend our usual attitudinal rules, pushing us to *break our ordinary procedure* and *experience something different.* This point is underpinned by the awkward, low typology of identification the game suggested and, on the contrary, the increased level of rage, frustration, fear of failing, and openness toward the topic. These scores attest that players who felt empathy were able to perceive to a higher degree some important, negative, and characterizing condition. In particular, players grasped the role that propaganda and strategic alliances can have in increasing the inequities toward a group. In those cases the victims felt powerless and simply hated.

According to the literature and the relevant analysis of Gee (2003), the term *identification* has a broad and layered meaning. Arguing that games create a tripartite play of identities, Gee declares that players can identify (1) as the player with a real-world identity, (2) as a member of a group with a *virtual* identity, and (3) with the in-game character as a projective identity. This simultaneous plurality of identifications can cause users to actively self- and meta-reflect on the construction of their own identities, and it acquires a further meaning when it happens in a game such as *DiscrimiNation*, which constantly put players to the test as ethical subjects, as part of a community, and as players performing roles.

Several times we noticed how the act of play actually explored the threshold between real and fictional (Turner 1982), empowering players to push the game borders as well as to swing between these two dimensions. In this regard, it was curious to witness the occurrence of some unexpected reactions by some players who actually belong to the in-game discriminated categories. For example, a female player was offended because Women were under constant attack. In that session there was only one female player, wearing the guise of a member from the Queer community, while Women were played by a young adult male. For the entire span of the game, the female player was actually and firmly answering to the accusations the others (all males) raised against Women (also played by a male). However, at a certain point she couldn't handle it anymore. When a player accused Women of having a smaller brain than men, and limited intelligence as a consequence, the female player's cheeks purpled, and she shouted "If you don't stop, I [will] throw one of my shoes on your head!" Then, when another player acted cruelly and insulted Women, one more time she felt the need to intervene, shouting with bitter sarcasm, "You're getting on my nerves. You should think a bit to your own rights—that, by the way, you don't have anymore!" Later she complained, "Women have always been the exhaust valve of humanity," attesting that the in-game dynamics portrayed thousands of years of history. Accordingly, it is interesting to notice how, for the majority of gameplay, she chose to not play any card against the Women's category. Over the sessions, we noticed analogous protective attitudes shown by other players who really belonged to the categories discriminated against in the game.

These situations confirm that, although players succeeded in discriminating against each other with strong and sometimes evil words, they could not completely forget who they were, being moral agents rooted in an ethical value system. This could explain why they constantly legitimized their immoral choices.

To explore the significance and impact of this game, it was necessary to explore several theoretical frameworks. Conflating some relevant definitions, it can be said that games are make-believe architectures (Caillois 1957; 1958) that involve players in artificial conflicts (Crawford 1984; Juul, 2005) accompanied by a special awareness of a second reality, or of a free unreality, where agency, interaction, and immersion take place (Murray 1997; Wolf 2001; Ryan 2001). Games allow for enactment, since players interact with and participate in the game and the representation(s) it engenders (Frasca 2007, 52). Moreover, while playing *DiscrimiNation*, players underwent a state of immersion that extended well beyond the end of the game. While players often became brutally sarcastic, being willing to make offensive statements in order to progress (reinforcing the idea that everyone possesses biased views), the players also experienced moments of broader, situated comprehension of what was actually going on. Shifting from the contextual in-game meaning of a situation to the real out-of-the game meaning, players often offered enlightened reflections. They revealed to be in a state we can call *critical immersion* (Mariani 2016), where they were immersed in the game, able to critically contextualize their own in-game actions. Sarcasm emerged as the only way players had to deal with the amount of bad things happening to them. For example, in the middle of the game, the man playing the Women-category said: "I'm a woman. Now I'm an object. I'm full of money. Oh, I'm a piggy bank!" which other players made clear was actually counterintuitive, since there is the prejudice that women spend money rather than save it.

Following the reasoning on immersion, we compared the difference in the level of agreement between who felt more engaged or involved and who did not. Fig. 14.11 shows the diversity between the increased levels of anguish and frustration due to the fact that players who felt engaged and involved were actually stressed. Analogously, they felt sympathy and incomprehension, sensations later explained (during the interviews) to be due to the difficulty of articulating pseudo-reasonable sentences related to themes and biased perspectives they didn't personally hold. On the contrary, the levels of shame and embarrassment or discomfort are

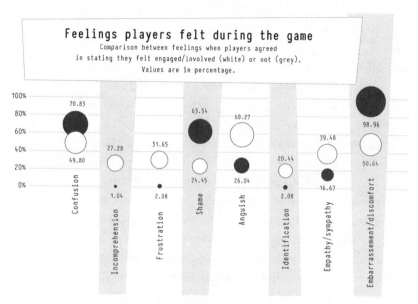

**Feelings players felt during the game**
Comparison between feelings when players agreed
in stating they felt engaged/involved (white) or not (grey).
Values are in percentage.

**14.11.** The values differentiate the diverse positions between who agreed in stating "I felt engaged/involved" (red) and who did not (blue).

lessened. We attributed that reduction to a simple statement: "I know what I did and why."

Most importantly, what emerged is that the arguments players used to justify and legitimize their discrimination toward other players and the groups they impersonated were similar to the ones actually employed and endorsed or supported by oppressors and those subscribing to prejudices and stereotypes. This shows that even if someone does not believe in such discriminating statements, certain ideas and arguments belong to a sort of collective legacy that some often make full use of. Racist, homophobic, misogynous, anti-religious messages could be adopted by all and easily recalled when prompted or provoked.

## CONCLUSION

This game invites us to interact and build the story of Discrimi—a story each time different, but always mean and biased. A story that varies according to the players, their creativity, and their prejudices that asks us to show our dark side. That's the great challenge that underpins *DiscrimiNation*: to make us act as repugnantly and unethically as possible in order to push us to realize and unveil the ludicrous absurdity that is prevalent in all discrimination. We are implored to interact and communicate, personally testing the most common justifications that have been used in human history to legitimize discriminatory ideologies. And it is in this process of pretending to be someone else that we can explore the other, as well as our authentic self (Winnicott 1971; Leonard 2006; Deskins 2013). What emerged from our analysis is a high level of immersion in the fictional world and a curious identification due to the ability of becoming invisible, hidden behind a category. This combination allows new levels of expression and comprehension of the processes that underpin similar practices.

This game is not easy, but its play is meaningful. Players are asked to perform roles very different from their own and experience the world from an unusual perspective. Experiencing the world of perpetrators who fabricate persuasive reasonings to support discrimination, they are pushed to explore and move through liminal thresholds (Turner 1982) where real and fictional dialogue overlap. This game enables players to embrace an ethical investigation of how discrimination is culturally present and active in our society, empowering players to put their morals and ethics into play, and meanwhile challenging dominant historical and ideological hegemony. It's a game imbued with exploration opportunities that asks players to use the game as a meta-communication (Geertz 1973), as a deception, an *illusio(n)* that focuses players on in-game objects to communicate real-life situations and serious meaning. In essence, it is an act of play meant not to cause a mere emotional identification with the characters but to provoke, on the contrary, a rational self-reflection, a critical view of the performed actions, on a subjective and communitarian level. In pushing and requiring players to make offensive and discriminatory statements, those who participate are prompted to explore their own ability to tap into an inner biased cultural legacy, becoming more aware of their own unconscious biases and prejudiced thoughts.

The reasoning behind discrimination is embedded in the game's mechanics. However, to grasp the broader meaning and significance within the games, players are asked to explore the boundaries between the fictional in-game actions and real ones. It encourages players to become conscious that the game portrays and mirrors a significant, scarring resemblance to reality. We found that players were very excited, engaged, and willing to be exposed to these issues. Players were also quite moved by the awareness they gained: discriminating is easy, and even easier when you have a sort of justification (as shown through the objective of the game).

The practice of using processes persuasively (Bogost 2007), with a continuous focus on understanding how players receive the game and its meanings (Sicart 2011), is central in this contribution. The game was first designed and then observed as an experiential way to communicate how things work (Bogost 2007, 29), providing a fertile source of further reasonings. It succeeded in exposing the psychological patterns that condition our critical thinking and in questioning the issues beyond diversity. Problematizing discrimination, *DiscrimiNation* affects players' attitudes, challenging their being moral agents. Arguing on the topic of inclusion and equal rights, it stealthily stimulates empathy and mutual comprehension to meaningfully interrogate discriminatory instincts that more or less consciously populate our daily lives.

## WORKS CITED

Alberello Conti, E. 2015. "Non ci sono giustificazioni: La violenza dei meccanismi discriminatori affrontata tramite il game design." MsC thesis, Politecnico di Milano. http://hdl.handle.net/10589/109591.

Antonacci, F. 2011. *Puer Ludens: Antimanuale per poeti, funamboli e guerrieri*. Milano: Franco Angeli.

Bateson, G. 1956. "'The Message' This Is Play." *Group Processes* 2: 145–241.

Bogost, I. 2007. *Persuasive Games: The Expressive Power of Videogames*. Cambridge, MA: MIT Press.

Brathwaite, D., and Sharp, J. 2010. "The Mechanic Is the Message: A Post Mortem in Progress." In *Ethics and Game Design: Teaching Values through Play*, edited by K. Schrier, 311—29. Hershey, PA: IGI Global.

Burgess, M. C., Dill, K. E., Stermer, S. P., Burgess, S. R., and Brown, B. P. 2011. "Playing with Prejudice: The Prevalence and Consequences of Racial Stereotypes in Video Games." *Media Psychology* 14 (3): 289–311.

Caillois, R. 1957. "Unity of Play: Diversity of Games." *Diogenes* 5 (19): 92–121.

Caillois, R. 1958. *Les jeux et les hommes*. Paris: Gallimard.

Crawford, Criss. 1984. *The Art of Computer Game Design*. New York: Osborne/ McGraw-Hill.

Creswell, J. W., and Plano Clark, W. L. 2007. *Designing and Conducting Mixed Methods Research*. Thousand Oaks: Sage.

Cross, N. 2006. *Designerly Ways of Knowing*. London: Springer.

Deskins, T. G. 2013. "Stereotypes in Video Games and How They Perpetuate Prejudice." *McNair Scholars Research Journal* 6 (1): Article 5.

Dourish, P. 2006. "Implications for Design." SIGCHI Conference. Quebec, Canada. April 22–27.

Frasca, G. 2001. "Rethinking Agency and Immersion: Video Games as a Means of Consciousness-Raising." *Digital Creativity* 12 (3): 167–74.

Frasca, G. 2003. "Simulation Versus Narrative." In *The Video Game Theory Reader*, edited by M. J. P. Woff and B. Perron, 221–35: New York: Routledge.

Frasca, G. 2007. "Play the Message: Play, Game and Videogame Rhetoric." PhD diss., IT University of Copenhagen.

Fron, J., Fullerton, T., Morie, J. F., and Pearce, C. 2007. "The Hegemony of Play." In *Situated Play: Proceedings of the 2007 DiGRA International Conference*, volume 4, edited by Akira Baba, 309–18. University of Tokyo, September 24–27.

Gee, J. P. 2003. *What Video Games Have to Teach Us about Literacy and Learning*. New York: Palgrave Macmillan.

Geertz, C. 1973. *The Interpretation of Cultures*. New York: Basic Books.

Goffman, E. 1974. *Frame Analysis: An Essay on the Organization of Experience*. Cambridge, MA: Harvard University Press.

Joy, M. 2003. "Psychic Numbing and Meat Consumption: the Psychology of Carnism." PhD diss., Saybrook Graduate School.

Joy, M. 2009. *Why We Love Dogs, Eat Pigs, and Wear Cows: An Introduction to Carnism*. San Francisco: Conari Press.

Juul, J. 2005. *Half-Real: Video Games between Real Rules and Fictional Worlds*. Cambridge, MA: MIT Press.

Kaufman, G., and Flanagan, M. 2015. "A Psychologically 'Embedded' Approach to Designing Games for Prosocial Causes." *Cyberpsychology* 9 (3): Article 5.

Laurel, B. 2003. *Design Research: Methods and Perspectives*. Cambridge, MA: MIT Press.

Lees, M. 2016. "What Gamergate Should Have Taught Us about the 'Alt-right.'" *Guardian*. December 1.

Leonard, D. J. 2006. "Not a Hater, Just Keepin' It Real: The Importance of Race- and Gender-Based Game Studies." *Games and Culture* 1 (1): 83–88.

Mariani, I. 2016. "Meaningful Negative Experiences: Design and Analyse Games for Social Change as Persuasive Communication Systems." PhD diss., Politecnico di Milano. http://hdl.handle.net/10589/117855.

Murray, J. H. 1997. *Hamlet on the Holodeck: The Future of Narrative in Cyberspace*. Cambridge, MA: MIT Press.

Myers, D. 2012. *Social Psychology*. New York: McGraw-Hill.

Ryan, M.L. 2001. *Narrative as Virtual Reality: Immersion and Interactivity in Literature and Electronic Media*. Baltimore: Johns Hopkins University Press.

Salen, K., and Zimmerman, E. 2004. *Rules of Play: Game Design Fundamentals*. Cambridge, MA: MIT Press.

Schell, J. 2008. *The Art of Game Design: A Book of Lenses*. London: Taylor & Francis.

Sicart, M. 2010. "Values between Systems: Designing Ethical Gameplay." In *Ethics and Game Design: Teaching Values through Play*, edited by K. Schrier, 1–15. Hershey, PA: IGI Global.

Sicart, M. 2011. "Against Procedurality." *Game Studies* 11 (3). http://gamestudies.org/1103/articles/sicart_ap.

Turner, V. W. 1982. *From Ritual to Theatre: The Human Seriousness of Play*. New York: Paj Publications.

Winnicott, D. W. 1971. *Playing and Reality*. New York: Routledge.

Wolf, M. J. P. 2001. *The Medium of the Video Game*. Austin: University of Texas Press.

# CONTRIBUTORS

**JENNIFER HELEN ALLAWAY** holds an MFA in game design at New York University Game Center.

**SHAUN-PATRICK ALLEN** is a student research assistant with the Games for Participatory Cultures Lab at Saginaw Valley State University.

**TAYLOR ANDERSON-BARKLEY** is an undergraduate at High Point University double majoring in computer science and interactive media and game design.

**THOMAS APPERLEY** is an ethnographer who specializes in researching digital media technologies. Tom is currently a senior lecturer at University of New South Wales.

**MARESA BERTOLO** is assistant professor of design in the Design Department at Politecnico di Milano.

**KRISTIN M. S. BEZIO** is assistant professor of leadership studies at the Jepson School of Leadership Studies at the University of Richmond in Virginia.

**ANDREA BRAITHWAITE** is a senior lecturer in communication and digital media studies at the University of Ontario Institute of Technology.

**ELEONORA ALBERELLO CONTI** is a recent graduate of the communication design program at Politecnico di Milano.

**AMANDA C. COTE** is assistant professor at the University of Oregon School of Journalism and Communication. She received her PhD from the University of Michigan.

**ROB COVER** is associate professor in the School of Social Sciences at the University of Western Australia.

**KIRA FOGLESONG** is a double major in computer science and interactive media and game design at High Point University.

**ROBBIE FORDYCE** is a research fellow on the Melbourne Network Society Institute project "The Domestic 3D Printing Initiative" and a research assistant on the Australian Research Council project "Avatars and Identity."

**ANTHONY GONZALES** is a student research assistant with the Games for Participatory Cultures Lab at Saginaw Valley State University.

**KATHRYN HEMMANN** is assistant professor of Japanese in the Department of Modern and Classical Languages at George Mason University in Fairfax, Virginia.

**MELISSA HOBART** is a student research assistant with the Games for Participatory Cultures Lab at Saginaw Valley State University.

**FENGBIN HU** earned his PhD in communication in Shanghai University in 2014. He is currently a postdoctoral fellow in the School of Journalism at Fudan University, in Shanghai, China.

**STEPHANIE C. JENNINGS** is a graduate student in the Department of Communication and Media at Rensselaer Polytechnic Institute.

**ILARIA MARIANI** is a PhD candidate in design in the Design Department at Politecnico di Milano.

**TIMOTHY NEALE** is a research fellow at the Institute for Culture and Society, University of Western Sydney.

**KYLE NOEL** is a student research assistant with the Games for Participatory Cultures Lab at Saginaw Valley State University.

**STEPHANIE ORME** is a doctoral student in the College of Communications at the Pennsylvania State University.

**SHERUNI RATNABALASURIAR** is an interdisciplinary scholar and assistant professor of criminal justice at Saginaw Valley State University.

**BRIANA REED** is a student research assistant with the Games for Participatory Cultures Lab at Saginaw Valley State University.

**TIMOTHY ROWLANDS** is an interdisciplinary scholar and assistant professor of criminal justice at Saginaw Valley State University.

**KAREN SKARDZIUS** is a PhD student in the joint communications and culture program at York University and Ryerson University.

**ZIXUE TAI** is associate professor in the School of Journalism and Telecommunications at the University of Kentucky.

**STANISLAV VYSOTSKY** is assistant professor of sociology and criminology at the University of Wisconsin–Whitewater.

# INDEX

**A**

AAA, 7, 71–72, 78n3, 157, 252, 258
activism, 20, 45, 194, 196, 208–9, 214; anti-racist, 233, 235, 252–66; clicktivism, 253–54; commodity, 253, 260; definition, 253; feminist, 103, 143; online, 253–54; slacktivism, 254, 261, 265
Administration of Industry and Commerce (AIC), 89–90
*Adventure of Link, The*, 214. See also *Legend of Zelda*
Afghanistan, US invasion of, 129
Africa, 244–45; African diaspora, 275
Alexander, Leigh, 193
Alibaba, 85
Allaway, Jennifer, 17
Allen, Shaun-Patrick, 16
Al Qaeda, 127
alt-right, 11, 28, 77, 119, 140, 176, 194, 217, 234
Amazon, 85
*America's Army*, 14
Anderson-Barkley, Taylor, 20
anonymity, 12–13, 176, 200–201, 203, 216
Anthropy, Anna, 7–8, 14; *Rise of the Videogame Zinesters*, 226
anti-feminism, 11–12. See also Gamergate; misogyny; sexism
anti-racism, 20, 231–47, 252–66
Aonuma, Eiji, 215, 226
Apperley, Tom, 20
Apple Store, 231

Aristotle, 47
*Assassin's Creed*, 15, 257
*Assassin's Creed: Black Flag Freedom Cry*, 15
assemblage, 29–30, 37–40, 43
asylum, 127, 235–36. See also refugees
Australia, 214, 221, 233, 236–38, 241; South Australia, 235
Australian Council of the Arts: New Media Arts Board, 236
avatars, 3, 33, 38, 185–86; gendered, 114, 161–62, 169; immersion and, 34–39, 43; racialized, 231–47
*Average Maria Individual*, 226
Avidan, Daniel "Danny Sexbang," 215

**B**

Bacon-Smith, Camille, 219
"bad behavior," 182, 204–5
Bahrain, 200
*Balance of the Planet*, 255
Balogh, Boglarka, 244–45, 247
Balsamo, Anne, 165
Bannon, Steve, 77, 194, 217, 234
*Barbie Fashion Designer*, 144–45, 148
*Battlefield 1*, 5–6
Bee, Aevee, 161
Behm-Morawitz, Elizabeth, 104
*Bejeweled*, 258
Belman, Jonathan, 261
Bergeron, Bryan, 261
Bertolo, Maresa, 20
Bessière, Katherine, 197

Bezio, Kristen, 17–18
*Big Bang Theory, The,* 202
*BioShock,* 136n5
*BioShock Infinite,* 136n5
Bishop, Jonathan, 184
Black Death, 6, 13
blackface, 243–44
Blackfulla Revolution, 235
Blackness, 3, 8
Blizzard Entertainment, 175, 177, 181–82,
    186, 190, 200–201, 203
Blodgett, Bridget, 234
Blumstein, Philip, 102
Boal, Augusto, 47, 50; *Theater of the
    Oppressed,* 58
board games, 20, 270–90; pencil-and-
    paper tabletop role-playing games,
    59, 240
Bogost, Ian, 136n2, 256, 272–73
"boy's club" of games, 110–12, 116
Braithwaite, Andrea, 18
*Breath of the Wild,* 226. See also *Legend
    of Zelda*
Brecht, Bertold, 47
Breger, Claudia, 123
Breitbart, 77, 194, 217, 234. *See also*
    Gamergate
Brenick, Alaina, 104
Brown, Janelle, 148
Brown people, 5–6
bullying, 11, 21, 41, 73
Burrough, Edgar Rice, 121
Bush, George W., 128, 130
Butler, Judith, 29–30, 38, 40–42, 177–
    78, 181
Byzantine Empire, 120, 128–29, 132

**C**

Caillois, Roger, 84
California, 256
"Call of Cthulhu, The," 165–66, 168–69
*Call of Duty,* 252
Campe, Shannon, 68
Canada, 162, 200, 219, 241
Canadian Game Studies Association
    conference, 162
capitalism, 17, 48, 85, 121, 143. *See also*
    gold farming; neoliberalism
Caraher, Lee McEnany, 143, 148
*Cards Against Humanity,* 272
Cartesian mind/body split, 30–31

catharsis, 45, 48, 58, 241
C-Change, 260
Chan, Dean, 14, 239
Chan, Queenie, 221
Charmaz, Kathy, 87
*Child of Light,* 65
China, 17, 82–86, 95–96. *See also names
    of individual cities*
Chinese people, 200
*Chop Suey,* 151
Christianity, 120–21, 126–32, 135, 136n7,
    164. *See also* Crusades; religious right;
    Vatican
citizenship, 19, 178–80, 188–90
*Civilization V,* 235
CNN, 260
co-creative media, 85
Cognitive Trio, 273
CoLiberation, 179
colonialism, 18, 122, 241; Australian,
    235; Canadian, 241; settler, 233; US,
    241. *See also* imperialism; White
    Man's Burden
Columbine High School, 258
Comedy Central, 232
comics, 8, 219–20, 227, 236–37, 265;
    *dōjinshi* (fan comics), 221–22
communities of play, 178–79, 187–90
community management, 194, 199–200,
    203, 206, 209. *See also* reputation
    systems
computer games, 5, 141, 149. *See also indi-
    vidual games*
Confucianism, 91
Consalvo, Mia, 6, 73, 106, 239
console games, 5, 59, 83, 136, 214–15, 226.
    *See also individual games and consoles*
Constantinople, 120, 131
Conti, Eleanora Alberello, 20
cootie approach to marketing, 148–49
Core Dynamics, 120
corporeality, 158; corporeal ethics, 27–43;
    docile bodies, 33
corporeal turn, 32
cosplay, 219
Cote, Amanda, 19
Council on American–Islamic Relations
    (CAIR), 119
Cover, Rob, 16
Crawford, Chris, 255
"Creepy Side of E3, The" 102

Crenshaw, Nicole, 202
criminalization, 6, 8, 16, 45–60, 68, 254
Critical Whiteness Studies, 231
Croft, Lara, 18, 119–37
Crowley, Kevin, 239
crunch time, 72–73, 103
Crusades, 119–20, 126–32, 136n7
Crystal Dynamics, 121, 123, 134, 136n4
Csíkszentmihályi, Mihaly, 179
cultural appropriation, 8, 121
cultural studies, 16, 32
cyberspace, 30, 34–35, 143

**D**

damseling, 213–14, 218, 223–25
Darfur, 256–57
*Darfur is Dying*, 256–57
de Castell, Suzanne, 181, 190
deindividualisation, 273
DeKoven, Bernie, 179
DeLappe, Joseph, 14
Denner, Jill, 68
DePass, Tanya, 15
de Peuter, Greig, 121
*Depression Quest*, 12, 14
DeVane, Ben, 239
DeviantArt, 110
dichotomisation, 273
Dietrich, David R., 239–40
DiMassa, Diane, 8
DiSalvo, Betsy James, 239
discrimination, 13, 20, 41, 232, 236–37,
    246, 270–90; in gameplay, 36, 42,
    194–96, 198–99, 204–9; in games
    industry, 65–78, 101–17. *See also*
    Gamergate; heteronormativity;
    heterosexism; homophobia; micro-
    aggressions; misogyny; patriarchy;
    racism; sexism; transphobia
*DiscrimiNation*, 270–90
diversity, 41, 158–59, 264–65, 290; attacks
    on, 8; complexity of, 18; in games
    industry, 7, 15, 47, 65–78, 102, 115, 136,
    152, 262–63; in player communities,
    83, 116, 163, 188, 195, 200, 208; in play
    styles, 160; race and, 40, 47, 120, 136,
    278; representation in games, 13–15,
    20, 65, 147, 149, 273, 275, 283. *See also*
    Everyone Can Make Games movement
    (ECMGM); #INeedDiverseGames
*Division, The*, 15

docile bodies, 33
Dolezal, Rachel, 244–45, 247
Don't Ask, Don't Tell, 182–83
*Doom*, 144, 149
Douglas, Susan, 71
doxxing, 12, 102, 117n3
*Dragon Age*, 238
*Dragon Age: Inquisition*, 241
Drew, Nancy, 18, 139–52
*Duke Nukem*, 141
Duncan, Theresa, 151
Dyer-Witheford, Nick, 121
*Dys4ia*, 7

**E**

*Edge*, 215
*Edge and the Light, The*, 221
Egypt, 134
*Electronic Gaming Monthly*, 215
Electronic Sports League (ESL), 76
*Elle Girl*, 149
Embedded Design, 124–25
empathy, 19–20, 127, 135, 243, 246–47, 259,
    261–62, 285, 290
epistemology, 18; feminist, 155–70
#EricGarner, 6
*Escape from Woomera*, 235–36
ethics, 16, 21, 136n5, 194, 205, 244, 273,
    278, 283, 286, 289; corporeal ethics,
    27–43; of nonviolence, 29, 40–41
ethnography, 187, 240, 279; autoethnog-
    raphy, 18
Europe, 68, 121, 215
European Union, 234
*Everyday Racism*, 20, 231, 233, 236–39,
    241–42, 246–47
Everyone Can Make Games movement
    (ECMGM), 65–78

**F**

Facebook, 235
Famicom, 214, 215
*Famitsū*, 215
Fangamer, 224
fans, 20, 84–85, 151, 177, 259; as creators,
    19, 213–14, 219–27. *See also* playbour
Female Link Jam, 226
femininity, 69, 103–4, 112, 150, 157, 160–
    63, 167, 170
feminism, 17, 143, 224–26; attacks on,
    10–12, 51, 103, 176, 216–17; Everyone

Can Make Games Movement and, 65–78; feminist epistemology, 157–63, 170. *See also* anti-feminism; post-feminism

Feminist Frequency, 51, 76, 216

Field, Deborah, 240

Filiciak, Miroslaw, 34

Fisher, Stephanie, 76, 78n1

Flanagan, Mary, 124, 157, 162, 261, 272

flow. *See* intersubjective flow

Foglesong, Kira, 20

Fordyce, Robbie, 20

Foucault, Michel, 180–81

4chan, 216–17. *See also* Gamergate

Frasca, Gonzalo, 45–48, 50–51, 58

Fron, Janine, 77, 122, 142, 151, 233–34

Fuchs, Christian, 85

**G**

Gaiser, Megan, 143

Galloway, Alexander R., 239–41

Game Boy, 215, 221

game developers, 78, 119, 126, 226–27, 254–55, 257; addressing harassment, 198–201, 205–9; diversity-minded, 14, 18; Gamergate and, 193–96; hiring processes and, 72; indie, 71–72, 75, 258; people of color, 3, 72, 136; trans people, 7; women, 3, 7, 21, 67, 69, 72–76, 102, 197, 216. *See also* game industry

*Game Grumps, The,* 215

game industry, 6, 16, 19, 83–85, 90–91, 93–94, 195, 215–16, 226, 232; discrimination in, 65–78, 101–17; diversity in, 7, 15, 18, 47, 65–78, 102, 115, 136, 152, 262–63; gender in, 7, 10, 12, 17–18, 65–78, 101–17, 122, 135–36, 139–52, 159, 181, 209n1, 233–34, 263–65; US game industry crash (1984), 141

game jams, 226

Game Maker, 7, 71

game programmers, 69, 72

Gamergate, 17, 28, 41, 59, 74, 216–17, 225, 264; aftermath of, 46, 66, 176, 193–94; relation to 2016 election, 10, 77, 234, 265; violence of, 5, 9, 11–14, 21, 28, 36–37, 51, 102. *See also* doxxing; harassment; misogyny; racism; sexism; sexual violence; swatting; toxicity; trolling

gamers, 7, 14–17, 20, 29–32, 34, 40–41, 48, 51, 53, 72, 74, 126, 186, 193, 195, 215, 216, 253, 255; Chinese, 82–83, 86, 96; of color, 4–6, 10, 68, 199, 234; feminist, 67; Japanese, 221; LGBTQ, 18–19; men, 4–5, 10, 12, 68, 176, 197, 263; white, 4–5, 10, 12, 68, 263; women, 4–5, 9–10, 21, 68, 140, 147–50, 176, 194, 196–210, 226, 252

Games for Change, 252, 255–56, 258, 260

*GameSpot,* 215

game studies, 16, 21, 37, 77, 159–60, 162, 176, 239

gaming culture, 17, 37, 39–41, 83, 85, 191, 195, 231; homophobia in, 7, 30, 176, 181, 234; margins of, 36; racism in, 65–66, 71, 74, 96, 121–22, 234, 265; sexism in, 7–11, 13, 28, 65–67, 71, 96, 101–22, 193–210; transforming, 4–8, 18–19, 30–32, 176, 205, 208–9

Gartner, 216

gaslighting, 11

Gee, James Paul, 58–59, 285

gender, 33, 39, 47, 158, 214, 240, 271; avatars and, 114, 161–62, 169; gender binary, 18, 105, 157, 160, 176; players and, 139–52, 193–94, 213, 226, 236, 243

Germain, Shanna, 101

Germany, 146

Gibson, William, 35

girls' games movement, 18, 139–52

Girls Make Games, 67

Girls Who Code, 76

Gjoni, Eron, 12

glass ceiling, 108

gold farming, 17, 82–96

Gonzales, Anthony, 16

Google, 66, 85

*Grand Theft Auto,* 14, 16–17;

*Grand Theft Auto: San Andreas,* 58

*Grand Theft Auto V (GTA5),* 46, 48–49, 53, 57–58

*Grand Theft Auto Online (GTA Online),* 45–60

*Grand Theft Auto 3,* 34; Creator Mode, 46–47

Gray, Kishonna L., 4, 46, 74, 77, 96, 121–22, 149, 176, 194–95, 199, 206, 234

Great Aussie Patriot, 235

Great Britain, 122, 200.

Grosz, Elizabeth, 32–33, 38–39
group cohesion, 179, 188
*Guardian, The*, 217
*Guild Wars 2*, 207

**H**

Hagström, Charlotte, 202
*Hair Nah*, 3–4, 4*fig*
Haiti, 15
*Half the Sky: Turning Oppression into Opportunity for Women Worldwide*, 260
*Halo*, 252
Hanford, Nicholas, 162
Hanson, Arin "Egoraptor," 215
harassment, 15, 18–19, 21, 140, 177, 181–82, 208–9, 237–38; anonymity and, 201–3; reputation system and, 203–6, 210n2. *See also* Gamergate; homophobia; racism; sexism; sexual harassment; transphobia
Haraway, Donna, 157–58
Hardin, Benjamin, 185
Harding, Sandra, 158
Harlem Hellfighters, 5–6
Harvey, Alison, 76, 78n1
hate crimes, 119
Heeter, Carrie, 68
hegemony of play, 77, 96, 136, 142, 147, 149, 151, 196, 233
Helix, 198
Hellman, David, 224–25, 225*fig*
Her Interactive, 139–43, 148, 150, 152; Teen Advisory Panel, 144–47, 149, 151
heteronormativity, 13, 123, 176–77, 180–81, 184, 187, 274. *See also* heterosexism; homophobia
heterosexism, 5, 148, 184, 272. *See also* heteronormativity; homophobia
heterosexuality, 7, 77, 104, 158, 183–84, 222, 263, 272
Higgin, Tanner, 15
Hinkley, Alexander, 204
"Hire Me" campaign, 76
Hitler, Adolf, 184. *See also* Nazis
Hobart, Melissa, 16, 53, 56–57
Höglund, Johan, 122, 126
*Homeless: It's Not a Game*, 259
homophobia, 187, 193, 199, 205, 208–9, 234, 288; in gaming culture, 9, 13, 19, 21, 30, 36; in *World of Warcraft*, 176–77,

184–85, 189. *See also* heteronormativity; heterosexism
homosexuality, 176, 183
Hu, Fengbin, 17
Huizinga, Johan, 36, 43, 84, 179
Humphry, Justine, 239
Hungary, 244
*Hyrule Warriors*, 226

**I**

Ice Bucket Challenge, 253
identification, 34, 77, 88, 147, 176, 285, 289; gamer communities and, 147, 179, 216–17; gendered, 67, 165, 183–85, 187, 200; racial, 5, 245; sexual, 183–85
identity tourism, 243
*IGN*, 215
Imagis Lab: Game Design group, 270
immersion, 3, 43, 46–47, 252–53, 262, 275, 281–82, 289; breaking of, 47, 50, 52, 55, 58–59, 203; critical, 287; and activism, 255–56; idea of, 34–35
imperialism, 7, 14, 17–18, 119–36. *See also* colonialism; White Man's Burden
implicit bias, 136n6
India, 237, 260
*Indiana Jones* (film series), 121, 123, 134
Indie Salary Report, 71
Indigenous nations, 235, 237–38, 242
#INeedDiverseGames, 15
Intercultural Innovation Awards, 246
International Game Developers Association (IGDA), 67–68, 72, 74, 76
intersectionality, 8, 18, 159–60, 163, 170, 234, 240
intersubjective flow, 179, 187
Iraq, US invasion of, 14, 129
Islam, 119. *See also* Crusades; Muhammad
Islamic Golden Age, 136n7
Islamic State (ISIS/ISIL/Daesh), 127
Islamophobia, 18, 119–20, 127, 131, 135. *See also* Crusades; Orientalism
Ito, Mizuko, 219
Ivory, James D., 6, 239
Iwata, Satoru, 78

**J**

Jansz, Jeroen, 105, 239
Japan, 164, 214–15, 219, 221
Jenkins, Henry, 142
Jennings, Stephanie, 18

Jenson, Jennifer, 181, 190
Jinhua, 87–88
Joffe, Helene, 87
Johns Hopkins University, 65
Jonestown massacre, 130
journalism, 28, 39, 76, 193; role of in
    Gamergate, 12, 21, 28, 194
Joy, Melanie, 273–74
Juul, Jesper, 195

**K**

Kafai, Yasmin B., 68, 240
Kanzeon, 183
Kaufman, Geoff, 124, 272
*Keep Me Occupied*, 7
Kelley, Robin, 177
Kennedy, Helen W., 162
Kickstarter, 102, 216, 224
Kollock, Peter, 102
Konami, 226
Kony, Joseph, 254
*Kony 2012*, 254
*Kotaku*, 231
Kristof, Nicholas, 260
Kunshan, 87–88, 90, 92

**L**

Laurel, Brenda, 143–44, 151
*LayOff*, 258, 262
*League of Legends (LoL)*, 206, 209n1; Social
    System, 204–5; Tribunal system, 205,
    210n2
Ledonne, Danny, 259
Lees, Matt, 11, 77, 217
*Legend of Zelda, The*, 19, 213, 218, 223–25,
    227; *The Adventure of Link*, 214; *Breath
    of the Wild*, 226; *Link's Awakening*, 215;
    *A Link to the Past*, 215; *Ocarina of Time*,
    215, 219–21; *Oracle of Seasons*, 221; *Sky-
    ward Sword*, 222; *The Wind Waker*, 222
Lentin, Alana, 239
Leonard, David J., 5, 46, 103, 125, 159, 194,
    232, 243
Levinas, Emmanuel, 40–41
Lin, Jeffrey, 205
linguistic profiling, 74, 234
*Link's Awakening*, 215. See also *Legend of
    Zelda*
*Link to the Past, A*, 215. See also *Legend of
    Zelda*
LiveJournal, 219

London, 127
Lorde, Audre, 8, 195
Lovecraft, H. P., 165–66, 168–69
ludology, 36, 45
Lyons, Jonathan, 126, 128–32

**M**

MacCallum-Stewart, Esther, 202
*Mafia III*, 15
Marcotte, Amanda, 10
Mariani, Ilaria, 20
marketing, 69, 71, 85, 101, 104, 139–40,
    150, 196; cootie approach, 148–49
Marshall, T. H., 180
Martin, Nancy, 143, 239
Martins, Nicole, 6, 239
Martis, Raynel G., 105
*Marvelous: Another Treasure Island*, 215
*Mary Sue, The*, 224
masculinity, 40, 156–58, 167, 170, 227,
    234; disrupting, 18; gaming and,
    27–28, 101–4, 110–15, 195–96, 199;
    geek, 11; hegemonic, 48, 105, 122;
    toxic, 9, 11, 105; white, 70, 122, 176.
    See also Gamergate
*Mass Effect*, 136n5, 238
mass shootings, 258–59
Mastro, Dana, 104
*Matrix, The*, 48
Mattel, 143–45, 148–49, 151
Maz, Alice, 226
McRobbie, Angela, 70–71
media studies, 16
media theory, 32
*Message in a Haunted Mansion*, 146.
    See also *Nancy Drew*
metacritic.com, 140
#MeToo, 9
microaggressions, 3, 13, 210n2, 235
micro-nooses, 13
Microsoft, 74, 131, 234
Middle East, 120, 128. *See also individual
    countries*
Mikula, Maja, 134
militarism, 14, 27, 217
minstrelsy, 8, 243
*Mirror's Edge*, 65
misogyny, 28, 41, 51, 74, 102, 105, 113, 176,
    193–94; in gaming culture, 4–5, 8–14,
    17–19, 30–31, 36–37, 65–66, 198; repre-
    sentation and, 46, 49, 51, 115, 164–65,

misogyny (*continued*)
216–17; transmisogyny, 107, 109–10.
*See also* anti-feminism; Gamergate;
gaslighting; sexism; sexual harassment; sexual violence
Miyamoto, Shigeru, 214–15
Miyazaki, Hidetaka, 156
modding, 16, 235, 257
Momo Pixel, 3–4, 4*fig*
Mongols, 128
Moreton-Robinson, Aileen, 242
Morgan, Piers, 260
MTV, 256
Muhammad, 131
multiculturalism, 10, 19
Muslims, 8, 119, 124, 126–32, 136n8, 237
*Myst*, 144

**N**

Nagle, Angela, 217
Nakamura, Lisa, 193, 243
*Nancy Drew: Message in a Haunted Mansion*,
146; *The Secret of Shadow Ranch*, 149;
*Secrets Can Kill*, 149; *Stay Tuned for
Danger*, 145–46, 148
Nanjing University, 91
Nardi, Bonnie, 176, 202
Nash, Ilana, 141
National Association for the Advancement of Colored People (NAACP),
244
Native Americans, 6. *See also* Indigenous
nations
Nazis, 134
Neal, Mark Anthony, 13
Neale, Timothy, 20
Near, Christopher E., 104
Nebliina, 185
*Need for Speed*, 144
Nelson, Jacqueline K., 242
neoliberalism, 17, 70, 76–77, 217, 241
*Never Alone*, 14
New Jersey Coalition Against Sexual
Assault, 9
Newman, James, 122
New York City, 146
9/11, 127, 129
*9 Minutes*, 260
Nintendo, 214, 226
Nintendo Entertainment System (NES),
214

Nintendo 64 (N64), 215
Nintendo Switch, 226
Nixxia, 184–85
Noble, Safiya, 15
Noel, Kyle, 16
non-player characters (NPCs), 48–49,
55–56, 144–45, 184, 224
Norwood, Roy, 239

**O**

Oakland, 7
objectification, 9, 42, 68, 113, 227, 273
*Ocarina of Time*, 215, 219–21. See also
*Legend of Zelda*
Occupy Wall Street, 7
Olympians, 113
#OneReasonWhy (#1ReasonWhy), 101
Ooyl, 175–76, 181–82, 184–85, 190
*Oracle of Seasons*, 221. See also *Legend
of Zelda*
*Oregon Trail, The*, 254
Orientalism, 121–24, 132–35. *See also*
Islamophobia; racism; xenophobia
Orme, Stephanie, 17

**P**

Paris terrorist attacks (2015), 136n8
Parsler, Justin, 202
patriarchy, 48, 103, 105–6, 109, 112, 116,
133, 135, 157, 160, 164–67, 169
Pearce, Celia, 85, 179, 188
pedagogy, 8–9, 13, 239, 253; anti-racist,
233, 241, 244, 246–47
performativity, 32–33, 163, 170, 178
Perreault, Greg, 126
#PhilandroCastile, 6
Phillips, Jonathan, 128
Phillips, Whitney: *This Is Why We Can't
Have Nice Things*, 217
philosophy, 32, 47, 157, 217, 280
Photoshop, 110
playbour, 85, 96. *See also* fans
Playboy bunnies, 113
player-characters, 156, 167–69, 218, 222
PlayStation, 53
PlayStation 3 (PS3), 136n1
PlayStation 4 (PS4), 54, 59, 136n1
playthroughs, 155, 160–61, 168, 214–15
*Pokémon*, 35, 219
*Pokémon Go*, 30, 33, 35–37, 39, 42
Polasek, P. M., 46

*Pong*, 254
*Portal*, 101, 136n5
post-feminism, 66, 70, 71, 76, 78n1
post-race discourse, 18–19, 47, 66
Powell, Adam Clayton, III, 243
Pratchett, Rhianna, 123
precarity, 16–17, 41–42, 76, 96, 177–78,
    181–82, 184–85, 190, 217
PricewaterhouseCoopers, 216
privilege, 5, 7, 13–14, 17, 20, 158, 188, 196;
    male, 66, 103, 106, 122, 194, 234, 237,
    272; white, 66, 122, 125, 194, 232–34,
    237, 272
procedural rhetoric, 256, 272
Proudmoore server, 177, 180, 187, 190
Proudmoore Pride Parade, 178, 185–86
psychology: applied, 242; social, 32
Pulos, Alexis, 176
Purple Moon, 143–46, 148–49, 151

**Q**

Qingdao, 87, 91
*Quake*, 141, 144, 149
queerness, 7–8, 182, 185, 190, 275, 286
queer studies, 8
Quinn, Zoe, 12, 67, 197, 216

**R**

race, 15, 19, 33, 38, 41, 47, 140, 157, 194,
    197, 200, 208, 265, 271, 274; in game
    industry, 3, 7, 18, 65–66, 68–71, 75–77,
    103, 105, 122, 135–36, 209n1, 233–34,
    263; racial stereotypes, 5–7, 10, 16, 27,
    40, 68, 72, 121–22, 125–27, 193, 242,
    281; representation in games, 3, 5–8,
    16–17, 27, 39–40, 57–58, 65, 68, 74, 119–
    37, 193, 231–47, 262–63, 265, 275–78,
    281. *See also* Blackness; whiteness
racism, 3, 13, 70, 106, 135, 231–47, 264,
    271–72, 278, 281, 288; in gaming
    culture, 4–8, 10, 19–21, 30–31, 36, 65–
    66, 71, 74, 77, 96, 121–22, 176, 193–94,
    196, 198–99, 205, 208–9, 232, 234, 265.
    *See also* anti-racism; Great Aussie
    Patriot; Islamophobia; microaggres-
    sions; Nazis; Orientalism; Reclaim
    Australia; United Patriot Front;
    White Man's Burden; white suprem-
    acy; xenophobia
rape culture, 8–10. *See also* Gamergate
Ratnabalasuriar, Sheruni, 16, 54–55

Ray, Sheri Graner, 105
Reclaim Australia, 235
Reebok Human Rights Foundation, 256
Reed, Briana, 16
refugees, 120, 124–25, 127, 129, 131–32, 135,
    163, 235, 256. *See also* asylum
religion, 17–18, 52, 119–37, 166, 238, 241,
    277–78, 288. *See also* Christianity;
    Crusades; Islam; Islamophobia;
    Muslims; religious right; Vatican
religious right, 125
*Re-Mission*, 257, 259
representation, 4, 27, 29, 31–34, 37–40,
    42, 48, 53, 55, 58, 69, 84, 147, 159, 195,
    202, 257, 261–62, 264; diversity in, 8,
    13–15, 18, 20, 40, 47, 65, 69, 120, 136,
    147, 149, 273, 275, 278, 283; gendered,
    3, 5–9, 17, 49–51, 57–58, 65, 68, 103–5,
    113–14, 119–37, 162, 170, 184, 193, 197,
    218–23, 237, 262–63, 265, 275–78, 281,
    286–87; racial, 3, 5–8, 16–17, 27, 39–40,
    57–58, 65, 68, 74, 119–37, 136n5, 193,
    231–47, 262–63, 265, 275–78, 281; reli-
    gious, 119–37, 275–78, 281; sexual, 5,
    7–9, 51, 68, 104, 113–15, 179, 187, 262–
    63, 275–78, 286
Republican Party, 10
reputation systems, 200, 203–6
*Resident Evil*, 141
Reskin, Barbara, 78n2
Richard, Gabriela, 186
Riot Games, 200, 204–6, 209
Rochester (NY), 140
Rockstar Games, 46
*RollerCoaster Tycoon*, 257
Room to Read, 260
Roos, Patricia, 78n2
Rowlands, Timothy, 16
Roy, Louisa, 219–21
Ruin Jam, 226
Ruiz, Susana, 256
*Rust*, 246
Rye, Angela, 21

**S**

Saklofske, Jon, 162
Sakura-kan, 222
Salter, Anastasia, 234
#SandraBland, 13
Sarkeesian, Anita, 13–14, 102, 197, 213,
    225; Feminist Frequency, 51, 76, 216;

Sarkeesian, Anita (*continued*)
"Tropes *vs.* Women in Video Games," 12, 216, 218
Scalzi, John, 231–32
Schwartz, Pepper, 102
*Second Quest*, 224–25, 225*fig*
second shift, 207
*Secret of Shadow Ranch, The*, 149. See also *Nancy Drew*
*Secret Paths in the Forest*, 144–46
*Secrets Can Kill*, 139, 145. See also *Nancy Drew*
Sega, 143, 148
Serious Games Initiative, 255, 257
sexism, 3, 70, 150, 157, 164–65, 264, 272; in gaming culture, 4, 7–11, 13, 18–19, 28, 30, 41, 66–67, 71, 96, 101–17, 140, 148, 176, 181, 193–210, 216, 232–34, 265. *See also* anti-feminism; Gamergate; gaslighting; misogyny; post-feminism
sexual harassment, 12, 77, 176, 198–200, 207, 217, 234; in gaming culture, 73–74, 102–3, 107–8, 112, 116, 117n1, 193–96, 265. *See also* Gamergate; sexual violence
sexuality, 12, 148, 194, 197, 202, 222; representation in games, 5, 7–9, 51, 68, 104, 113–15, 179, 187, 262–63, 275–78, 286; in *World of Warcraft* communities, 18–19, 175–90
sexual violence, 18, 19, 48–50, 73, 103, 107, 112, 115, 116, 117n1, 119, 164–65, 198–99, 234; Gamergate, 5, 9, 11–14, 17, 21, 28, 36–37, 41, 46, 51, 59, 66, 74, 77, 102, 176, 193–94, 196–97, 216–17, 225, 264–65; rape culture, 8–10. *See also* #MeToo; sexual harassment; toxicity
Shanghai, 87–89, 91, 94
Shaw, Adrienne, 147, 159, 187, 239, 243
Shiroyui, Hiromi, 222–23, 223*fig*
Siberia, 120, 123, 127
Sicart, Miguel, 159, 272–73
*SimCity*, 144
situated knowledge, 157–59
situated play, 160
Skardzius, Karen, 18
skill, 67, 69, 72, 75, 88, 96, 108, 126, 142, 156, 199, 207, 227

*Skyward Sword*, 222. See also *Legend of Zelda*
Snelling, Michael, 236
social justice, 43, 124, 134–35, 206, 209, 243; fighting for, 7–8, 21, 196, 23, 235–36; gaming and, 27–30, 32, 36–37, 46–47, 57–58, 65–66. *See also* social justice warriors
social justice warriors, 8, 10–11, 51, 77, 176
social media, 3, 6, 12, 216, 236, 253. *See also individual platforms and hashtags*
*Souls: Bloodborne*, 155–70
South Park, 202, 232
Southpark Digital Studios, 232
*South Park: The Fractured but Whole*, 232
Squire, Kurt D., 239
*StarCraft*, 240
*Star Trek*, 219
*Stay Tuned for Danger*, 145–46, 148. See also *Nancy Drew*
stereotypes, 58, 88, 124, 131, 136n6, 186, 195–96, 202–3, 207, 262, 263–65, 271–72, 278, 288; gender, 5, 10, 13, 27, 69–70, 72, 101–2, 104–5, 112, 122, 139, 149–50, 193, 242; racial, 5–7, 10, 16, 27, 40, 68, 72, 121–22, 125–27, 193, 242, 281; religious, 125–27
Stream, 71
Strong Museum of Play, 140
strong objectivity, 158–59, 170
Sudan, 256–57
Sundén, Jenny, 187
*Sunset*, 15
*Super Columbine Massacre RPG (SCMRPG)*, 258–59
Super Famicom, 215
*Super Mario Bros.*, 214, 252
swatting, 102
Swift, Kim, 101
Syria, 125, 127–28
Syrian Civil War, 127

**T**

Tai, Zixue, 17
#TamirRice, 6
*Tarzan of the Apes*, 121
Taobao, 89
Taylor, T. L., 85
Terranova, Tiziana, 46, 85
terrorism, 8, 11, 125, 127–28, 130, 136n8

Tezuka, Takashi, 214
*Thief of Wind, The,* 222–23, 223*fig*
Thomas, Douglas, 261
Thompson, Tevis: *Second Quest,* 224–25, 225*fig*
Tolkien, J. R. R., 241
*Tomb Raider: Rise of the Tomb Raider (RotTR, 2015),* 17–18, 119–36; *Tomb Raider* (1996), 123, 125; *Tomb Raider* (2013), 120, 123–24, 133, 136n4
Tönnies, Ferdinand, 179
toxicity, 5, 66, 113, 115, 177, 186, 193, 195, 199–200, 204, 209. *See also* Gamergate
toxic masculinity, 9, 11, 105. *See also* Gamergate
transphobia, 21; transmisogyny, 107, 109–10
#TrayvonMartin, 13
trolling, 184, 201, 217
Trump, Donald, 10–11, 17, 28, 77, 217, 234
Tumblr, 217, 219
Twine, 7, 71
Twitter, 12, 101, 107, 162, 216–17, 235

**U**

Ubisoft, 232
Uganda, 254
United Nations PEACEapp awards, 246
United Patriot Front, 235
United States, 9, 49, 68, 73, 105, 127, 182–83, 200, 214–15, 233, 235, 241, 244, 263. *See also* US presidential election (2016)
United States Census, 239
Unity, 72
University of Southern California, 256
Urban II, 128
Uruguay, 45
US game industry crash (1984), 141
US presidential election (2016), 5, 8, 119, 265; roots in Gamergate, 10, 77, 234, 265
Ustream, 59
Utah State University, 13, 216

**V**

Vatican, 120, 123
video game genres: action-adventure games, 141, 143; activist games, 252–66; adventure games, 124, 139, 141, 143, 146, 224, 235; arcade games, 7, 196; battlefield combat games, 84; casual games, 28, 104, 195, 208; combat games, 141; drill and practice games, 257; educational games, 254–55; fantasy games, 7, 122, 241; first-person shooters, 27, 35, 258–59; games for health, 233; games for social change (G4SC), 46, 243, 252, 255–56, 270–71, 285; kung fu games, 84; massively multiplayer online games (MMOs), 28, 114, 190, 197, 201, 204, 207; massively multiplayer online role-playing games (MMORPGs), 86, 197, 202; military games, 5, 13, 27, 122; mobile games, 28–29, 110, 208, 233, 236, 238, 246, 260; mystery games, 139, 151; persuasive games, 20, 256–61, 266, 273; point-and-click adventure games, 235; serious games, 20, 45, 233, 235, 255, 257, 259, 266; social games, 27–28, 27–29, 110, 195; war games, 5, 14, 162, 263
vulnerability, 15, 20, 29, 31–32, 35–37, 40–43, 178, 184
Vysotsky, Stanlislav, 17

**W**

Wachowski sisters, 48
*Wake Up!,* 222
*Warcraft,* 240
war on terror, 128
Warriors of Aboriginal Resistance, 235
Washington, DC, 146
*Watch Dogs 2,* 15
*We are Chicago,* 14
Weaver-Hightower, Rebecca, 134
Westboro Baptist Church (WBC), 52, 56
White House, 77
White Man's Burden, 121, 132
whiteness, 3, 6–7, 122, 231
white possession, 242, 246–47
whitesplaining, 242
white supremacy, 3, 6, 13, 119, 194, 217, 241. *See also* Nazis; Reclaim Australia; United Patriot Front
*Whyville,* 240
Wii, 222
Williams, Dmitri, 6, 68, 82, 186, 206, 239

*The Wind Waker*, 222. See also *Legend of Zelda*

Winslow, J., 232

Women in Games International (WIGI), 67, 69, 75

women-in-games (WIG) projects, 76

Woomera Immigration Reception and Processing Center, 235–36

*World of Warcraft (WoW)*, 18–19, 175–79, 181–84, 201–2; Real ID, 201–3; The Spreading Taint, 180; The Stonewall Family (TSF), 180, 185–90

World War I, 5

World War II, 122

Wu, Brianna, 12

WuDunn, Sheryl, 260

**X**

Xbox, 53

Xbox Live, 74, 200, 203–4, 206, 234

Xbox One, 59, 136n1

Xbox 360, 136n1, 203–4

xenophobia, 4, 19, 135. *See also* Orientalism; racism

**Y**

Yee, Nick, 114

Yiannopoulos, Milo, 217

Yoder, Janice D., 102

Young, Filamena, 74

Young, Helen, 7, 239

YouTube, 51, 54, 59, 102, 215, 217

**Z**

*Zelda: The Dark Mirror*, 219–21

Zeus, 164

Zhengzhou, 87, 91, 93

*Zoe Post, The*, 12